Wild and Fearless

THE LIFE OF
MARGARET FOUNTAINE

By the same author
An Amazon and a Donkey
The Amber Trail
Chickenbus Journey

❀ Wild and Fearless ❀

THE LIFE OF
MARGARET FOUNTAINE

Natascha Scott-Stokes

PETER OWEN
LONDON AND CHESTER SPRINGS

PETER OWEN PUBLISHERS
73 Kenway Road, London SW5 0RE

Peter Owen books
are distributed in the USA by
Dufour Editions Inc.
Chester Springs
PA 19425-0007

First published in Great Britain 2006 by
Peter Owen Publishers

ISBN: 0 7206 1276 4

A catalogue record for this book is available from the British Library

Printed and bound in Great Britain
by MPG Books Ltd, Bodmin, Cornwall
Jacket printed by Windsor Print Production Ltd,
Tonbridge, Kent

For Charity Scott-Stokes

Acknowledgements

I will never be able to thank Dr Tony Irwin enough for his generous gift of time and help. Without his superbly efficient and precise response to all manner of queries, much of the research for this book would have been impossible. Without the commitment of everyone at Peter Owen Publishers, this book would never have been published, and I am very grateful. I first discovered Margaret Fountaine through the edited version of her diaries presented by W.F. Cater, whose introduction provided me with an excellent starting point for my own researches.

Thanks are also due to the curators and library staff at the following institutions in London: the Natural History Museum, the Royal Entomological Society, the British Library, the University of London Library and the Royal Geographical Society Map Room. Many thanks also to Jane Mygatt at the Museum of Southwestern Biology at the University of New Mexico, Paul Smith at the Thomas Cook Archive in Peterborough and Stella Brecknell at the Hope Library, Oxford University Museum of Natural History.

Finally, my heartfelt thanks to Benoit LeBlanc, for never suggesting I should get a proper job; to my mother, Charity Scott-Stokes, for her much-valued critical eye; and to both parents for their help in funding my research.

I will never forget the kindness of Mike and Kim Krupnick, who came to my rescue in Albuquerque, but a great many others gave their time and knowledge, not to mention practical support and positive criticism. I thank them all:

Phillip Ackery (Natural History Museum), Patrick Boston, Benny Bytebier (*East African Journal of Natural History*), Daniele Calinon (Institut universitaire d'histoire de la medicine et de la santé publique, Lausanne), W.F. Cater, Matthew Cock, Mrs Jodye Cowper, Julie Early, Henry Elwes, Charles and Susan Fountaine, Melville and Elnora Fountaine, Fr Hildebrand Greene, Dr Dulcie Groves, Otared Haidar, Mrs Hardcastle, Keith Harris, Louise Haysey (Durham University), Francis Herbert (RGS), John Hewson, Brian Hodkinson (Limerick Museum), Anne Jaquet (University of Lausanne), Betty Keane (Limerick Tourist Office), Caroline Knox, Michael Maguire (Limerick Library), Andrew W. Moore (Castle Museum, Norwich), Trevor Mostyn, Rev. Stuart Nairn, Berit Pedersen, Abbot John Pereira, OSB (The Abbey of Our Lady of Exile, Trinidad), Julie Prebel, Dame Miriam Rothschild, Chris Starr, Susannah Tarbush, Colin G. Treadaway (Forschungsinstitut Senckenberg, Frankfurt am Main), Alex Shoumatoff, Professor Karl H. Schwerin (University of New Mexico), Mrs Betty Sutcliffe, Peter Tuckwell (Quebec Hall), Mark Whatmore, Mark Williams and Pat Wolsely.

The author gratefully acknowledges permission from Norwich Castle Museum, which owns Margaret Fountaine's private diaries, to use their contents for this biography. Times International and W.F. Cater own the copyright in the diaries, and thanks are due to them for permission to quote in this book. Please note that all quotations are taken from the original diaries and not from the edited versions published previously.

Margaret's sketchbooks are courtesy of the Natural History Museum, London. All other illustrations are courtesy of Norwich Castle Museum or the author, with the exception of photographs of Nanny Hurley and Arthur Fountaine's wedding, which are courtesy of Elnora Fountaine, and the group photograph of the Entomological Congress in 1912, which was supplied by the Hope Library, Oxford University Museum of Natural History. The photograph of 100A Fellows Road was supplied by Dr Dulcie Groves.

All illustrations are either reproduced by kind permission of the owners or are out of copyright.

Please note: The scientific nomenclature for butterflies has changed since Margaret Fountaine's day. Butterfly names in this book are normally those used during her lifetime.

Contents

❧

BUTTERFLIES: 1928–1940

POSTSCRIPT:

APPENDIX I:

APPENDIX II:

APPENDIX III:

Illustrations

Between pages 160 and 161

South Acre Church and Rectory
Nanny Hurley
Melanargias (Marbled White)
    butterflies
Bruno Galli-Valerio on Lake Como
    in 1895
Butterfly-collecting friends in Hungary
Trieste Dockyard in 1898
Margaret, aged thirty-seven, with her
    bicycle
Diary entry with pressed flowers given
    to Margaret by Khalil Neimy in
    1901
Khalil aged twenty-four and in Amasia
Horse-drawn yileys in Anatolia/Turkey
Margaret butterfly-hunting in Turkey
    in 1903
Henry Elwes, Margaret's butterfly
    mentor
Margaret and Khalil horse-riding
    in Algeria
Khalil setting a butterfly in Algeria
Margaret, aged forty-four
Margaret's brother Arthur and Mollie
    Williams on their wedding day, 1910
Group portrait, including Margaret
    and Khalil, at the Second
    International Congress of
    Entomology in Oxford, 1912
Margaret's delegate badge from the
    Entomology Congress in Paris,
    in 1932
Margaret in her West Hampstead
    studio, 1910
Papilio ulysses butterfly caught during
    Margaret's time in Queensland,
    Australia
The ill-fated house in Myola,
    Queensland, Australia
Lee Fountaine, aged five in 1917

Papilio turnus caught during Margaret's
    visit to Virginia in 1917
Making bandages for the French Red
    Cross in Los Angeles in 1918
Cunard liner *Aquitania* on which
    Margaret travelled from New York
    to Southampton in 1921
Margaret aged sixty in 1922
Margaret camel-riding near Cairo, 1922
Philippine early butterfly life-cycles
    recorded in Margaret's sketchbook,
    volume 2, and the butterflies she
    bred from eggs found in the wild
Brazilian early butterfly life-cycles
    recorded in Margaret's
    sketchbook, volume 3, and the
    butterflies she bred from eggs
    found in the wild
The only known portrait of Khalil and
    Margaret together

p. 12 Margaret aged nineteen, from
    the frontispiece to her diary of
    1881
p. 18 Margaret aged twenty-four,
    from the frontispiece to her diary
    of 1886
p. 60 Margaret aged thirty-two,
    from the frontispiece to her diary
    of 1895
p. 128 Margaret aged forty, from the
    frontispiece to her diary of 1903
p. 232 Margaret aged sixty-six, from
    the frontispiece to her diary of
    1928
p. 265 Front page of *The News-
    Bulletin*, Belen, New Mexico,
    5 December 1974 reporting
    the continuing search for Denis
    Cowper

Margaret aged nineteen, from the frontispiece to her diary of 1881

INTRODUCTION
Death in the Forest

On a humid April day in 1940, Brother Bruno found a shrunken white woman collapsed in the rainforest near his monastery. She was wearing a crumpled man's shirt with outsize pockets and a long skirt covered with the same, all filled with an assortment of glass jars and small boxes, but the lady was no mystery. She had stayed in the monastery guest-house several times before, and Brother Bruno knew her as the English butterfly collector, Miss Fountaine. By the time he carried her uphill to the guest-house, there was little left to do but administer the Last Rites, and so she died, 'a stranger in a strange land', just as she had always predicted for herself. She was buried the next day and lies in an unmarked grave outside Trinidad's capital, Port of Spain.

Home for Margaret Fountaine had been wherever her work had taken her – a guest-house in Singapore or a forest station in the Amazon, it made no difference. As long as she had her natural-history tools and a good supply of tobacco, she was content. Nor did the thought of death frighten her. In spite of her intense relationships, she was fundamentally an individualist and wanted nothing more than to die without fuss and suffering, and in that she succeeded.

Yet Margaret Fountaine did always intend to leave her mark on the world, even if she did not show it during her lifetime, and in that, too, she was successful. One hundred years after she had first started writing them, her private diaries were unsealed at the Castle Museum in Norwich, where she had decreed they must stay after her death, to be opened on 15 April 1978. In fact, they were opened two days late, on 17 April, as the appointed day fell on a Saturday. But no matter, the surprise for those assembled was considerable, as they had no idea what was about to emerge.

No one knew, either, why the box should have remained sealed, and no one in the decades after her death bothered about it. It was assumed there would be a quantity of personal papers in there, but nothing of any significance. After all, the main body of Margaret's work was her butterflies and artwork, which was already publicly available. Her superb collection of 22,000 butterflies was kept at the Castle Museum, while her exquisite paintings and sketches of chrysalids and caterpillars were available for study at the Natural History Museum in London.

The diaries inside the box were no ordinary document either. They did not follow the usual format of regular entries throughout any given year but instead contained a continuous narrative written up annually from notes, letters and mementoes. Idiosyncratically, each year begins on 15 April, which her family celebrated as her special day, almost like a birthday.

Alongside the twelve identical bound volumes of densely written text was a covering letter, written on 5 September 1939, the last time Margaret sealed the box:

> Before presenting this – the Story of my Life – to those, whoever they may be, one hundred years from the date on which it was first commenced to be written, i.e. April 15th 1878, I feel it incumbent upon me to offer some sort of apology for much that is recorded therein, especially during the first few years, when (as I was barely 16 at the time it was begun) I naturally passed through a rather profitless and foolish period of life such as was, and no doubt is still, prevalent amongst very young girls – though perhaps more so then – a hundred years ago, when education of women was so shamelessly neglected, leaving the uninitiated female to commence life with all the yearnings of nature quite unexplained to her, and the follies and foibles of youth only too ready to enter the hitherto unoccupied, and possibly, imaginative brain. Some writer has said (I think it is Bulwer Lytton) that 'a woman's whole life is a history of the affections – the heart is her world!' And indeed, there is alas much that is only too true in this statement, for are not these loves so fondly cherished and so dearly clung to, often merely as it were, so many gates leading on through paths of sorrow to ultimate disaster and final loss?

Margaret was concerned that her colourful personal life might detract from a serious consideration of her work, and she was right. For even when an edited version of her diaries was published in the 1980s, it was her passionate love life that caught the imagination. She was presented as an eccentric Victorian with an indiscriminate passion for men. Yet there is so much more to Margaret Fountaine than her queue of would-be lovers, and this biography will present the full picture of her life for the first time.

Margaret Fountaine was a natural-born hunter: whether it was love, adventure or butterflies, her pursuit was relentless and her energy legendary. Born in rural Norfolk in 1862, she emerged from an unremarkable Victorian upbringing with an extraordinary drive to self-determination which defined her entire life. Unconventional by nature, she was never cowed by society's strictures or by what was expected, which provided her with many exciting opportunities, but was also the cause of her most painful failures. A highly strung and passionate teenager, she fell in love easily, with a particular liking for curates. But it was a handsome young chorister at Norwich Cathedral who came to obsess her, and she loved him passionately from a distance for several years. Tragically, he never felt the same about her.

When Margaret was twenty-seven a surprise inheritance unexpectedly gave her the freedom to choose her own path without recourse to her domineering mother, who had struggled to provide for eight children after their father died, when Margaret was fifteen. Naturally her mother wished for suitable husbands for her daughters, but Margaret insisted on using her new-found independence to pursue her Irish chorister, who had run away from his debts, back home to Limerick. The humiliation and broken heart he inflicted on her when he withdrew from their engagement was never forgotten and produced a certain hard edge in her, for which many subsequent suitors paid the price.

Travel to the Continent was Margaret's initial diversion from her sorrow, and she also chose to study singing in Milan for a couple of years, punctuated by regular adventures around Europe. At first she travelled with one of her sisters or cousins, but she soon developed a taste for freedom and male company which made travelling alone a more enticing prospect. Men found her irresistible, and Margaret was delighted, exploring the possibilities with a Corsican bandit, an Italian doctor, several barons and a variety of guides and fellow travellers.

Yet in her heart she was always yearning for the perfect mate, and she found him in the most unexpected place: a hotel in Damascus, in the shape of a lowly interpreter and guide. His name was Khalil Neimy and he was hardly more suitable than the wretched Septimus from Limerick. Not only was he married, but there were also the significant barriers of language, class and culture, not to mention their difference in age. Margaret was thirty-nine when she met Khalil, who was just twenty-four at the time.

Khalil turned out to be her ideal companion, however: devoted, passionate and totally committed to his role as assistant to her chosen vocation as lepidopterist (butterfly expert), which she had been pursuing for several years by the time she arrived in Damascus, in 1901. There was also no possibility of Khalil dictating the terms of their relationship or indeed Margaret's life. She was the one with the money and she was therefore the decision-maker, and he accepted his role without question for almost the entire time of their twenty-seven-year relationship, not least because he had a wife and children to support. The impossibility of marriage was a further advantage to Margaret, because it released her from a conventional woman's role – even though they both preserved the fiction of wanting official status and went to a great deal of trouble in their attempts to achieve it.

At first, Margaret and Khalil travelled together posing as relatives – though it is doubtful a Syrian with American-learnt English will have been very convincing. Later he was assumed to be a fellow naturalist; and later still he was her husband in all but name, having become 'Charles', even in Margaret's private diaries. Theirs was one of the most productive working relationships in science, though their love life was less satisfactory in the long term – fatally flawed by the reticence of both parties. Yet Margaret was devastated when Khalil died and gave him equal credit for their work by naming her collection the Fountaine–Neimy Collection. She continued travelling the world alone for another twelve years after Khalil's death, her energy and enthusiasm driving her to the very end, and her obituary in *The Entomologist* recognized her not only as a respected lepidopterist but also as an indefatigable traveller.

Her travels coincide with the history of early tourism, and the methods she used to reach her destinations are almost as various as the places themselves. Margaret rode everything from mules and horses to camels and oxen, though she loved the bicycle best, taking herself over the Apennines with her Coventry Humber and to many other places as well. Steamships and trains were her most common form of transport, but as soon as the motor car was invented she thought nothing of buying one to cross the swamps of Uganda. If she had had the time, she would undoubtedly have learnt to fly as well.

It would be easy to see Margaret as one of those dreaded 'New Women' who made themselves so unpopular with the male establishment at the turn of the nineteenth century, but she was far too much of an individualist to fit neatly into that category. In fact, one of the most remarkable aspects of Margaret Fountaine is the degree to which her unconventional life has universal appeal to women now. She was amazing for the times she lived in and remains so, even by today's standards. Any woman who has travelled alone will relate to the astonishing adventures Margaret survived, and any woman who has ever battled with the conflicting demands of love and personal freedom, children and career, will recognize the agonizing choices she had to make.

Her writing is also a revelation: here is a traveller who considered the effects of tourism on native populations and environments long before anyone else, and she also developed ideas of sustainable research long before others had stopped culling species for the world's museums. The price of freedom was high, but she never regretted her choices – except perhaps on one occasion – and was proud to end her covering letter, 'To the reader, maybe yet unborn, I leave this record of the wild and fearless life of one of the "South Acre children" who never grew up and who enjoyed greatly and suffered much.'

The abbey where Margaret Fountaine died is dedicated to Our Lady of Exile, which was an extraordinarily apt place for her to expire at last. She had been travelling the world for nearly forty years, exiled from her homeland in body and spirit for most of her adult life and profoundly unsure of her place in heaven as well. Only time will tell if her rank among the world's finest naturalists can be assured, but in the meantime it is still as easy as ever to fall in love with Margaret.

Margaret aged twenty-four, from the frontispiece to her diary of 1886

PASSION
1862–1890

❊ 1 ❊

CHILDHOOD IN NORFOLK

THE SCHOOLROOM AT South Acre rectory was a very busy and crowded place, when the children could be persuaded to attend. A huge bell was mounted above the back door to call the children in – it is still there today – but there were birds' nests to hunt for in the woods, hedgerows to explore for butterflies and insects, and meadows to roam for wild flowers and rabbit food. Margaret, the second oldest child, was especially difficult to rein in, a determined and headstrong girl who readily spurred her beloved black pony in the opposite direction whenever she heard the German governess calling.

There were eight desk-lids to slam in the schoolroom, and Fräulein undoubtedly had her work cut out getting everyone to behave like the genteel and well-bred girls and boys they were supposed to be. Perhaps she succeeded in getting John, the eldest, to help her shame his gaggle of six sisters and baby brother to cooperate, but it must have been a struggle. A strict routine will have helped, beginning with the morning register. The names of John, Margaret, Rachel, Constance, Evelyn, Geraldine, Arthur and Florence would have been called, no doubt in order of seniority, and then they would have been expected to settle down to their lessons. French and German were taught by reading and translating the literature; English composition, literature and improving texts were studied, and there was also painting and music. Margaret found the French and German lessons a trial, but she adored music and enjoyed painting, too, especially if it meant sketching outdoors first.

When the children were not in lessons they were expected to amuse themselves and not bother the adults, especially not Mama, who was very strict and seems to have found her children rather tiresome. Margaret was, by her own account, especially good at annoying her mother, and one of her minor crimes is still there for all to see, in the glass of what was once her bedroom window: *Margie, November 1870* reads the etching in large wobbly writing. Mother ought to have counted herself lucky. Many of the women in her family were prodigious breeders, confined a great many more times than she was. Her own mother produced fourteen offspring, and her sister Anne gave birth to eleven children in fifteen years. All three had reverends for husbands.

Margaret's father was the Reverend John Fountaine, who had taken his time starting a family, getting married to Mary Isabella at forty-four, in the winter of 1860. She was not as young as she might have been either, being twenty-eight, which was virtually an old maid in those days. Both came from highly respectable and ancient Norfolk landed gentry. John grew up at Narford Hall, near King's Lynn, one of many younger sons and daughters who would not inherit the family seat. His bride, meanwhile, grew up in the even grander environs of Walsingham Abbey, daughter of the Reverend Daniel Henry Lee Warner, and some thought she could have done better than end up in a remote provincial rectory. Certainly her sister did rather better with her husband, the Reverend Atwill Curtois, who provided her with the very fine residence of Washingborough Manor, near Lincoln.

Yet John's and Mary's home was by no means humble. South Acre Rectory is a magnificent country house, set in beautiful grounds and looking across the lovely Nar Valley to Castle Acre and its ruined priory. Nor was Margaret's mother burdened with any more onerous duties than running a large body of staff to serve her family's needs. The children were cared for by their beloved Nanny Hurley and a succession of slightly less beloved governesses, while the house and gardens were serviced by all the usual servants of a respectable Victorian household: a cook, a parlour maid, at least one or two servant girls, and a gardener and stable boy to take care of the outdoor jobs, as well as the animals, which included pet goats, dogs, rabbits and ponies.

The eldest child, named John after his father, was born in 1861, within a year of his parents' marriage. Margaret arrived the following year, born on 16 May 1862, the first of six daughters who almost all arrived at annual intervals: Rachel in 1863, Constance in 1864, Evelyn in 1865 and Geraldine in 1867; the following year a second son was born, named Arthur, after whom Florence trailed by three years, born in 1871. No wonder Mother was strict – it was the only self-defence she could muster against being entirely devoured by her children's needs.

Father preferred country pursuits to chasing glory or fortune in his own right, and when his oldest brother, the Squire of Narford, gave him the living of South Acre he was happy enough to settle there. He made no effort to advance to higher office in one of Norfolk's towns, much less to any great position at Norwich Cathedral, which his wife might have hoped for, considering the family connections and her father's example. Instead, John senior was happy to remain an obscure country rector for his entire career, practising benevolent neglect on his parishioners and gaining a reputation as a great shot, once bringing down a pheasant, a partridge and a woodcock with a single blast from his gun.[1]

An inspection of South Acre church and its parish records suggests there might also have been a less salubrious reason for John Fountaine's failure to advance his career than a mere lack of ambition. The church is remarkable for an extremely rare absence of any commemorative plaque to a rector who served the parish for nearly thirty-two years. Nothing at all remembers him to posterity, even though his predecessor enjoys three separate stone plaques and his successor an elaborate memorial near the altar. Furthermore, his grave lies obscured under a mass of brambles at the back of the graveyard, which no uninitiated visitor would ever find. No information has survived to tell us why the parish chose to forget John Fountaine so thoroughly, though its registers of baptisms and funerals may hold some clues. For example, no children born outside wedlock are recorded prior to 1846, when John Fountaine became the rector of South Acre church, yet after this date the baptisms of illegitimate children almost outnumber those born in wedlock.

These unorthodox arrangements may have had something to do with the fact that John Fountaine was a bachelor for his first fourteen years at South Acre. Or they might have had more to do with the fact that South Acre was an important base for migrant agricultural workers at that time. At any rate, there are no records of illegitimate children being baptized after his marriage to Mary in 1860. Perhaps her influence had something to do with this, but it seems clear he preferred free-and-easy country living to promoting religion.

Considering his wife's deeply religious background, this may also be another reason why Margaret describes her as very strict and somewhat bad-tempered. Her mother's husband was more than likely a profound disappointment to her, and it must have been a great comfort to be able to escape to the vast network of relatives throughout East Anglia and beyond whenever she craved more congenial company. We know from Margaret's diary that visits were not only regular but also lengthy, often running to several weeks. Favourite destinations were Mother's sisters, especially Anne Henrietta at Washingborough Manor, and Mary Anne at Québec House, outside East Dereham, who could easily be reached in less than a day's travel by train and horse-drawn carriage.

John's heritage did, however, give at least one of her children something no amount of money can buy, though Mary never thought to value it. For the Fountaines are one of the greatest art collectors and connoisseurs of England, generation after generation producing individuals of profound artistic sensitivity. Margaret inherited this sensibility, which may have accounted for her highly strung temperament, and certainly expressed itself in her artistic talent, which was sufficient to allow serious consideration of two possible careers in her twenties, as a painter or a singer.

The tradition was begun by Andrew Fountaine I (1632–1706) and firmly established by his son, Sir Andrew Fountaine II (1676–1753), who filled Narford Hall with some of the country's finest private collections of art and antiquity, especially Italian majolica (tin-glazed earthenware) and paintings. He was perhaps the luckiest country squire of his generation, combining excellent contacts with good looks, charm and education, which ensured entry into the highest society at a very early age. We know this from the letters of the German philosopher Gottfried Wilhelm Leibniz (1646–1716), who was a personal friend. For example, when he wrote to Fountaine to let him know the latter had been accepted as a member of the Royal Society of Berlin, in 1701, he could not resist commenting on his effect on the ladies, writing: 'your wit, your good looks, or rather your beauty, remains engraved in their imagination, and makes as much noise at Court as your learning does among our *Savants*, who have had the advantage of your acquaintance'. Margaret was no beauty, but she, too, was to become irresistible to the opposite sex.

Knighted by the time he was twenty-two, Sir Andrew Fountaine quickly rose to become a successful banker, close not only to the English Court but also to several European ones, such as at Hanover and Florence. He made most of his contacts during two Grand Tours, each taking several years, but he was very successful at keeping in with society at home as well: he was a favourite of Princess Caroline, who appointed him Vice-Chamberlain in 1725 and Master of the Mint, when she was Queen, in 1727. He succeeded his friend Sir Isaac Newton who died that year.[2]

The vastness of his collection becomes clear when one looks at the inventory made on Sir Andrew's death which included a list of a total of 3,327 prints in one eleven-drawer cabinet alone, not to mention paintings by great artists, such as Canaletto, Rubens and van Dyck. One of the most famous paintings, still at Narford Hall today, is the canvas *Sir Andrew Fountaine and Friends in the Tribune*, by Giulio Pignatta (1715), significant because it is the earliest known depiction of the Tribune Gallery in the Uffizi Palace at Florence, which paid homage to the Medici. It has pride of place in the Music and Ball Room, among the family portraits, and as a child Margaret would have had many occasions to study it, along with all the other cultural treasures at Narford Hall.

Sir Andrew also loved books and literature, perhaps encouraged by his friendship with Jonathan Swift, with whom he even collaborated on one of his publishing ventures, and the library he created is significant not only for its collection of books but also for being one of the finest early-eighteenth-century interiors still in existence today. All along the walls, above the bookcases, a total of thirty-one literary portraits gaze down at the visitor, images of contemporary and historic icons whom Sir Andrew particularly admired.[3]

The title died with Sir Andrew, who never had children, but the family tradition of art patronage was continued by his niece's son, Andrew Fountaine III (1770–1874), who was a key figure in the thriving artistic scene of Norfolk throughout his lifetime, active not only as patron but also as a collector. His major contribution to the family's collections was in painting, which was also the great achievement of his son, Andrew Fountaine IV (1808–74), who ensured Margaret would have been able to see original works by many European Masters but especially by Dutch and Flemish ones, including Brueghel, Jacob van Ruisdael and Jan van Huysum, just four miles down the road from her own home.[4]

Margaret's early childhood was therefore characterized by a unique combination of high culture and nature. Her exalted family connections meant she was accustomed to mixing with Norfolk's high society on occasion, familiar not only with the treasures of Narford Hall but also with those of other great houses in the county. Yet she also had the freedom of being a country girl, running wild in the woods and fields with her brothers and sisters. From any perspective it was an idyllic childhood, safe and secure from hardships or worry and embraced by Nanny's firm but caring love.

This Arcadian life was shattered, though, when John Fountaine died intestate in 1877, when Margaret was just fifteen. It left her mother a widow at forty-six, with eight children to bring up, no home and no money of her own. The Married Women's Property Act, which gave women the right to administer their own property and money, was not introduced until 1884, and anyway the rectory at South Acre belonged to the Narford estate and was not available for inheritance. The children were therefore dispersed to a variety of in-laws while their mother tried to make arrangements for a new life elsewhere.

It was decided to move to Norwich, which was a big step for everyone, not least the children, who found the idea of city life very intimidating. For Margaret, however, it was also incredibly exciting. As a teenage girl on the cusp of womanhood, she was thrilled and terrified in equal measure. At least two of her sisters felt the same, and together they composed a poem for the frontispiece of Margaret's very first diary:

> Those dreams, of the far distant future,
> Whose mysteries, are yet unsealed,
> Oh! Could I but pierce through its shadows
> And gaze on its untrodden fields.
> What scenes of vexation and sorrow!
> What moments of heart-rending anguish
> Would instantly burst to my sight.

Written by Margaret, Constance and Geraldine, it inaugurated Margaret's first entry, on 15 April 1878, the day the family moved to Eaton Grange, in the parish of Eaton, two miles from the centre of Norwich. It was a momentous event, not only because it marked the beginning of a new era but because it was the day she began Volume I of what was to become a body of twelve volumes, each a meticulously neat, handwritten record of her long and remarkable life.

Judging by the care she took, it seems obvious she always intended the diaries to be read by others one day, and she created each volume with as much clarity and precision as possible, including numbered pages, an index of illustrations and even the amount of time required to read each account. Perhaps this also explains the remarkable omission of any mention of her father. Considering the move to Norwich was precipitated by his recent death, it is extraordinary that he gets no mention, not even in reference to how Margaret might have felt about the bereavement. In fact, there is only one passing mention of him in the entire twelve volumes. A heavy Victorian silence hangs over his memory, and the inescapable conclusion is that she felt the need to protect her family's reputation by leaving John Fountaine out of her story. Like the parishioners of South Acre, she felt it best to say nothing.

At first, she intended to write up just one day each year, 15 April, which was her special day, and the one day when she could expect to take precedence over all her siblings, receive small gifts and get away with pushing her luck with Mama. Thus, the first entry is marked as requiring just nine minutes to read and records her thoughts and feelings for the day of their move to Eaton Grange.

The girls excitedly pumped Nanny Hurley for information as they headed for Thorpe Station, in Norwich. What did Eaton Grange look like? Did it retain any of the country atmosphere they cherished so much? Margaret certainly did not think much of the streets she saw on their way out to Eaton, taking a particular dislike to New Eaton Church, which looked more like a chapel than a church to her, owing to its 'very small spire'.

On arrival, Margaret was relieved to find everyone was dressed just the same as they had been at South Acre. Somehow she had imagined they would all have to wear their Sunday best in the city, but everyone was as 'countrified' as ever.[5]

The girls ran about the house in a noisy clatter which grated on their poor mother's nerves, but the carpets were not yet down so the racket of echoing footsteps was inevitable. Everything was still in chaos. The bookcases were not yet filled, and the dining-room was crammed with furnishings which meant supper that evening was served in the school-room. But Margaret was happy enough. She liked the dining-room because it was very similar to the one at South Acre, and she approved of her freshly papered bedroom, which she was going to share with Rachel and Geraldine.

In fact, the house was almost as large as the one they had left, a fine Victorian mansion with plenty of room for the entire household of South Acre, including the staff. The grounds were large enough to accommodate a tennis court and the smaller pets, so life looked very good to Margaret at the end of her first day there.

'I wonder what I shall be doing this time next year,' she asks herself at the end of her first diary entry. But she is not worried. The present is far too interesting to bother about an unknown future, and she ends her diary with a blasé 'good bye for three hundred and sixty four days'.

The roller-coaster of Margaret's eventful life was about to start, the lows lower and the highs higher than her wildest fancies could have imagined. Not only that, but the next decade of her life was going to mark her for ever and set her on a course no one could possibly have predicted for this spirited provincial girl from Norfolk.

❦ 2 ❦

UNLADYLIKE BEHAVIOUR

'OH! WE NEVER knew at South Acre what real happiness was! We might have been excited and pleased about some new discovery in the woods or fields, or some fresh plan that seemed likely to turn out well, but what was that to the joy I have felt at Evening Service in Christ Church, when my heart has seemed almost bursting with happiness, and I have felt almost carried away with delight at the sound of music and singing, and only because *he* has been there.'[1]

'He' was the local curate, Charles Woodrow, the object not only of Margaret's passion but also that of her sisters Constance and Geraldine.

Margaret's worries about town life were a distant memory as she and her sisters threw themselves into the new adventures Norwich offered. 'How little we think of deceiving Mamma at every turn, in order to carry out our own ends, and how much goes on amongst us, without her having the slightest idea of it,' she confessed with only a dutiful hint at a guilty conscience; '. . . only one thing is certain, and that is that I will always, as long as I live, love Charles Woodrow,' she gushed, though this did not stop her and her sisters from making extended 'shopping trips' into Norwich town centre, where they might chance to bump into other male acquaintances. They even devised a colour-coded notch card, on which each girl marked the number of gentlemen spotted on any given day, according to their assigned colours. A Mr Reggie Fellowes was red, while Mr Ludlow was blue.

There was reason for passionate grief as well, though, as the sisters' much-loved older brother John died within months of the move to Norwich, and Margaret was briefly shocked into contemplating the cruelty of fate, before her own irresistible vitality quickly swept her back to the 'rapid stream' that was her teenage life.

Geraldine's infatuation with Mr Woodrow wilted under the disapproving comments of Mother, who referred to him as 'that vulgar boy', but Margaret persisted, spending most of her eighteenth year swooning over him. Yet she began her entry for 1881 with a dramatic change of heart: 'Oh! How little is it possible for us ever to tell how very great may be the change that will come over us, only in the space of one year.' A garden party was the reason, for there she first danced with Gerry Bignold, whose forebear founded Norwich Union. But Gerry, though eminently suitable from the point of view of class and money, was too worldly for Margaret's spiritual tastes. There were plenty of others, though, and the sisters happily shared their infatuations, since men were little more than props in the romantic dramas they constructed in their imaginations.

'What I suppose I *ought* now to have done, instead of allowing these silly thoughts and foolish fancies to pass through my mind, was to have turned away from all such follies and to have gazed steadfastly on the stern realities of life . . .' But how much more fun it was to dream instead, and Margaret had a tremendous need and capacity to love, though she knew perfectly well how ridiculous it was to fall at the feet of complete strangers.

'I long to go forward and act my part on the great stage of life,' she wrote, a happy, vibrant teenager, impatient to see what the future would bring. She closed her diary entry for her nineteenth year in a romantic haze, tinged with novelistic foreboding: '. . . at present it all looks so bright, there appears to be no cloud in my sky, but the brightest warmest days are often those which end in the most terrible thunderstorms; I can only hope that this will not be the case with me. I feel at this moment so very happy and everything in this world appears to me so very very lovely, that alas I only fear I love it too well.'

After four years of writing her diary up on her special day, only recounting her thoughts and feelings on that day, Margaret decided instead to write up each year as one continuous narrative, to provide a detailed history of her whole life, 'be it one of success and happiness, or of repeated follies'.

The follies were already plenty, including falling in love with Mr Swindell, a curate who had claimed her sister Evelyn's heart. For once, she was not willing to share her object of desire and shamefully admitted to an entire summer of deceit, accompanying Evelyn to sermons at Holy Trinity church, ostensibly to lend her moral support, when all the time she was secretly in love herself. 'Oh! It is no use to disguise the fact any longer,' she confessed only to her diary. 'I knew but too well, that I – I loved Mr Swindell far more than Evelyn . . .'

Of course, Mr Swindell probably had no idea he was the object of such overheated passions, since neither sister had ever spoken to him. They lived in an era where relations between middle-class men and women were so limited that to speak with a man to whom one had not been introduced was out of the question. Young women could find their reputations ruined just for being alone in a room with someone of the opposite sex, if malicious gossip was the result, and no respectable woman expected to leave her house without a chaperone.

In fact, the Mr Swindell love story was not spoilt by wagging tongues but by Geraldine, who could not resist telling her sisters one day, 'Of course, you heard him say *his wife.*' Evelyn was sad, but Margaret was devastated. 'I felt as if all the sunshine of my life had died,' she mourned, and yet she could not resist torturing herself with continued visits to Mr Swindell's sermons, displaying a dangerous masochistic tendency for the first time. Not only did she burn his initials into the palm of her hand with iodine, she also stalked him, spying on him and his wife at home, commissioning photographs of his house and the church where he served. Instead of moving on, she became obsessed and began her twenties 'reconciled to the shame of being in love with a married man'.

Mama, no doubt aware of her daughter's intemperate feelings, decided that a change of scene might help and took Margaret and Rachel to Cheltenham for a few months, sending the other siblings to a variety of relatives in Norfolk and Lincolnshire. The young ladies were very bored, since it was not the 'season', but Margaret nevertheless managed to fall in love with one of the musicians playing in the park each afternoon. 'Don't laugh,' she implored the reader in one of her very rare asides. 'I blush at the thought of it,' she confessed, though she could not resist claiming that he was 'remarkably good-looking', adding that even Rachel had admitted as much.

Back home in Norwich, her holiday fancy forgotten, Margaret had nothing better to do than resume her infatuation with Mr Swindell. She was cursed – like almost all unmarried women of her class – with a life of unutterable boredom, denied an education or meaningful employment and forced to while away the endless hours of the day with a repetitive routine of piano, tennis, reading, diary-writing and copying out hymns and bible texts. The sheer pointlessness of her existence was crushing, and she had far too much time to think, with no father figure or older brother to temper the enclosed female perspective.

Poor Mother got the brunt of Margaret's moods, and frequent rows were regularly followed by periods of not being on speaking terms. Margaret took to staying in bed late in order to miss family breakfast and sought comfort from Nanny Hurley, who soothed her with long hair-combing sessions. She spent many hours in her room, pouring her heart out to her diary, which began to read like the worst romantic novel imaginable. She burnt with 'a mad consuming fire', and love was an 'unquenchable fury' in her bosom. Yet the fire went out as suddenly as it flared up when she decided she loved Gerry Bignold better after all and devoted almost a hundred pages to him, racked by passionate feelings and haunted by images of his 'dazzling beauty'.

By the time Margaret approached her twenty-first birthday she had realised something must be done or else she would lose her mind completely, though she had no concrete idea how to change her life:

> I am entirely wanting in all ambition, having often been told that my talent for drawing is such that I might be an artist and yet no ambitious love of notoriety has ever moved me with the desire to excel either in that or anything else. A few months ago, I heard that Mr Muriel, our doctor, had said that both Evelyn and I had got a monomania on one subject, and that was the love of men! It seems a dreadful thing for him to have said, and still more so as I am certain he was not mistaken, though I think Evelyn's monomania is restricted to curates *only*! But I know that with me it is not even that; for very often when I find myself in the presence of a man, even one whom I am really perfectly indifferent to, I feel my monomania raging and burning in my brain, I am bound with a spell which I cannot resist before the object in whose company I am.
>
> Sometimes I feel afraid when I think how desperately, how awfully wicked I am, while at others my heart is so hard, that I do not even deplore my sins.

It ought now to be my greatest wish, that before this time comes round again, I shall have grown in grace and in the knowledge of Jesus Christ, but alas! There is one other wish in my heart which I fear is far greater. Oh! How I long that it may please God to grant me *that* wish! *That* desire!

Tragically for Margaret, her greatest drama of unrequited love was about to engulf her. It would not only consume the rest of her twenties but also leave a wound in her heart and soul from which she would never entirely recover. So far, she had only cast herself in the role of lovelorn woman in her private dreams and fancies, where she could always comfort herself with the cliché that it was better to have loved and lost than never to have loved at all. The reality of her actual public humiliation was an experience for which there was no solace, and she carried an air of sadness with her that was clearly recognizable, even to complete strangers, for the rest of her life. Norman Riley, Head of Entomology at the Natural History Museum in London, remembered his first impression of her, in the summer of 1913, when she was fifty-one:

A summer afternoon at the Natural History Museum, July 1913 or thereabouts. 'A lady to see you, Sir: Miss Fountaine.' Having heard something of Miss Fountaine's exploits the announcement conjured up visions of a well worn battle-axe about to assault me. Instead I met a tall attractive, rather frail-looking, diffident but determined middle-aged woman. She was pale and looked tired, but the strongest impression she gave me was one of great sadness, a sadness that seemed to envelop her entirely.

Yet her irrepressible zest for life had not left her either, as Riley also wrote: 'it was not long, however, before I discovered that this veil of sadness could be penetrated by self-deprecating flashes of humour that quite transformed her'.[2]

Some time in the autumn of 1883, when she was twenty-one, Margaret heard Septimus Hewson singing in Norwich Cathedral Choir for the first time and was entranced. Music always inflamed Margaret's most passionate feelings, and the voice she encountered now was the 'very breath and soul of music'. Soon, to hear and see him again was all that mattered, and she quickly established a routine to ensure this could happen as often as possible, making the cathedral the focus of her sketching and painting.

Every day she walked the forty-five minutes it took from Eaton to the cathedral with one of her sisters and spent hour upon hour sketching and painting, one eye always open for Septimus, a lay chorister employed by the cathedral, who might have cause to pass by at any time. The cloisters were an especially promising spot from this point of view, as the choristers often practised in the adjoining rooms. On Sundays she even persuaded her sister Geraldine to accompany her to both morning and evening service, Mother being under the impression they had suddenly become very devout indeed.

She was only ever happy in the cathedral now, a place where she could 'dream away the long hours of those still, autumn afternoons' and be transported daily into a song-inspired reverie of love. By the following summer Margaret's swooning obsession with the cathedral had become cause for concern, and her mother persuaded her to spend a few weeks in Hunstanton, on the Norfolk coast. But the fresh sea air failed to clear Margaret's head, much less her heart, and she descended into a severe gloom instead, which may well have been depression. She describes to her diary how she felt trapped by a melancholia she was unable to escape from: 'in vain I strove to awaken from the deep slumber into which I had fallen; my brain was on fire, either burning with a slow, consuming heat, which destroyed my every thought of happiness, or else bursting into a bright raging flame, making me feel an excitement so intense as to be almost painful to endure'.

On her return to Norwich she simply resumed her routine of sketching and attending services at the cathedral, where the magical world of silence and music allowed her to live out her fantasy of love and fulfilment, and she could 'behold the face of him whose spirit alone [had] haunted me'. Afterwards she would stumble home enraptured. Occasionally she would bump into Gerry Bignold, which caused cringing embarrassment all round, but to her mother's eternal disappointment Margaret persisted in ignoring the perfect catch he might have been.

Meanwhile, her mother did not even know the true source of her daughter's obsession, and it seems none of her sisters betrayed her either, though the secret must have weighed heavily on them. Certainly Margaret felt guilty, not only for deceiving her mother but also for what she perceived as her personal hypocrisy. 'I felt it was all sin, from beginning to end – the long practiced schemes of deceit to hide from Mother my real motive for going there, as well as the continual gratification of that unholy love, carried on within the house of God.' Yet she could not desist, and though she did not burn Septimus's initials into her palm she slept with his photograph under her pillow – or, rather, under her mattress, since Geraldine had an annoying habit of pulling her pillow out from under her head each morning.

All of 1884 and 1885 were taken up by musings on Septimus, her diary entries now requiring hours to read, rather than minutes, and taking up several hundred pages. When she failed to spot him among the choristers, she tormented herself with awful reasons for his absence, picturing him mortally ill and all alone or in some horrible accident. Aunt Anne came to take her away to Québec Hall, outside Dereham, for a few weeks of country air, but that did even less good than her spell in Hunstanton. She was miserable and intolerably morbid, to such a degree that her uncle insisted she be packed off home again.

'I hated myself and I hated him,' she wrote in a fit of self-loathing, but she found it impossible to move out of the shadow of her inner life, especially after Septimus acknowledged her in the cloisters one day. Perversely, his friendly smile was interpreted as a slight on her, as she imagined he knew her feelings and was laughing in the face of her infatuation. His smile seemed mocking to her, yet she could not resist coming back for more, hot with fantasies of submitting to him physically: 'it would seem as though he came to me, and I would imagine that I felt his breath upon my forehead, as he leant over me, and spoke to me with his eyes'.

It must have been hard to miss two young ladies sketching in the cloisters day after day for several years, only natural to stop and look, even if convention forbade conversation. In fact, Margaret became such a feature that one of the vergers even kept a water jar for use with her paints, and it was only a matter of time before she was deliciously tormented by the presence of Septimus one day, whistling softly behind the pillars while he watched the sisters at their work. If only she could have plucked up the courage to speak to him! Alas, he was gone before she finally turned.

One day she spotted him walking with a young woman and was crushed by his perceived betrayal. 'Oh, Septimus! and you never told me that there was one other who you truly loved!' she cried to her diary. 'Ah! He never told me, but he never spoke to me, so how could he tell me?'

Reality only got a quick look in before she threw herself utterly into despair. By now she was well and truly beyond reason, even self-respect, as she admitted to her diary, and it was not unusual for her to hang around the streets beyond the cathedral gates in hope of spotting the object of her desire, though a glance in her direction was instantly perceived as mocking humiliation.

'No one else saw the worm beneath – the worm which fed like a poisonous canker upon my inner life – I deceived the world, and the world smiled upon me,' she wrote melodramatically in her diary. Aged twenty-four, she had now spent almost three years in the grip of her obsession with a man she had never spoken to. Yet she persuaded herself they shared a profound intimacy and that she 'knew and understood him better than any other man I had ever known'.

At last they spoke. But this time it was not his perceived arrogance that pained her – as with the smile a couple of years earlier – but his undeniable servility. In the absence of the verger, she had plucked up the courage to ask him for her usual glass of water for the painting, and his alacrity in getting it offended her. He had done no more than was expected of him, yet that was precisely what spoilt the occasion. '. . . I had without meaning it ordered as a servant the man who in my secret heart I had sought to think of as a lover.' The moment she had been awaiting for years was spoilt by the social chasm between them, and she was genuinely ashamed of herself, especially when she recalled the society wedding she had only just attended in London for her cousin Mary, who had married a lord, no less, while she was ready to stoop to the poverty and lowly position of a working man's wife! She gave him the cold shoulder the next time he tried to make polite conversation, and he no doubt concluded that this strange woman was best avoided.

'I wish I had a key or an index that would explain to me the meaning of this part in my life; I cannot understand it,' she wrote sadly. 'I am so tired, so weary, that I sometimes almost long for death . . .' She had no idea how or why this great obsession had taken hold of her, and no way of extricating herself either. She was completely alone with it, her sisters long since bored with the subject of Septimus, and her mother had never been taken into her confidence. 'Oh! It is so hard to bear! The only man on earth who has the power to touch or move me is one whose society my own best judgement, beside many other obstacles, commands me not to seek. The dark barrier of rank and position has placed him far, far beneath my reach, and so I may not go to him even if he calls me.'

There was never any danger he would have called her, but Margaret's incorrigible persistence led her ever closer to disaster. She forced Septimus to acknowledge her once more by writing to him before leaving on a four-month visit to Winchester, thus ensuring her holiday with Geraldine was spiced by secrecy and furtive visits to the post office, in case of a reply. At last a reply did come, his letter still in her diary today, a much-read treasure, though its formality was far from what Margaret had wished for. 'I thank you for your kindly feeling towards me,' he wrote politely. 'We are having very beautiful weather here and I hope you are enjoying the same pleasure in the South,' he ended, which sent Margaret into a fury of disappointment for its lack of passion.

A year later her folly reached new heights when she wrote to him again, this time driven to action because she had heard a rumour that he was engaged.

Dear Mr Hewson, Having heard of your approaching marriage, I hope you will allow me to send you this little breast pin as a wedding present, if it is only to show you that you have my most sincere wishes for your future welfare.

If I am making a mistake, having been misinformed, will you please excuse the error, and I should like you to accept my present all the same, which I hope you will wear sometime when perhaps for the passing moment, you may give a lingering thought of pity for one 'who loved, not wisely – but well, ah, but too well'.

I trust it will reach you safely, but I neither wish or expect to receive any answer.

She was duly punished by receiving not even a thank-you note.

At twenty-six Margaret continued to be trapped in her pointless routine of sketching, church services and a bickering home life, though there was much to enjoy among the tedium and loneliness. Highlights were trips to

London's theatreland and long visits to Washingborough Manor and the Norfolk coast, as well as energetic walks with her pet goats, which she liked to take out on leads while the dogs roamed free. On a good day, when the sun was shining and the lanes were alive with birdsong, life did not seem so bad.

'Am I right in thinking that I stand on the borders of a happy future?' she could write in the spring of 1888, ending her annual write-up. 'Is it possible that I shall yet after all these years of exile be the wife of Septimus Hewson at last? Ah! Maybe it is but a false hope, never to be realised. Then there is that other life, when hardened and embittered, I shall find myself a homeless wanderer – unloving and unloved – destined to live as a stranger among strangers, and to die a stranger in a strange land.'

Her words were prophetic, though her fate was not going to be as loveless or embittered as she imagined a life without Septimus might be. In fact, she was already able to envisage another, more positive, life story for herself, which would also prove an accurate forecast. She understood that women could lose themselves in their role as wives and mothers, failing to achieve what their own potential might offer. 'All women can marry, and live only in the love of their husbands,' she wrote. 'Might I not weary of that phase of existence so common to all. And gaze with restless yearning eyes upon the dim visions of that strange dream: life I have now more than made up my mind, that it will be my lot to lead.'

She had cast herself as wandering painter, the most realistic role so far, since she was already beginning to sell her cathedral sketches and watercolours. She would be an artist – unconventional and earning her own money. It was a much better dream than the one about Septimus, which was about to engulf her in a full-blown nightmare.

✸ 3 ✸

THE SECRET PASSION

ARGARET'S INDEPENDENT VISION of herself was strengthened over the coming year when it became apparent that Septimus had taken to drink. Mortified to witness him arriving intoxicated at a private garden party one day, she was truly shamed when he refused to sing until supplied with more beer. Her love had become the object of gossip and ridicule, and she was disgusted enough to make a serious effort to forget him. From now on, she promised herself, she would seek 'a life of constant change, of travel and of incident, of new faces and fresh scenes' to blot out his memory.

Poor Septimus. He had neither asked for nor encouraged Margaret's devotion. The role she had given him was entirely to her own design, right down to the thoughts and feelings he was deemed to have, and gave no thought at all to the real man, who must have found life in Norwich very lonely. His beautiful singing voice had given him the chance to earn a living, but he was far away from his native Limerick, in a society that was very cold compared to the Irish life he had left behind, where everyone was in and out of each other's houses and nobody was too good to speak to. Cut off from his family except for the occasional trip home, it was only natural that he would spend most of his free time at the pub, especially if there was music and singing to be done.

Sadly, Margaret's good intentions disintegrated when Septimus stopped to chat with her at the cathedral one day, and not even an heir to £30,000, whom Mama had found for her, could bring her to her senses. On another occasion Septimus even held her hand and thanked her for the precious breast pin. Margaret was elated, though not so much as to believe he really did write the letter of thanks he claimed to have sent. The important thing was that he was not engaged, nor ever had been, and poor mother was written off as 'match-making Mamma'.

The inescapable fact was, however, that Septimus had given himself up to the bottle. Increasingly he failed to turn up for his singing duties, and one day he even fell out of the pub door straight into Margaret's arms, which made for a very awkward walk to service indeed. It was madness to throw away her chances for this sorry man, and Margaret became more steadfast in her plan to earn enough money to stay away from Norwich. She had already spent time sketching the cathedrals of Ely and Rochester, and now she decided to go further afield, to Chester and Liverpool.

Each lodging away from home required at least two references and time-consuming arrangements, but Margaret enjoyed discovering new places on her own and especially the chance to observe other people's way of life. In Ely she had adored the Crosby family's children and felt her own childlessness deeply for the first time. In Rochester her unmarried lady hosts had sent shivers down her spine at the thought of 'perpetual spinsterhood', while in Chester she was deeply moved by the happy marriage her hosts seemed to enjoy. No matter that they only had one apparently dim-witted, servant. Margaret was getting privileged glimpses of a range of society she could never experience at home and getting excellent practice at her independent lifestyle.

'I certainly derive great pleasure from travelling,' she wrote, 'I liked the idea of knocking about the world, and getting used to the ways and customs of men.' But she flattered herself if she thought she was ready for independence. A letter from her sister Geraldine telling her Septimus was to leave Norwich instantly dissolved her conviction to follow her own path, and she wept uncontrollably into her host's maternal bosom. Mrs Henderson was everything her mother was not: warm and unquestioningly affectionate. 'I know you have received a letter that disturbed you, dear,' she said soothingly, but never pried into Margaret's obvious grief.

Back in Norwich, her mother had come to need a glass of wine before the 'fatigues' of morning service with her daughters and had all but given up on getting any sense out of her secretive eldest. Margaret, meanwhile, wrote a desperate letter to Septimus:

Dear Mr Hewson, I hear you are leaving Norwich. Please write to me by return, and tell me if this is true. I know you have scarcely ever answered my letters, but you must answer this one.

Perhaps you do not know how much I really care for you . . .

Do please let me keep up your acquaintance even if you really are going, there is nothing in the world I would not do for you at any time, for I shall never care for anyone, but you, as long as I live.[1]

Her letter went unanswered and Margaret forced herself to attend her love's final performance at the cathedral. He avoided eye-contact, but the burning gaze upon him must have been inescapable as Margaret sat tormenting herself with regret and shame. She had thrown away six years of her life for a man sacked from his job for drunkenness.

'And is the dream of nearly six long years to end thus? Is this the last chapter in the story of my life? Oh! How sad and meaningless has it been throughout – how sad and meaningless is the ending now.' She stumbled home blinded by tears, but worse was to follow. Not only did Septimus leave without so much as a goodbye for Margaret or anyone else, he also absconded in the night, leaving a paying audience without a performer and creditors without their money. Her love had become a common criminal, and Margaret was profoundly shocked. She took to her bed and her diary and became physically ill from the torment raging inside her. She had lost her life's purpose.

'For six long years it had woven itself into my every thought,' she mourned, 'actuating my every action, it had been the dream of my life to marry Septimus Hewson – my one and only hope. What else had I lived for? What else had I longed for? What else had I prayed for? If I went away it was only for the sake of the moment when I should return! God only knew how I had loved that man! God only knew how I loved him still,' she confessed.

Her incorrigibly romantic nature yearned to share his burden with him, even now. Yet sometimes, for brief moments, she was able to see her dream for the obsession it was. She admitted to her diary that it had poisoned her life and barred her from everything that was wholesome and desirable, yet she was powerless to leave it behind her. 'Why then did I not want that it was removed, rejoice at the release, instead of longing for it to come back again?' she wrote. 'I don't know what to say! I was an enigma to myself.'

The opportunity to move on was missed. Instead, she decided to send Septimus five pounds of her own money to help with his debts, having secured an address in Ireland from someone at the cathedral. It meant no more travelling for her for the time being, and the unwelcome thought forced itself upon her that he would more than likely pocket the money without so much as a thank you, much less a letter in return.

But a letter did arrive. What is more, it arrived on 16 May, her twenty-seventh birthday, and she was agog with delight. He thanked her for her generous gift of money – the equivalent of several months of his salary at Norwich Cathedral – and promised to write a longer letter soon; and, though it never came, his short communication made Margaret's spirit blossom. Like the desert after rain, her dream revived into a myriad of colourful visions in which she imagined herself his wife in Limerick, picturing 'the quiet routine of daily life'.

Her devotion to Septimus burnt more fiercely than ever, and his failure to write again was an intolerable torment. She became restless and dissatisfied, going for long walks with her goats and dogs, but there was no escaping the searing disappointment. God had not answered her most desperate prayers and she began to doubt her faith, becoming increasingly morbid. If not even God would hear her cries, what was the point in living? News of her beloved Uncle Edward's death threw additional gloom over the whole family, and Margaret sincerely wished she could join him in the grave. One of her father's brothers, Edward Fountaine had often had his fatherless nieces to stay with him at Easton, west of Norwich, and the bereavement was a deep blow for all of them.

But God or the fates did have a caring hand in the girls' lives, even if Margaret doubted it for the time being, for a letter arrived announcing that Uncle Edward had left his entire fortune to the six Fountaine nieces and one of their cousins. By the terms of his will, his money was to be held in trust for their benefit, providing each of them with an independent income for life. It was news that struck like a 'thunderbolt among us', wrote Margaret, and the realization soon dawned that Uncle Edward had given her the freedom to make her own way in life, free to leave Norwich on sketching trips whenever she liked. It was only small comfort at first, since she was feeling so extremely depressed, but she tried to divert herself with singing lessons from a handsome sub-organist from the cathedral. Sadly, his 'lovely face' did nothing for her, and she felt frustrated at her perceived inability to enter into the spirit of her beloved music. Years of unfulfilled yearning had left her emotionally numb and her failure to respond even to music increased her despondency enormously.

Sir John Lawes, her Aunt Caroline's husband and sole executor of Uncle Edward's will, came to visit and carry out the necessary paperwork. He was businesslike but kind, and the sisters were amazed to find he had no desire to side with Mama and control the way they spent their money. They could do whatever they liked, he informed them – travel the world or buy fancy dresses: 'Only don't come and tell me how you spend it, that's all!' he announced to disbelief all round.

'We thought you said £20,000, Uncle Lawes,' they gasped.

'Oh, yes,' came the brisk reply, 'but it was impossible to tell within a few thousand till I looked into it.' In fact, the capital was a stunning £30,086 10s. 9d., fifteen times more than their father had left.

He gave them an initial cheque for £60 – the equivalent of a grammar-school teacher's annual salary at the time – to be divided equally among them, and left for London. A millionaire who had invested his brother-in-law's money well, he was far too busy to get involved in these young women's lives beyond administering their allowances.[2]

Margaret decided to head north again, returning to the homely welcome of Mrs Henderson's house in Chester, which was also a convenient base for experimental trips alone. The first was to Liverpool, where it thrilled her to move among the heaving crowds on the banks of the Mersey, though the city also gave her a quick lesson in travel basics when she left her purse unattended while sketching in the cathedral. But the big adventure was a journey to Dublin and the homeland of her ideal.

'There are some things in life which make an impression upon us, which we feel will never quite be obliterated,' she wrote of her first rail journey along the North Wales coast. The sight of the Welsh mountains rearing up on one side and the vastness of the blue seas on the other was unforgettable, all the sweeter for bringing her ever closer to Holyhead, and the steamboat to Ireland. 'Ireland, the land that I so often visited in my dreams, the native country of the only man in my whole life I had ever known what it was to truly love.'

Margaret could barely contain herself. 'I can see that scene now,' she recorded, 'the midnight stars in the dark sky above, and the red harbour lights upon the dark waters below. But it was cold and chilly, and I was not sorry when the signal of approach was heard, and a red light larger and brighter than any of the others was seen shooting rapidly along, coming towards the pier. Everyone said it was "the boat" and everyone was right.'

She was intrigued by the ragged poverty of some of those leaving the boat and amazed at the huge number of mail sacks arriving on men's shoulders. As soon as they were allowed to embark, Margaret retired to her cabin, where sleep evaded her. She was taut with anticipation, and there were too many strange noises. The boiler needed coal, which seemed to take for ever to load, and then there was the endless racket of new passenger arrivals and the noisy scrum for berths. At last she must have fallen into an exhausted sleep, and the boat made its journey, for her next waking moment was filled with the consciousness of arrival. She lay in her narrow bunk savouring the moment:

I felt an intense pleasure in lying there, looking out of the little round cabin window . . . it brought such a sense of pleasure to me to feel that I had reached Ireland at last. And I shall never forget my first sight of that place, when later on I stood on deck and saw the green trees and the houses, and I longed to land that I might press the ground of that dear country beneath my feet. Oh! How silly and foolish we are sometimes, we grown up people with our full maturity of years, and all the undeveloped thoughts and dreams of childhood still there.

Margaret was only in Dublin for one day before returning on the next night ferry, but this one day was a flawless pleasure, a day when she could savour her dream and imagine that the warm winds from the west were coming straight from Limerick. She wished her spirit could travel back on those winds to meld with Septimus.

Her companion for this adventure was a lady she had joined at Anglesey, but Margaret spent most of her time exploring alone, only meeting Mrs Williams for shopping and lunch near O'Connell Bridge. She took horse-drawn trams to explore – from the great Phoenix Park to the north to St Patrick's Cathedral to the south. The most memorable part of the day, however, was a street market, the description of which could come straight from any developing country today:

> I call it a bazaar, but perhaps it might better be described by saying that it looked as though the shops had overflowed, and heaps of merchandise, principally in the form of old clothes, lay in the street, and also vegetables, by which the old Irish women were sitting nursing their babies, and singing wild Irish ditties, but what struck me as being most strange was that there were no customers, neither did the numerous sellers at all seem concerned at this rather unfortunate deficiency for the advancement of trade.

She was not sorry to leave behind the poverty and dirt she encountered, though it was hard to tear herself away from Ireland so soon. She had found Septimus's homeland both lovely and downtrodden and compared it to a beautiful girl fallen destitute and grovelling in the dust of 'violence and unconquered hate'. Nevertheless, she returned to Norwich with the hunger in her soul unsatisfied, her short visit to Dublin only giving her fresh scenes to brood over. 'The memory of his country was left written on my heart,' she wrote.

Autumn in Norwich was not all bad, though. Mother was absent for several months, which made for a much more relaxed atmosphere at home. 'If the absence of pain is pleasure, then indeed was the life I led then one of pleasure,' Margaret wrote grimly, though she also admitted to actual joy when she described her singing lessons. Music was, as always, her solace, and though she still felt unable to unlock sincere passion for it she could at least enjoy its language.

The year which had filled her heart with sorrow and her pockets with gold ended with a severe bout of influenza and renewed depression. She suffered feverish dreams haunted by Septimus and what might have been and was crushed by the realization she herself had thrown away the key to happiness. Her religious upbringing had taught her that pride is a sin, and the idea became deeply embedded in her psyche that she was damaged goods. Pride and arrogance had led her to believe she could manipulate fate and go against society's rules. Her punishment was the meaningless existence she led now, 'like a plant that neither germinates nor yet falls into decay'.

However, Margaret's indomitable drive revived in the spring, and she hatched a new plan. The irresistible thought had come into her mind that as a 'monied lady' she might yet prevail with the penniless Septimus. The role reversal amused her, and she hatched a plan to seek her man out one last time, inconvenient humility effortlessly suppressed once more. Her cousin Louie Curtois tried to talk some sense into her but failed dismally. Plain speaking was no doubt very 'improving', Margaret recorded in her diary, but she stubbornly refused to take any advice. Instead, she relied on another cousin to help find her a family to stay with in Dublin the next summer, and life seemed worth living again. The cherry trees shed blossom 'like summer snow', the dogs and goats gambolled on the sun-drenched lawns, and Margaret could think of nothing but the fact that she would gladly never set eyes on this bucolic loveliness again for the chance to make her life in Ireland.

✵4✵

MISSPENT YOUTH

ESPITE HER MOTHER'S best efforts to get Sir John to oppose the planned Irish visit, Margaret's will prevailed and anticipation was only slightly marred by a weak moment when she agreed that her sister Evelyn could accompany her. She had no desire for companions on her journey to destiny, but even Margaret could admit support was never a bad thing, especially if her true purpose came to nought.

The sisters were to stay on the estate of Lady Rowan Hamilton, on the southern outskirts of Dublin, and Margaret made discreet preparations to dispose of her affairs in Norwich, improve her wardrobe and even have her letter paper engraved with the family crest. She was not coming back, that much was clear, and when it came time to say goodbye Margaret felt strangely elated. All her senses were heightened, and she felt an extra-ordinary awareness of imminent happiness, much as pregnant women often describe: fulfilment was to be hers very soon, she believed, only in her case it was a phantom.

Margaret wasted no time initiating her campaign and sat down on her first day in Ireland to write to Septimus. No matter he had not responded to the newspaper clipping of her uncle's will she had sent last year. This time, in his own country, he would surely not ignore an invitation to renew their 'acquaintance'. Yet her letter was strangely brusque for someone trying to kindle romance:

> It is now more than a year since I last heard from you, but in the meantime Fortune has (quite unexpectedly) favoured me in other ways. I shall never really be happy without you – that I know – but no matter. It is something

to be well off and independent as I am now . . . So you see I shall soon have every reason to forget you.

She asks casually, 'Do you ever come up to Dublin? If you did happen to during the next few weeks, I could easily meet you there.'[1]

It was an altogether extraordinary letter. As a love letter it failed to convey any warmth of feeling whatsoever, and from the point of view of conventional behaviour at the time it was utterly outrageous. There was no legitimate reason for a lady of Margaret's position to be inviting a known petty thief to meet her socially. If anyone in England had had the faintest idea of Margaret's real intentions they would more than likely have had her certified and locked up for her own protection. Yet Margaret had no difficulty in ignoring the facts and pursuing her objective, and he at least had the decency to reply within a week. As with almost all her correspondence, his letter was neatly copied into her diary:

> My dear Miss Fountaine,
>
> I was more than delighted when I received your letter last evening. I thought you had quite forgotten me, as I wrote you after you had written to me last year and I had no answer. I would be very proud indeed to renew your acquaintance. I daresay you thought me very cool towards you when in Norwich, but to tell you the truth, I always had a great liking for you, though you may not have thought so from the way I behaved. Of course our positions in life were different, and I thought it better not to be seen much with you, as it would only make people talk, and perhaps get you into trouble, but now as you say you are independent, I should be delighted to see you, but am greatly afraid I cannot go to Dublin, as I have only just returned from my holiday and any spare cash I had is gone.

Margaret no doubt had no idea that a return train ticket from Limerick to Dublin cost the best part of a week's wages.

> I wish I was in a position to settle down and have a nice little home of my own, I know what I should do. But – God Willing – all will come right some day. I am very pleased indeed you have been so fortunate. I wish I were like you. I am so glad you are pleased with Ireland. I knew you would like it.

He suggests Margaret might like to see Ireland's beautiful West Coast and visit Limerick *en route* so they could meet in his own home town. He tries to assure her of his respectability, too, claiming he no longer touches alcohol and never 'walks with ladies'.

> I must finish now my dear. I must be off to service. Please excuse the dirty letter, as I was in a great hurry. Hoping you are quite well and happy, with love,
>
> I remain, yours ever,
> Septimus Hewson

Ten handwritten pages! No matter it arrived in a gaudy orange envelope, it was the longest and most personal communication Margaret had ever received from her ideal man. She read it again and again, feasting her eyes on her beloved's handwriting, concentrating on the good bits – like being a total abstainer now – and quickly moving on from her disbelief regarding no girlfriends or his supposed letter to her last year. She was in love, but she was not stupid. The only part that really jarred was his familiar turn of phrase towards the end. She did not feel they were quite at the stage where he could call her 'dear', even if she was prepared to ignore their different social positions. She decided to mull things over for a while before her next move but soon persuaded herself that Septimus's letter was God's answer to her prayers. To doubt his good intentions was to doubt God, and a reply was quickly posted to Limerick. She tried not to be too effusive – hardly her style beyond the privacy of her diary – yet assured him of her everlasting love and friendship which no barrier of class or money should ever impede. To prove it she even offered to pay for his ticket from Limerick, pressing him to come to her, rather than the other way around.

This time a reply arrived within a day of post and the tone was even more personal than before. He asks if he can call her by her first name in his next letter and assures her he would rather walk across Ireland to Dublin than miss seeing her even for just a few minutes. He complains that his uncle is keeping all his wages – no doubt for good reason – and also rather warily asks if Margaret's mother or anyone in her family knows she is writing to him, which of course they do not. He signs himself with a familiar 'Sep' and leaves no doubt in Margaret's mind that he loves her, too. Surely, Margaret thought, she stood at the Gates of Heaven now. Her object of desire was hers at last and Ireland the most beautiful country in the world.

Every letter brought Margaret's meeting with destiny closer until she finally threw all caution to the wind and decided to travel to Limerick alone. Septimus had made it clear he was unable to visit Dublin, and though Margaret was somewhat concerned that he had not returned the money for his fare she nevertheless booked herself into Cruises Hotel in Limerick and sent a message that he should meet her at the station. The sisters agreed to lie to their hosts about their true intentions, and it was arranged that Evelyn would visit Mrs Williams in Anglesey while Margaret was away.

'I had a very difficult game to play,' she wrote. 'I wondered if he would be for my coming to Limerick or no. But my nature is one that loves to scheme and plan, to control action, and subjugate events to the power of my will,' she added in a moment of clarity. But almost in the same sentence she also persuaded herself they were engaged now, deciding it was an understood thing between them, even though they had not actually ever discussed it. In fact, by the time she arrived in Limerick she was sincerely convinced they were to be married.

But disappointment was all Margaret's devotion ever yielded, and Septimus was not there to greet her at Limerick station. Instead of the open arms – or at least open smile – she had hoped for, she stood alone on the platform, strangers pressing past towards a place she did not know, feeling more vulnerable and terrified than ever in her life before. A porter helped find the luggage she had imagined Septimus carrying for her, and she sat on the hotel omnibus in a stupor of mortification.

'I do not think in the whole of my life I had ever felt so lonely and dispirited as I did now,' she wrote later.

Margaret had never set foot in a hotel and had no idea how to book into her room, much less where to find a meal. Cruises Hotel, which until the mid-1980s was the largest and most famous hotel in Limerick, was a mighty building on the town's central thoroughfare, full of men. William Thackeray stayed there in 1842, describing the street outside the hotel as being busy with idlers hanging around in every doorway and dandies parading alongside the clatter of carriages. 'After you get out of the Main

Street,' he wrote, 'the handsome part of town is at an end, and you suddenly find yourself in such a labyrinth of busy swarming poverty and
squalid commerce as never was seen,'[2] which was undoubtedly still the
case in 1890, when Margaret found herself being taken there. Even today
dereliction and poverty abound in Limerick, and it is easy to see why so
many of her inhabitants have left a place still known as 'stab city'.

What would Mother have said if she could have seen her daughter
now! Margaret could only shudder and tried to gather her thoughts over a
five-course dinner ordered to her room. She debated with herself whether
to go out for a walk or go to bed and cry into her pillow but decided instead
to take a book to the Public Reading Room, where she cut a lonely figure
by the window. She tormented herself with visions of Septimus drowned
in the Shannon, since she knew he had been on a river trip that day, but
then he turned up after all. He seemed angry that Margaret had not confirmed which train she was arriving on, but Margaret was just grateful she
had not given herself over to tears in bed. Now there was still time for a
stroll together and a chance to find out all about her beloved's home and
background. Every snippet of information was eagerly received and filed
in Margaret's fertile brain. He told her about his huge family: six brothers
and one sister, thirty nephews and nieces, and numerous aunts, uncles and
cousins. Enough to make a congregation on their own, he joked.

Margaret was most interested to know about her love's employment
now and soon discovered he was working in his uncle Massey's coach-
making factory on Roche's Street. He was strangely touchy on the subject,
though, no doubt eager to avoid precise details. By the time they reached
Cruises Hotel again it was nearing ten in the evening, but Septimus
surprised Margaret by suddenly deciding he wanted to show her some
'Limerick life'. Exhausted though she was, she could not refuse him now,
and so they set off for Irish Town, the city's notorious slum, which is
hardly a picture now but must have been terrifying then.

Crowds of unwashed men and women surged along the darkened
streets, and Margaret gripped Septimus's arm tighter as they neared a
brawling crowd outside a tavern.

'Oh! Here's a row going on,' he said, dragging her towards the jeering
multitude.

He and his brother liked nothing better than to watch an Irish fight, he told her, while Margaret was appalled to see the row was between a man and his wife. She almost fell when the mass of bodies surged against them, and even Septimus seemed to realize this was no place for a lady.

'What did you think of that?' he asked, almost intoxicated by the violence, but Margaret could only whisper she found it dreadful, especially to see a woman being beaten by her drunken husband.

'That happens every night of the week in these parts,' he informed her, and she could only marvel at the horror of it. It was almost as if he was trying to warn her off.

Septimus had not breathed a word of love to her, much less kissed her, but she consoled herself with the thought that it was only natural reserve and fell into bed. Every fibre of her being was exhausted, and yet she was eternally happy to have once more set eyes on her beloved, who was even better-looking than she remembered him.

The following morning it was pouring with rain, and Margaret hardly dared hope that Septimus would turn up for her on such a day. But he did, and they walked out into the foul weather without raincoats or umbrellas, dashing towards St Mary's Cathedral, where he managed to secure a key for the tower. The view was not much considering the weather, but Margaret managed to slip in a question about Septimus's sister, which was much more interesting to her anyway.

'She is very good, you know, very religious. All my people are. They are all good, except me – I'm the bad one!' he sighed without elaborating, and Margaret wished she could think of something cheering to say.

The rain continued all day and the damp atmosphere depressed Margaret, not least because Septimus had to leave her on her own for the rest of the day. She was also irritated to find people treated her with less respect than she was used to, though it never seems to have crossed her mind that her association with Septimus might have had something to do with it. However, her mood lifted in the evening, when she was treated to a private concert of singing at Septimus's brother's house, where she could sit dreaming of how lovely it would be to live in a little house like this one, Septimus at her side while she played the piano and he sang. He called her 'Miss Fountaine' in front of his family, which she found upsetting, but he assured her he would always call her 'Margaret' in private. It did seem odd, though, that he had not mentioned their engagement to his brother, when she so wished to be treated on the level and not with the deference she had found so lacking from others in Limerick; even odder that his parents should be 'on holiday' just when she was coming to visit for the first time. Alas, Margaret's alarm bell was firmly switched off.

The following day she was given the even greater honour of a day trip by pony cart with the dreaded uncle and his wife, who turned out to be as attentive and kind as Margaret could have wished for. Uncle Massey proudly regaled her with his knowledge of the local landowners and where they all lived, and Margaret could not help thinking that, in other circumstances, she would have thought nothing of visiting the high-born inhabitants of those grand houses. Yet she was happy as she was, trying out a different station in life, so to speak, and getting ever closer to realizing her dream of becoming plain Mrs Hewson of Limerick.

The reality of life in the Hewson family came as something of a shock, however, when she found herself being invited to his uncle's tiny flat above his workshop. Even her lodgings in England's cathedral towns had not prepared her for the humble and informal surroundings she found herself in now.

'He knew what my position in life was,' she wrote, 'so he knew to a certain extent what I must be feeling like, but I don't think he quite understood the full extent of the shock it gave me, to know that I was about to spend a friendly evening in the dwelling house over a shop!' The gentility of South Acre was indeed a distant memory. 'I simply hate myself for the thoughts that came into my mind,' she admonished herself, but no amount of kindness could hide the social gulf between them, though by the second evening she had almost persuaded herself it was the most normal thing in the world to stroll through a shop to the flat upstairs.

By the third evening the weather had lifted sufficiently for a moonlit walk along the banks of the Shannon, where Septimus finally drew Margaret closer and closer until, at last, he pressed his lips on hers for the first time. It was a long, long kiss, and her emotions reeled at the thought she had waited seven years for this moment, this kiss.

'That's the first kiss I have ever had,' she confessed, and then felt rather silly, considering she was twenty-eight.

More kisses followed, and all the years of sorrow and yearning disappeared into a world of darkness she hoped never to encounter again.

'That's worth waiting seven years for!' she could not help herself admitting.

'Seven years!' he repeated. 'Is it as long as that? Why didn't you tell me?'

'How could I tell you when I never spoke to you?' came the simple reply, and we can only guess at the shock Septimus must have felt to know this strange woman had been in love with him for all that time, though her confession was not too shocking to stop him kissing her many more times that night, and it was past midnight before an ecstatic Margaret swept past raised eyebrows at the hotel.

The roller-coaster of emotion Margaret found herself on took a dip the very next day, though, when she was bemused to find Septimus cool and preoccupied. Much worse, she thought she could smell alcohol on his breath, but the thought was too horrible to contemplate. She quickly decided it must be impossible. The strain was not eased, either, by Margaret pressing Septimus to correct his entry in her birthday book. She forced herself not to look over his shoulder during the tortuously long time it took for him to make his corrections, but she was incapable of not pointing out yet another error.

'Oh', he said, 'let me write it again underneath', and Margaret inwardly winced at the disorder he made of her entry system.

She let him flick through the rest of the book to see who else was in there. He thought he recognized an ex-colleague's name from Norwich Cathedral, and this time Margaret was sensitive enough not to point out that it actually said 'Countess Kersenbrock' and, furthermore, she was not in the habit of entering vergers' names in her private birthday book! But she told her diary.

The tension between them never quite went away, and Margaret found their last evening especially awkward. She had remained 'Miss Fountaine' to the Hewsons, even though by this time Septimus and she had exchanged the most personal details about each other. They had discussed her inheritance as well as his claim to be in line for the childless Uncle Massey's coach-making factory, and they had also shared many more intimate kisses. Septimus had even encouraged her to come clean with her mother. 'I'm sure your mother would like me,' he had said, conveniently forgetting his name was dirt in Norwich. Yet nothing was publicly mentioned about their engagement.

At least their parting was how she had imagined it ought to be. Septimus arrived early to escort her to the station, and she adored the way he took charge of her travel arrangements. 'How I loved the way he took care of me,' she wrote, 'and how I longed for the time when I should have him always to look up to and lean upon through life.'

Nothing she had seen or heard in Limerick had changed her conviction that Septimus was the man for her. One last squeeze of the hand through the carriage window, and she was off. 'All I thought was that I had never seen his eyes look so beautiful before, and we watched each other, till the crowd closed around him, and he was lost to my sight.' Septimus had been unable to disabuse his ardent lover face to face and sent her on her way believing her dream was coming true and they would one day be together for ever more.

'I've seen one magpie sitting just in front of your window several times lately' was the frosty reception she got back at her lodgings outside Dublin. 'You may depend upon it, it means trouble ahead!' her landladies (two sisters) pronounced rather unnecessarily, but they were furious to have been duped and wasted no time threatening Margaret and Evelyn with sending news to their mother, which, thankfully, they did not.

However, the big adventure was over now, and all Margaret had to look forward to was the terrifying prospect of coming clean with her mother. She tried to persuade herself it was nothing to worry about. 'Why need I fear?' she wrote. 'Only a few more struggles, a few more hours and days of suspense and agony, I thought, and then, and then I would be his for ever. And he would come for me and take me home with him, back to his own beautiful country!'

But the reality of facing her mother was hugely daunting. 'My Dear Septimus,' she wrote plaintively, 'I feel so far away from you now.'

Almost the whole family was gathered in Ilkley, below the Yorkshire Moors, where Mother had rented a house for the summer, so there was little chance to see her alone. By the second evening, though, Margaret plucked up the courage to invite her mother for a walk on the moors. The sky was suitably wild. A summer storm seemed to be nearing and the wind blew strong from the west. Margaret's heart thumped, not only from trudging up to the high ground, but also at the thought of the thunderclap she herself was about to impart on her poor mother.

As luck would have it, her mother turned the conversation in the right direction herself.

'Of course, some people think the great thing is to be married,' she said.

'I do,' Margaret quickly countered, and before she knew it she had admitted she was engaged to be married as they spoke.

'You really are, Margaret!' her astonished mother said simply. 'Well, I'm very pleased to hear it.'

'Wait till you hear who it's to,' her daughter rasped with a dry throat.

'I suppose it's someone you met in Ireland?' her mother asked, assuming she must have met someone at a garden party at Lady Hamilton's.

'No, not at Mrs Rowan Hamilton's garden party,' Margaret sighed. 'It's someone I've known for years.'

'I can't think who it can be,' said her mother, as the torment continued. 'Do make haste and tell me!'

'It's nothing you will be glad to hear,' whispered Margaret. 'It's Mr Hewson. I'm engaged to Mr Hewson, the man who used to sing in Norwich Cathedral.'

'Mr Hewson,' came the slow reply, as her mother tried to take it in. 'But he's not the least in the same position of life as you are!' came the shocked reply. 'But you can't marry him,' she said after a moment's thought, repeating his low status and reminding Margaret he had left Norwich under a cloud. 'Did you not know he did?' she asked incredulously. 'But where have you seen him in Ireland?' came the most dreaded question of all. 'I don't understand any of it.'

Now Margaret's nerves snapped, and she collapsed in floods of tears. She would always love Septimus no matter what, she sobbed into her mother's arms, who wisely said no more on the subject.

Margaret was amazed at how easily she had passed the first hurdle of confession and felt humbled by her mother's obvious efforts to show understanding and forgiveness. She made nothing of Margaret's betrayal of trust and even seemed to be trying to see things from her daughter's point of view. For Margaret's sake, her mother tried to imagine that Septimus was indeed a trustworthy character, and she was deeply ashamed to think how she had talked her mother down as a foul-tempered tyrant in front of Septimus.

Both Sir John and her mother were persuaded against their better judgement to support Margaret in her choice of husband, not least by her sincerity and assurances that she fully understood the social implications of her actions. It was more than Margaret could have hoped for in her wildest dreams, so she was quite unprepared for the obstacle to happiness which now transpired: silence from Limerick.

By the time the family was installed back in Norwich six weeks had passed without a single letter from Septimus, even though he had received many from Margaret and even one from her mother and another from Sir John. All went unanswered, and Margaret was at a total loss for an explanation. She was wracked with grief and disappointment to discover the dream she had cherished for the past seven years seemed to be slipping through her fingers at the very last moment, just when she least expected it.

After the best part of two months she could stand it no longer. On the verge of complete mental breakdown, she made her final attempt to gain an explanation by writing to Uncle Massey Hewson. Her letter was a cry from the heart and received an immediate answer from his wife:

My dear Miss Fountaine,

I am extremely sorry to hear you have been treated so badly by our nephew Septimus. I told him the contents of your letter, and he has promised me to write this evening and explain, but I can gather that he has no idea he ever entered into any engagement – how indeed could he, for he is totally without means.

The letter went on to explain in detail how Septimus had squandered every opportunity given to him after leaving Norwich and had only been taken on temporarily – and reluctantly – by his uncle this past summer to give him a final chance to get on the right path and prove his character.

Dear Miss Fountaine, you need not wonder at his not replying to your letters for when in Norwich and his Mother (as we thought) dying, both his sister-in-law and I wrote begging him to write even a line to ease her mind about him and he never did! Although her youngest and pet. I think the very best thing you can do, is banish all thought of him from your mind. He is not in any way worthy of you, and I scarcely think him capable of caring much for anyone but *himself*.

Mrs Hewson ended her letter with an appeal to Margaret to forget about Septimus for ever and an offer of deepest sympathy for her distress.

The final humiliation was having to write to Sir John Lawes, but he was as kind as ever – no doubt relieved, too – though not nearly as much as the Fountaine sisters when they found he had also sent them a cheque for £300. The fear had been that Margaret's misadventure would cost them all and that Sir John would cut them off.

'Reader, whoever you may be, may you never know what it is to crave for the pity of one human heart, and to crave for it in vain,' wrote Margaret in an unusual aside, noting that her entry for 1890 takes nine hours and thirty-nine minutes to read. It was the year she felt her heart had died, and only her indomitable spirit carried her forward.

The best part of Margaret's youth had been consumed by an obsession which almost destroyed her, but the money her uncle left her gave her a unique opportunity to escape the limits society had set. In time the same intelligence, resourcefulness and courage that had brought her shame and humiliation would be the foundation for an extraordinarily productive yet unconventional life.

Margaret aged thirty-two, from the frontispiece to her diary of 1895

ADVENTURE
1891–1900

✣ 5 ✣

FLIGHT TO THE CONTINENT

A FTER THE IRISH disaster, life in Norwich could never be the same again. Every corner reminded her of the vision of the future she had lost, and the bereavement was as real as for any physical death. She struggled to keep bitterness at bay, but the burden of her thoughts and feelings often threatened to crush her. She needed to get away, where she might 'forget sometimes', forget the past and not worry about the future which yawned before her like a black chasm.

Margaret's youngest sister Florence had the answer: they would take up Thomas Cook's invitation to become tourists and explore the Continent. They chose a round-trip ticket to Switzerland, via Belgium and France, and set about planning the adventure. Cook's guidebooks were the obvious source, and they did not mince words. The company's guide for travelling ladies advised:

> In choosing each item of travelling costume, care should be taken to avoid everything *outré* or conspicuous. It will be a good day for Englishwomen when, instead of the remark 'So English' being applied by foreigners to the most awkward and unsuitably-dressed lady they may meet, it will be to the best and most appropriately attired.

Margaret was sure she could never be accused of bad taste! Most important of all was to be in possession of the distinctive green ticket-holder with which all Cook's travellers were issued, not only guaranteeing passage on the relevant boat or diligence (horse-drawn carriage) but entitling the bearer to the free services of Cook's agents, stationed at every major port and railway station in Europe. 'I would never undertake a journey without these passports to civility,' wrote the author of the ladies' guide. 'To all ladies travelling *alone*, I consider this system absolutely necessary.'

Of course, no amount of advice can replace personal experience, as the sisters soon found out. At a stop-over in Brussels they were so eager to explore that they completely forgot to take note of the station, much less the route needed to retrace their steps. Which station had they arrived at? The Gare du Nord or the Gare de Luxembourg? By the time they reached the right one their onward train had left. No matter, they took the next departing train to Namur instead and pushed on south early the next morning.

In Strasbourg they paid so handsomely for lunch at the Hotel National that they vowed never to eat there again, while in Berne they made the mistake of arriving for the annual carnival. Not a room was to be found anywhere, but Margaret was entranced by the crowds of Swiss country folk in their holiday costumes. The sisters joined the parades and happily paid a fortune to sleep in a hotel wash-house for the night. How lovely was the August moon above glittering Berne, thought Margaret; how beautiful the hotel porter, thought Florence. Nevertheless, they tore themselves away next morning, for Mademoiselle Lassalle was expecting them in Geneva, where they were booked into her boarding-house for the duration of August and September.

'Switzerland, the land of wild loveliness, extolled by poets and over-run by tourists!' wrote Margaret in 1891. But the Alpine beauty all around had her hooked just the same. The cobalt skies and glistening peaks lifted Margaret's spirit like nothing else before, and she suddenly realized how beautiful the world could be and how little of it she had seen. She took long rides along the shores of Lake Geneva in the company of a smart young groom called Jean and found 'the gap' in her life filling up fast. 'I might never forget the love that I had lost, but other loves and other pleasures were fast entering into my life, to stand between me and that past – so sad and yet so fondly prized.'

This first journey abroad was also an opportunity to rediscover the delights of butterfly-catching – a childhood pastime which now became an all-absorbing pleasure. A young schoolgirl spending her summer learning French was Margaret's willing companion, and together they spent many happy hours dashing about in the scorching sunshine. The girl brought back laughter and games, and Margaret was thrilled to catch butterflies she had only known as illustrations in her childhood books. 'I little thought years ago, when I used to look with covetous eyes at the plates representing the scarce Swallowtail or the Camberwell Beauty, that in after years I should see both these butterflies in a valley in Switzerland . . . the love of natural history was strongly implanted in me then. I was a born naturalist, though all these years, for the want of anything to excite it, it had lain dormant within me.'[1]

If Margaret's exile from England – as she herself already thought of it – was to be in such places as the Swiss mountains, life was not going to be all bad. 'If it were to be in scenes such as these, I thought, that my wandering years of exile should be passed, I could not but feel in my heart a yearning adoration for this new world in which I found myself.'

The attentions of a Dr Ross were also a balm to Margaret's wounded pride, but she regretfully found her heart felt very little beyond the pleasure of letting him down when it came to say goodbye. She had enjoyed his rowing lessons on the lake, but he was from Norwich, of all places, and she was determined he would not know her there. His departure left her restless, though. Haunting memories crept out of the shadows to touch her 'with their cold fingers', and she felt a pressing need to move on; '. . . how could I feel sorrow at leaving any place when I could look back upon the moment that I left the place I had been told "some day" should be my home?'

So off they went to Dijon, where the summer lasted a little longer and the autumn cold had not yet reached, and then on to sinful Paris, where the bird market was busy within sight of Notre Dame, even on a Sunday, Margaret noted disapprovingly. The sisters enjoyed the hustle and bustle of the French capital and admired its monuments, especially the Eiffel Tower. But Margaret was not one for city sight-seeing, especially not museums. Of the Louvre she wrote, 'Of course we went to the Louvre, but alas works of art are lost, or nearly so upon me.' She was equally baffled by Wagner's opera *Lohengrin*, though she knew she ought to have enjoyed it, but the language barrier spoilt it for her.

Back in England, she felt nothing but disdain for her own country. 'Why,' she questioned her diary, 'when life can be made so joyous and happy, do the English seem to convert it into a thing so dull and depressing?' Her one desire now was to leave England again. 'I was not living then, I was merely existing. But I had learnt that life could be worth living, and that was enough.' Her first journey abroad had taught her to enjoy life in a new way. Far away from the grey skies and dreary society of England she could be free and enjoy her latest sport: tormenting men. 'I believe it is a terrible pain to a man to love a woman who scorns him, after having encouraged his affections for a time, and it was the pleasure of inflicting that pain that my soul was craving for. I could do it – I had the power. I had learnt it now at last. Neither do I believe that I am the only woman who has ever known her power, till she is no longer on the verge of youth.'

She spent the long dark months of winter brooding by the fireside, bored and dissatisfied with her old pursuits of walking and music and endlessly planning her next transformation from 'miserable, brooding woman' to gay, carefree tourist. She longed for the foreign life, 'the ways and customs of foreigners, and above all the foreign climate; the sunny skies and soft warm air'. The winter was not even over before she had arranged to escape the English fogs once more, this time with her favourite cousins, Louie and Edith Curtois, who would join her on a round trip to Italy via the south of France.

What a joy to introduce them to Paris! The city was hers, and she felt she knew the place and owned its pleasures. Secretly she also enjoyed listening to Edith's broken French, which invariably produced replies in English. Further south, her spirit soared at the sight of fruit trees already in blossom near Avignon, and the biting winds of Norfolk were a distant memory once they reached the purple seas of the Côte d'Azur. But Margaret was not quite the expert traveller yet. In her excitement she had forgotten the lesson of Berne, and the ladies arrived in Nice in the middle of the February carnival. Prices for the few remaining rooms were exorbitant, but there was nothing to be done but pay.

Sometimes anticipation is sweeter than arrival, and that was certainly the case for Margaret with the Cote d'Azur. Her image of the lovely Mediterranean seas did not fit with the tourist traps of Monte Carlo, Nice and Cannes, and she did not relish the pranks of carnival season either. She wrote in disgust, 'La Fête de Confitures was on the day following, and I can only say of it, that to have walked out minus an umbrella on that occasion would have been no less inconvenient than to have made a similar omission during a severe and prolonged hailstorm. "*Une Anglaise!*" would be the unanimous cry from each carriage as it drove by, and down would come a relentless shower of pellets.'

Before the cousins knew where they were Margaret had decided to travel onwards without them. They had quickly found they had very different interests anyway, Louie and Edith wanting to visit every sight recommended in their guidebook, while Margaret just wanted to live a little after the endless years of her dreary youth. 'The idea of some people in these wonderful days of travel is to visit place after place in rapid succession, to see all there is to be seen, to take everything at a rush, to make themselves thoroughly overtired and to enjoy nothing!' she wrote rather grumpily in her diary.

Margaret was a born solo traveller, temperamentally unsuited to group decision-making and hanging around for others to catch up. Rather, she enjoyed being a 'stranger in a strange land' and could think of nothing more pleasant than to drink in the wide world and the experiences it had to offer. She set off along the coast to Italy, only stopping to change trains in Genoa and Rome, before arriving in Naples bathed in the early evening glow of a fading sun. 'See Naples and die!' the saying went, and Margaret set off without a backward glance.

Nothing she had ever seen was as beautiful as the Bay of Naples, 'plunged in sun and wickedness, yet fairer than words can tell'. She climbed the slopes of San Martino with a Scotsman she had met at her boarding-house and flirted with him mercilessly, allowing him to pay for everything before a chaste goodbye that same evening. No sooner had he left than he was replaced by a Signor Scafidi, who made preposterously romantic gestures which Margaret had no hesitation in rebuffing with fits of frivolous laughter. It was good to be light-hearted, but when her new friend got too close she recoiled. Her emotional scars were not yet tough enough to withstand too much pressure. The memory of Irish kisses was too fresh, and the Italian was astonished to find his romantic appeals had the very opposite effect to the one desired, sending Margaret into a trough of morbid self-loathing. Not for long, though. There was far too much to see and do, and when the Curtois cousins finally caught up with her Margaret did nothing to stop them having Signor Scafidi turned out of his room to make way for them. Her zest for life was flourishing, and she took off with her cousins without another thought for her ardent Italian.

They visited Pompeii, a major tourist attraction even in 1892, but Margaret was once again out of sympathy with her fellow tourists, pining for living nature rather than dead history. 'It is difficult to realise that one is in a city of the dead when troops of modern tourists meet the eye at every side. The time to visit Pompeii and feel a true sense of its ancient glory, now crumbling into dust, would be at night, and alone, then the spirits of the mighty dead would again haunt its courts and temples, and the imagination would draw a vivid picture of the pomp and grandeur of past ages.'

The drive by horse-drawn carriage through the slums of Naples was more memorable to Margaret than their final destination. There were curious and distressing sights in equal measure: fresh pasta hanging on the washing lines, and desperately abused and underfed animals. It seemed to Margaret that not a day had gone by when she had not witnessed yet another atrocity of beating or deliberate maiming, and it upset her deeply. Someone told her the open sores on almost every horse and mule were purposefully left untreated to give quicker results for drivers' whips, and she blamed the Italian priests for not teaching the children to love God's creatures.

While the cousins ticked off all the sights on their list, Margaret made it her project to sketch Naples Cathedral. It was still second nature to her to study every cathedral she encountered, though the project was not quite the same in Italy as it had been in the sedate towns of England. Back home people had discreetly ignored her, but in Naples Margaret needed courage and determination to set up her easel. Men would gaze impertinently and a horde of beggars would insist on exposing every deformity and disease-ridden body part to arouse her pity. Failing that, the more persistent tried to pick her pockets, and Margaret found herself sitting uncomfortably on top of her purse. She began to draw such crowds each day that the sacristans soon objected. Her audience was failing to reach the intended destination of morning service, and such competition within the very walls of the church could not be allowed to continue. Margaret was asked to stop coming, and she willingly obliged. Her picture was finished anyway, and her next adventure already beckoned: an Italian woman with fluent English had kindly acted as interpreter with the sacristans, and this chance encounter now led to an invitation to visit her at home.

It seemed like a good idea at the time, though Margaret's and Louie's courage wavered when they found themselves being driven to a humble apartment block far from anywhere they recognized. Soon they were spending the afternoon in a cramped apartment with the Signora's extended family, and poor Louie found herself inching further and further away to avoid nudging male kneecaps under the table. Their hostess insisted they look through the family albums, and her guests were astonished to discover them full of English royals. 'I was in England two years you know, when I was a girl,' the Signora said, claiming to have met the Duke of Edinburgh, no less. Margaret and Louie could hardly fathom it, until it dawned on them that they had been to tea with the ex-mistress of some English nobleman.

Beautiful, wicked Naples and her smouldering volcano energized Margaret like no other place she had encountered so far, and her cousins had difficulty tearing her away. But the sights of Rome were still outstanding, and it was time to move on to the 'gaunt arms' of the capital, as Margaret wrote regretfully. 'The tomb of the mighty dead', she called it, finding the weight of history had crushed the city's spirit under a pile of ancient ruins. The vastness and complexity of Roman history is a challenge for the most dedicated tourist, and Margaret freely admitted she was not up to it. It was all too overpowering, and the crowds got on her nerves.

'At the time I was there it was overrun with tourists, the season of Easter being the time most chosen by the travelling multitudes . . . in its streets and piazzas the sound of English, German and American voices were far more often to be heard than the sweet tones of the Italian language.' She likened the multitudes of foreign visitors to 'swarms of flies feeding upon the dead carcass of some wild beast', and not even sketching St Peter's brought any joy. Suddenly she could hardly believe she ever spent so much time and energy painting and sketching cold and draughty buildings. Never again would the dead stones of a cathedral inspire her to make art, though she could admire their beauty still. 'What pleasure could I have found in facing the bitter blasts and freezing winds, as I would turn out into the streets of some painfully uninteresting provincial town in England after my morning's work,' she wondered and realized for the first time that though her talent was for painting her true love was music.

Try as she might, Rome did not touch her. The grandeur of Vesuvius or the delicate beauty of a rare butterfly meant so much more, and her cousins rightly identified her as a 'born naturalist'. They agreed to let her go once more, and Margaret took off for Florence, where she thought nothing of neglecting its fabulous museums and palaces for the vineyards and olive groves in the hills beyond. 'My soul died within me,' she wrote rather melodramatically of her efforts to appreciate Michelangelo's masterpieces, but she simply had no faculty to enjoy them as much as the view from the top of Giotto's Tower at the Duomo.

It was too early in the year for many butterflies, so her heart skipped a beat when she spotted a large Camberwell Beauty dancing just above her head. It strayed tantalizingly beyond her butterfly net, but the thrill of seeing its purple and cream-edged wings was worth a thousand monuments. Nature's art was most glorious to her, and the solitude of the Tuscan countryside brought an inner peace impossible to find among the crowds.

She pitied the other guests at her *pensione*, who came home tired and exhausted while she was vital and refreshed after a good day chasing insects. Nor did she find being alone difficult. She was becoming a confident traveller by now, at ease with strange scenes and unfamiliar people. 'How many rooms have I had in the course of the last few years to call my own,' she wrote, 'and occupy just for a few weeks, and then leave never to see again. How well I knew now the way on arriving in new quarters.' And how different from just a few years ago, arriving terrified in Limerick. It was only a year since she had first set foot on the Continent, but she was utterly hooked.

Uncle Edward's money put the world at her feet, and she intended to make full use of it. Eight weeks passed before she left Florence – not least because she suffered a nasty bought of rheumatic fever there – but there was still enough cash for a stay on Lake Como and a return to Switzerland, and Louie and Edith finally left her to it, travelling home without her. How much better it is to travel alone, Margaret discovered, free to make her own way and choosing company or solitude just exactly as it suited her.

She returned to the scenes of her happy summer the year before, in Geneva and the highland valleys beyond, and learnt yet another traveller's lesson: that it is rarely a good idea to return to a place where one has been so happy before, with other people and in other circumstances. Even an admirer who shared her love of butterflies failed to excite her, though the natural wonders all around were as thrilling as before. 'I don't wonder Switzerland is called the Entomologists' Paradise. The elegant Apollo was an everyday sight for my eyes to behold, and many a bright, flashing Fritillary would fall victim to my net.' Only the killing of these lovely insects worried her sometimes, though not enough to deprive her pocket box of any particularly fine specimen.

Reluctantly Margaret returned to the place she no longer thought of as home, though even she was weary after six months of travelling. And even though Norwich held no pleasures for her now, it was still comforting to find Hurley, her old nanny, sitting by her window darning stockings, just as she always had. The bond between them was as strong as ever, unclouded by expectation or disappointments, and Margaret loved her more than any other. But what to do? She could not possibly contemplate a future in England now, already feeling a stranger in her own country.

She decided to study singing in Milan. She had met an American girl in Geneva whose crystal voice and enthusiasm for music had galvanized her decision, and nothing her mother could say would change her mind. True, she was a little old to begin a singing career at thirty, but she would study with the best Milan could offer, and her mother's opposition only hardened her resolve. Butterflies and painting were mere pastimes. Singing was to be Margaret's true purpose.

❀6❀

MUSIC AND MEN

REST DID NOT suit Margaret. She found the 'vegetable existence' of a Norwich winter more fatiguing than six months of travelling. 'To spend a lifetime in one little spot of the great world', she wrote, 'is to render the mind feeble and contracted, the intellect crippled and deformed – unless of course that life is spent in study . . . but even then the ideas must necessarily become contracted to a certain extent.'[1]

By April she was ready to study singing in Milan. She took lodgings with a Signora Tagliaferri and was soon firm friends with her teenage daughters, Angelina and Maria, and the children, too, Ceci and the orphaned Lina. She liked her new role as La Signorina, drinking rather too much wine at dinner and joining in with the family's music-making. She enjoyed the jesting and teasing, especially with Lina, who abused her tragic position mercilessly by being very naughty.

She was entranced by the apparently easy-going nature of relationships in Italy, not least those of her landlady, who was receiving regular visits from a certain Signor Avocato. 'I cannot quite make out the nature and purpose of this gentleman's visits,' she wrote rather naïvely; 'daily, sometimes hourly, he comes, and when he comes he stays, thinking nothing of going into Signora Tagliaferri's bedroom.'

Most thrilling of all, though, was to be told by her singing professor, Signor Guadagnini, that she had the voice to sing professionally. A descendant of one of Italy's greatest violin makers, his impression of her musical talents was praise indeed.[2] Her lessons in the Via Monte Napoleone were the highlight of her day, though she was also racked with self-doubt, concerned she might not have the physical or mental strength for a life on the public stage. Developing her singing voice was one thing. Competing for a livelihood was quite another, and it was not long before she needed a rest from the intense pressure of studying in Milan.

A butterfly expedition to Corsica, famous for its flower-filled meadows in spring, was just what she needed. No matter the island was also famous for its bandits – that just added to the thrill, and her mother was appeased by the fact that Rachel agreed to join her. Her sister arrived in Bastia, the island's capital, by boat from Nice, while Margaret travelled south for a boat from Genoa. Those Cook's agents were wonderful. They could arrange travel and accommodation to almost every corner, no matter how remote, and the sisters met high up in the Corsican mountains, at Vizzavona.

The hotel was full of English guests with similar plans to Margaret's, and she found that 'to have come here for the purpose of collecting butterflies was at once to find myself completely in the fashion, at least amongst the male visitors of the place'. Most intriguing among the other guests was a Mr Raine, accompanied by a Mrs Cooke. The other English ladies at the hotel tended to shun Mrs Cooke, but Margaret made a point of cultivating her friendship, determined not to show prejudice to a social misfit, as she herself might have been. She identified with a woman who had chosen to rise above the malicious whispering of strangers and admired her constancy as well. 'I believe she had loved this man all her life – loved him with a persistency that only a true good woman can love,' she wrote, admitting in the next sentence the story she had constructed around Mrs Cooke might not be absolutely authentic. Officially, at any rate, she was Mr Raine's housekeeper and tireless catcher of butterflies for 'the master', as she liked to call him.

But the chilly heights of Vizzavona were no good for butterflies, and Margaret descended to the semi-tropical warmth of Ajaccio, on the island's west coast, where swifts darted among the cacti and eucalyptus trees and the butterfly prospects were glorious. She threw caution to the wind and set off alone and quickly found herself accosted by a wild fellow who looked liked a gypsy. He insisted on carrying her basket and was soon trying every trick in the book to hold her hand or clasp her to him, but she resisted, surprising herself by jumping over ditches unaided. When she unwisely admitted to not being married he became almost severe, lecturing her on the nature of things and advising her to note how the butterflies joined together *comme ça*, 'and he illustrated what he meant with his fingers, in a manner that was quite unmistakable'.

She took an early train to Mezzana the next morning and spent an entire day hunting there. This time she evaded incident until the end of the day when she arrived back at the train station hot and tired. She ordered some wine on an empty stomach and quickly found herself 'getting more intoxicated every minute'. In no time at all the regulars at the station bar had persuaded her to try the local spirit as well, and a tipsy Margaret was mortified to find herself travelling home third class with the man who had bought her a drink.

Happily, she made it back to her hotel unscathed, but since the water was unsafe she had to drink yet more wine with dinner and fell asleep in her room fully dressed. Margaret, the rector's daughter, had been drunk! Thank goodness she had been alone, she thought, filled with pious regret the next morning. Perhaps it was best if her sister stayed with her after all, she thought, and quickly persuaded her to leave the gossiping ladies in the mountains and join her by the sea, at Ajaccio. Together they could have plenty of adventures which 'feminine confidence' would keep on the right side of decency.

'As regards the Brigands – or rather Bandits,' she wrote knowingly, 'they were merely outlaws, not necessarily robbers, men who by some act of violence, probably murder, had escaped the sentence of the law by "taking to the Macchie", as it was termed, the Macchie being a prickly shrub growing in great profusion all over the mountains, with a strong and most characteristic smell, which seemed to pervade the whole island.'

The most famous bandit in Corsica at the time was a certain Jacques Bellacoscia, whose career as an outlaw had started with the shooting of the Mayor of Ajaccio some twenty-five years prior to Margaret and Rachel's visit. The poor man had objected to Bellacoscia keeping three wives instead of the usual one, and at least half a dozen gendarmes had lost their lives since that argument, trying to bring him to justice. An immense reward was set on his head, but no one had yet succeeded in catching Bellacoscia, who had the mountains and their inhabitants on his side.

The sisters were thrilled to bump into the man himself in the forests around Vizzavona one day. They shared a drink with him in the July sunshine, and Margaret noted how handsome he was and how at ease, though armed to the teeth and alert to danger at all times. An old woman with a grey beard took care of his every need, and Margaret soon cast her as one of his three wives, loving him with the devotion and loyalty 'only a good woman can provide'. He drank wine out of her painting glass, and Margaret was delighted to receive a gift of heather from him, which still adorns Volume IV of her diaries to this day: 'picked July 12th, 1893', it notes meticulously.

Margaret and Rachel spent almost three months in Corsica, but at last it was time to leave, and they took a boat for Marseilles. A fierce Mistral wind tossed and heaved them over huge waves, and Margaret was so weak from seasickness by the time they arrived that she needed two men to carry her to shore. But the agony of their journey was nothing compared to the fetid heat of Marseilles during a cholera epidemic, and Margaret immediately came down with a violent fever.

Fortunately it was not cholera in her case, but she could not bear to part with her favourite sister just yet and needed little excuse to accompany her as far as the French Alps before turning back to Milan. They spent some days in Chamonix, fully intent on resting. Instead, Margaret almost got them killed by deciding that she and Rachel could cross Mont Blanc's famous glacier without a guide and with nothing but tennis shoes and the butt end of their butterfly nets. 'However, no accident occurred,' she wrote blithely.

The quickest route from Chamonix to Milan, on the northern plains of Italy, was over the dreaded 2,005-metre Simplon Pass, which Margaret reached by diligence along rugged tracks rising ever higher above gut-wrenching precipices. The cliffs glistened black under the torrent of waterfalls cascading from above, and the struggling horses were often soaked in freezing water. Wordsworth, travelling here over a century earlier, thought this desolate place must be the face of the Apocalypse, and the gloomy heights draped in shifting swirls of mountain cloud are eerie still.

It was a journey of a good ten hours, prolonged by a breakdown shortly after the pass, but Margaret did not mind. One of her fellow passengers was a Dr Bruno Galli-Valerio, with whom she whiled away the hours sharing common interests. 'I found in this man not only one who was agreeable and intellectual in his conversation,' she wrote, 'but also of somewhat similar tastes to myself. He possessed a great love of natural history, and a profound admiration of nature, more especially in her sterner and grander moods, as seen upon the Swiss mountains . . .' She describes him as 'rather below middle height, with a thin, spare figure'. But she also noted a 'well cut nose and mouth' and was clearly drawn to him, because she speculates that he 'may be going to figure largely in the story of my life, and he may not'. The doctor turned out to be practising in Milan, so there was ample opportunity to continue the acquaintance, and she arrived with his card in her pocket.[3]

Margaret resumed her role as music student, though her doubts about her singing talent and ability to survive in the professional world of music continued to worry her. 'I was too sensitive by nature,' she wrote, 'too apt to shrink within myself.'

She had second thoughts about the doctor, too, whose earnest demeanour now seemed 'without chic'. It was all very well having an escort who could be trusted not to jump on you, but it left little room for romance to blossom. Perversely, she found him too respectable after the company of the louche musical set she was used to. But he persevered with her, and she rewarded him with regular trips to the opera.

She tried hard to remind herself that respectability was a good thing, having finally understood the basis on which most women achieved their artistic success at that time. 'Let a girl of moderate talent and mediocre ability gain favour in the eyes of the Impresario, and consent to become his mistress, and her success is secured. Whereas another . . . clinging to purity in her heart and life, would find for her no opening to mount the ladder of Fame.'

The doctor's chaste attentions irritated her nevertheless, and his graciousness somehow brought out the poison from her past. She behaved capriciously by wilfully missing agreed rendezvous or not answering his letters. She imagined him waiting in vain and rather enjoyed it. 'Now at last I shall be able to have my revenge,' she wrote grimly. 'I too know what it is to wait for letters that do not come . . . I chuckled with satisfaction to be able to feel at last that it was in my power to revenge in some degree, at least upon this man, the wrong done to me by another long ago. Was I a devil? Or was I only a woman?' she wrote, knowing full well she was being unjust.

Margaret flattered herself, however, if she thought the doctor was in love with her or suffered a fraction of the pain she had known. He merely enjoyed her company – perhaps it was an opportunity to improve his English – and he must have found her behaviour an unwelcome mystery. Once more Margaret was imposing on a man a role he had neither asked for nor encouraged, but thankfully this time things were brought out into the open much sooner. She received a letter from him during her Christmas holiday in Norwich, asking her to confirm that there was no misunderstanding between them, that they were friends not lovers. It was a disappointment, not least because Margaret was embarrassed to think he might have thought *she* was chasing *him*, and she quickly banished her limp fantasy of becoming the respectable Mrs Bruno Galli-Valerio. Her mood was not helped by being in Norwich, though, surrounded by reminders of past humiliations. Eaton Lodge felt like a 'living tomb, sodden with the tears of melancholy'. Memories hung 'like mildew' on the walls, and she struggled with her old enemies, self-pity and depression.

It was no wonder she had felt tempted to see herself as Bruno's wife. She was in a state of confusion after having decided the life of a singer was not for her, and she naturally sought a comforting alternative. But Margaret was not born for comfort, and in her solitude she began to realize how much better she loved the world of nature than that of man. Travelling and collecting butterflies was a pursuit she could safely control in almost all important aspects, and that meant a lot to a person who could not bear uncertainty in her life. The strain of success and the threat of failure as a performer would have been too much for her highly strung nerves, and she had enough self-knowledge by now to realize it. She also needed to steer clear of the 'waves of passion, sin, temptation and anguish' she had such a propensity for. 'Liberty is a treasure not to be relinquished for a trifle,' she admonished herself. 'What more could I wish for?'

Finally, all self-indulgent thoughts were banished by the news that her favourite cousin, Louie Curtois, had died of influenza in London, and her sister Constance was gravely ill in Menton, in the south of France. Action was required, and she had no more time for brooding. Her sisters needed her, doctors had to be found and travel arrangements made, and it was just as well she was kept busy. Louie was one of the very few women Margaret had really trusted and cared for – a confidante since childhood – and she could easily have given way to morbid introspection if she had had time.

'Sin would seem less ghastly' without her cousin's influence, Margaret wrote sadly, 'vice less revolting and virtue and self-respect less essential'. She proved her point by developing a serious gambling habit in the flesh-pots of Monaco, just a stone's throw from her sister's hotel in Menton.

Margaret's duties with Constance were shared by Florence and Rachel, so there was plenty of time for the delights of sin and contrition, and Margaret indulged both to the full. Most of all, though, she spent her thirty-second year going around in circles, searching for a way forward. She returned to Corsica and the Swiss Alps for butterfly-hunting expeditions but found her heart was not in it. There was no purpose to what she was doing, and though she enjoyed the camaraderie of other naturalists she met along the way it was also wearisome tramping the hillsides ten to twelve hours each day.

Back in Norwich the sisters discovered that their mother had decided to sell up and move to Bath. The doctors had advised it might be a better climate for Constance, who was believed to be experiencing the early stages of tuberculosis, and everything at Eaton Lodge was to be sold. Everything the girls had known since childhood was to go, even the piano, Mother's most prized wedding gift.

Margaret was more than ready to let go of the past, though. Her travels on the Continent had put distance between her and her obsession with Septimus, and she no longer considered Norwich her home anyway. It made no difference to her where her mother was based, and Bath seemed as good a place as any. The city enjoyed one of the liveliest 'seasons' in the country, and the cultural life was much less provincial than in Norfolk.

Of course, Bath could hardly compete with cosmopolitan Milan, and it was less than a year before Margaret was back among the familiar piazzas and streets of her second home, so much more enjoyable now that she spoke fluent Italian. Bruno had loyally kept up his correspondence with her the whole time she was away, and it was very pleasant to receive his gallant attention once more. He was the first man with whom Margaret developed a genuine friendship, though both had clearly considered taking things further. Margaret admitted as much in her diary, and, though Bruno denied it, his eyes filled with tears when she finally announced her decision to leave Milan. Was it just excess of emotion, or did it signify more? Margaret did not have the confidence to hazard a guess. 'I never do know any of the secrets that come into my life,' she wrote. 'I conjecture and speculate as to what things may mean, but to know, and in knowing to be blest, is what is for ever withheld from me.'

Signor Guadagnini could not persuade her to continue her lessons. Margaret was quite clear by now she had neither the temperament for singing professionally nor the will to share the lives of her musical friends. What had seemed so exciting in previous years now appeared sleazy and pointless. 'What do these people live for?' she asked rhetorically. 'What is the meaning of their daily life? With the women especially, they dress, they take their meals, they laugh and joke, but there is no real gladness in their laughter.'

Margaret was determined not to be judged by the man on her arm. She took herself off to the hamlets on the plain south of Milan and Venice to gather her thoughts in the sun-drenched countryside of the Po Valley. Only the occasional bullock-wagon disturbed the peace here, and she spent a quiet week chasing butterflies along winding streams and open fields. But peace did not come to Margaret, and she found that the loneliness and poverty of her surroundings just magnified the 'depression and contortion' of her thoughts. She wanted to make her own way in life, but solitude did not suit her, and she admitted to her diary that after a week alone she was so desperate for company she even accepted an invitation by the waiter of her hostel to 'go down into the kitchen in order to enjoy the unique and exceptional advantage of making the acquaintance of the cook'.

She fled to Lake Como and the resort of Tremezzo, where she knew from her previous visit with Edith and Louie she would find plenty of English tourists. She felt a need to be around her own kind and thrived on light-hearted rowing escapades and civilized dinners. Margaret loved her food, and there was nothing better to revive the spirit than a hearty five-course meal washed down with a good Italian wine. Even better, as soon as Bruno heard she was in Tremezzo he insisted on coming to join her.

They agreed to meet again in the Swiss Engadine Valley the following month, and Margaret steamed up to the northern end of the lake to discover yet another corner of her beloved Switzerland across the nearby border. A combination of train and diligence took her towards Switzerland's loveliest valley – home of the now famous resort of St Moritz and a renowned hunting ground for butterflies. She was developing a much more professional eye by now, seeking out particular species for her growing collection back in England, and she enjoyed nothing better than to compete with fellow naturalists for the best specimens. She knew from reading the standard works at the time that each butterfly was known by at least two names, just like people, only in science the surname comes first. Thus, the surname (genus) of any butterfly was always followed by the Christian name (species), and if a third name was added it was either to denote a subspecies with uniquely different markings or to identify the person who first described it. Beautiful colour plates in her reference books helped Margaret with identification.

'The entire female population of *Pieris napi* was represented by var: *Bryoniae*. Directly I saw the males on the wing, I conjectured that at this elevation the females would most probably be of this variety, and I was glad to find I had conjectured rightly,' she was pleased to report on her catch of Green-veined Whites. 'But it seemed so brutal to rob them of all their little wives – and mothers of the next brood – but then there was no choice but to take a "good thing" when I saw it, or give up collecting altogether.'

She moved from one village to the next on foot, sending her luggage ahead by diligence and carrying nothing more than a small knapsack and her butterfly net. 'It was a charming way of travelling,' she wrote, 'on foot through all that wonderful scenery. I really did feel like a traveller then, especially when arriving at some wayside inn, to partake of a simple, but hearty meal, before resuming my tramp.'

She walked thirty kilometres, from the Maloja Pass to Pontresina, along the pebbly shores of the Silser See and past the farms of St Moritz and St Moritz Bad, which were quiet villages then. 'I don't think in my life I had ever felt so independent before,' she wrote happily.

At Pontresina there was also the Morteratsch Glacier, which added extra adventure, though she knew to show it respect after her experiences on the Mer de Glace of Mont Blanc. She would wait for Bruno, who was an experienced alpinist. He had written to say he would set off from his home town of Sondrio, climbing the great Pizzo d'Argento (3,950 metres high) before descending the glacier on the Swiss side. It seemed thrillingly dangerous, and Margaret awaited his arrival on the appointed day with a combination of fear and excitement. She was not in love with Bruno – she knew that – but she was so happy in the mountains that she allowed herself the fantasy of lasting happiness with a man once more and persuaded herself he, too, might change his mind and come to see her as his ideal wife. They had so much in common and shared such carefree times, it was easy to forget they had long ago agreed to be platonic friends.

But when it came to love the fates were not on Margaret's side, and Bruno failed to turn up, much less propose. Agonizing days went by before news reached her that Bruno and his guide had spent seventeen hours lost on the glacier before turning back to Italy. The many hours of gazing into the blinding light coming off the ice had given Bruno snow blindness, and he was condemned to weeks of darkened rooms and painful recuperation. When finally he was able to see well enough to write himself it became eminently clear he shared none of Margaret's secret fantasies, and she choked back bitter tears of disappointment in a way she had thought never to do again.

She returned to England and lodgings in Bath, to set her butterflies and regale the ladies with her adventures. She needed care with both: her stories needed editing for the ears of 'polite society' and her butterflies needed rehydrating so their delicate wings could be spread on to purpose-built setting boards. Each butterfly had to be carefully laid on damp sand in a closed jar to loosen the muscles but not for too long or the whole thing would start to rot.

While travelling Margaret placed most of her catches in special tri-angular envelopes, with their wings closed to protect them from damage and exposure to light, which soon bleaches the bright colours of wings. But too much handling during rehydration and setting risked breaking off delicate antennae, so undoing the effects of rigor mortis and opening up the wings was not easy without spoiling the insect's body and required patience and a steady hand.

Christmas was spent making music and playing cards until midnight with fellow residents of her boarding-house, and Margaret was flattered to find that a rather serious and high-minded gentleman, a Mr Lockie from Kensington, had fallen in love with her. Naturally she did not want him. 'The love of a true, good man is for ever denied to me,' she wrote. 'It's no use for me to try and imagine anything else, therefore I will just get all the pleasure in life I can, from intercourse with the *bad* men that I meet – that is to say going to the very edge of the precipice, but without falling over it!' she wrote grimly.

The winter of 1895/6 was the longest and severest on record – even the Thames froze over along its London stretch – and Margaret did her best to stave off a 'sea of undefined, unuttered desires'. But the safe monotony of Bath gave her far too much time to think and let her fears run away with her. 'But why should I, who from my earliest childhood had ever been the spirit and essence of independence, now at my age (33) begin to feel an unquenchable terror at facing the dangers and temptations of life – alone?' she admonished herself. 'But of course I was not going to give way to myself.' Her mother's prayers for her brought tears to her eyes, though she could not think why. Perhaps for innocence lost.

❧ 7 ❧

SICILIAN ADVENTURE

T HE PERSONAL FREEDOM Margaret had discovered in the last five years gave her a completely new perspective. She relished the liberties she could take beyond the shores of Victorian England. Abroad, her social horizon was far wider, unconstrained by divisions of class or the limited world of respectable ladies at home. Hiking alone from village to village without a chaperone in Switzerland had been intoxicating; sharing wine with Corsica's most famous bandit even more so. She had ventured deliciously close to the precipice and survived unscathed, and her confidence in handling herself in the wider world was secure by now.

Like many women who have travelled alone, Margaret had quickly discovered that a single woman is in no more danger than the average male, safety having very little to do with physical strength. In fact, she considered, women were often safer than men because they had the double advantage of being able to use their feminine guile without being regarded a threat by anyone. It is a unique advantage she learnt to use well in the shortest time, and she had the imagination and spirit to contemplate journeys few others would have dared to consider at the time.

So far, however, her restless spirit had got in the way of focusing on a specific enterprise, and Margaret was only just beginning to realize where her true interests lay. After three years of studying singing in Milan she had had the strength of character to admit it was not for her. But recognizing her true vocation was much harder. 'I am entirely wanting in all ambition,' she had written as long ago as 1883, aged twenty-one, yet a passionate woman like Margaret needed to have something. If it was not going to be a husband or a life on the stage, what should it be?

A visit to Henry John Elwes's butterfly collection was pivotal in finding the answer. Until then butterfly-hunting and collecting had been a mere pastime, something to add interest to her holidays abroad and a useful topic of conversation with fellow hotel guests, but Elwes inspired her. He was a giant of a man with a 'fog-horn' voice, who caused dread in less exalted contemporaries, yet Margaret was enthralled by his superb museum, which housed the largest private collection of lepidoptera in the country, including over 11,370 specimens of Palaearctic butterflies, which now form a substantial part of the Natural History Museum's collection in London.[1]

The visitors' book at his estate in Colesbourne, Gloucestershire, records that Margaret visited with her sister Rachel on 27 October 1895 and stayed three days. It was an honour secured via Margaret's contact with the Norfolk entomologist James Edwards, who was employed as Elwes's curator and secretary.[2] The sisters thus enjoyed an extended period of the great scholar's hospitality, during which he regaled them with exotic tales of collecting trips all over the world but especially in the Orient. Margaret was gripped, and what had once been just for fun was now a much more serious subject. Furthermore, her competitive nature was roused. Her own collection was paltry compared to what she had seen here, and her ambition to become a serious collector was born.

Margaret's chance to make her mark came soon after her visit to Colesbourne, when she decided to spend the following May and June in Sicily. She knew from her books that the island's mountains were home to some of the finest butterflies to be found in Europe, and, even better, it seemed no English collector had been there before. She would be the first, braving Sicily's notorious brigands to capture the island's famous range of *Melanargia* (Marbled Whites), easily distinguished by their striking wing patterns in black and white and exceptional within their family of Satyridae butterflies, which are normally coloured somewhere between black, brown and orange. The dual prospect of danger and rare butterflies was simply irresistible: 'any hesitation I might previously have had . . . was quite at an end,' she was to boast in her first article for *The Entomologist* a year later.

There was plenty of help available for her new passion, too, because Margaret's interest in butterflies was hardly original. In fact, butterfly-collecting had been a fashionable pursuit since the early 1700s, and quite a few of the earliest known collectors were women. Lady Margaret Cavendish Bentinck – later the Duchess of Portland – amassed a substantial private collection, as did Mary Somerset, widow of the first Duke of Beaufort. But the 'Golden Age of Natural History' was undoubtedly the nineteenth century, and by the time Margaret decided to dedicate herself to butterflies regional natural history societies were commonplace, and there were also a number of specialist journals, such as *The Entomologist's Monthly Magazine*, which was founded in 1864 and continues to this day.[3]

New guides and books encouraging the Victorian fad for collecting and naming flora and fauna had come out at regular intervals since Darwin's *The Origin of Species* was published in 1859.[4] 'How many tourists are there who, passing a short time on the Continent, would be glad to add to the interest of their stay by making a collection of the lovely insects which are met by the wayside or in the mountain top?' trilled Mr Vismes Kane, leading Irish entomologist of his day, in *European Butterflies*.[5] Conveniently, he pointed out, many of the top tourist destinations of the time, such as the Swiss Alps and the French Côte d'Azur, are also some of Europe's finest butterfly-hunting grounds. 'The best-known passes, the Simplon, St Gothard, and Albula, are perfect treasuries of insect beauty,' he claimed. No wonder Margaret's first journeys abroad were to these very places. Another popular source at the time was H.C. Lang's two volumes of *The Butterflies of Europe*, which Margaret had already studied closely, especially the second volume, which is entirely made up of beautiful colour plates identifying species.

The craze for amateur natural history was quickly capitalized upon by Victorian entrepreneurs as well, and by the time Margaret became serious about butterflies one could find suppliers of every kind of collecting tool one might desire. Firms such as Watkins and Doncaster, established in 1874 and still going strong today, supplied everything from custom-made butterfly nets with collapsible rings and handles to purpose-built killing jars, either from their shop at 36 The Strand, London, or by mail order. Margaret may well have used their services herself, as there was no supplier in Norwich at that time.[6]

Despite William Swainson's advice to hire a small boy for carrying a naturalist's kit in his popular 'how to' guide of the day, Margaret liked to travel light, as far as possible, so her collecting kit was limited to her hunting net and what she could easily carry in one bag: a cigar box to store her catches in their triangle envelopes, a handy guide for identifying them and a repair kit for sewing up ripped netting.[7] Back at the hotel, her luggage would also have included setting boards and pins, as well as larger storage boxes for safe transportation. She already knew that setting specimens was far more onerous after rigor mortis had set in, so she bought specially designed travelling cases which could hold up to a dozen boards, each a small cork-covered wooden block with a groove down the middle to hold insect bodies in place.

The business of killing butterflies was the only aspect of entomology that Margaret did not relish, though it was not the killing she objected to but the guilt she felt for ending the life of something so delicate and beautiful. Yet she was already an expert at crushing their little thoraxes between finger and thumb to ensure a quick death, and each was then quickly popped into its envelope and annotated with the specimen's name, if she knew it, and when and where she found it.

She set off for Gibraltar on 3 April – Good Friday – departing from Tilbury Docks on the *Ormuz* and spending five miserable days being seasick in the Bay of Biscay. Predictably, she arrived in dismal mood, not improved when British soldiers garrisoned to guard the Rock refused to let her climb it. 'I soon felt thoroughly disgusted with Gibraltar, which really seemed little else but a gigantic prison, where the English government bore rule in a most tyrannical and despotic manner,'[8] she grumbled in her diary and was very glad to cross the Bay of Algeciras to meet her sister Evelyn in Spain instead.

Together they visited Seville and Cadiz, but Margaret did not take to Spain. In Cadiz the streets smelt so bad that the sisters walked about with carnations under their noses, and that was nothing compared to the horror of the bullfight. 'Never shall I forget the horror of that spectacle!' she wrote.

To see all those poor, dumb animals brought in there to die in agony and torture of the worst that man could devise . . . the horses were literally torn to pieces, their entrails, their lungs, their bowels gushed out and hung down, sometimes almost trailing on the ground, for, alas, they did not always die. If a vital part had not been touched they were forced to get up, while the Picador remounted his disabled steed, and unmercifully spurred the trembling animal again and again to meet the fury of the bull – again to be pierced and torn with his long sharp horns till at last perchance some vital part is touched and the poor worn out horse sinks down dead upon the sand . . . even the Spanish ladies of high rank smile approval behind their fans, the more revolting, the more horrible the atrocities they witness.

It was a relief to leave Spain, and the *Oruba* took Margaret from Gibraltar to Naples, thankfully providing her with a calm Mediterranean crossing, and she changed boats for Palermo refreshed and confident. Her few hours in Naples were invigorating, but her arrival in Palermo made her spirits soar. The city was 'a glittering diamond in a setting of gold, as it lay along the blue bay, with the sunlit mountains enclosing it on all sides'.

She booked herself into the Hotel de France, recommended in her trusty Cook's Guide, and then quickly set off to find Signor Ragusa, Sicily's leading authority on the island's butterflies at the time. Mr Elwes had kindly written her a letter of introduction, and, happily, he was not hard to find, as he was also the proprietor of the Grand Hotel des Palmes.[9]

She wasted no time charming him into sharing his best hunting grounds with her. Conveniently, these were just five miles from the city, on the slopes of Monte Cuccio, and Margaret soon settled into a daily routine of setting off early by horse-drawn carriage to reach the little hamlet of Bocco di Falco. The countryside was in full bloom, and she marvelled at the hedges of pink roses lining the roads and the meadows filled with yellow marguerites and orange marigolds. If the locals thought her unusual, they did not show it, and Margaret was left to scatter hens and goats as she gathered up her net and knapsack to scour the mountain for her treasure.

What a thrill it was to skip among the boulders giving chase to the finest butterflies she could spot. What a dusty tangle she would find herself in, skidding on loose stones and caught in prickly heathers. No matter! The hot aroma of mountain herbs filled her nostrils, her hair was loosened by the breeze, and she was free. Mind and body were united in her butterfly endeavour, and she sometimes found it hard to adjust to any humans she encountered, especially those gawping at her on her journey back to the hotel. 'I will not say I altogether cared for the attention I attracted when I walked along the Corso in butterfly attire,' she admits in her diary.

Evenings among gentlemen in the hotel were another matter. Having washed and dressed for dinner, she rather enjoyed being the only woman among fifteen to twenty men. She was a rare butterfly herself, and she enjoyed the attention, 'always trying to make myself agreeable to anyone I happened to be sitting next . . .' She was not beautiful – she knew that – but she could tell a good story and hold her own in intelligent conversation, and men found her fascinating. Her apparent confidence and rather manly butterfly-hunting were an irresistible provocation, the aphrodisiac effect spreading right across the social spectrum, from Palermo's dissolute youths to lonely barons. 'A new epoch was beginning in my life which I attributed almost entirely to my having discovered a new and very becoming way of doing my hair,' she mocked in her diary, though this may well have added to the interest she aroused.

Three young men attached themselves to her on her very first day in Palermo, even having the nerve to enter her hotel and knock on her door.

'What time do you go to bed?' one asked.

'Very early,' she replied.

'I knew an improper proposition was coming, and soon enough out it came,' she recorded later. Did she go to sleep quickly, the impertinent youth had enquired, and, when that line of enquiry seemed to lead nowhere, he asked to see Margaret's butterflies, assuming he would need to enter her room. She defeated him once more by offering to bring her butterflies to the salon downstairs and never saw him again.

A tall, bearded Italian who spoke excellent English was more successful. He persuaded Margaret to spend an afternoon with him, taking her to the half-ruined gardens of the Villa Belmonte. The rain came down soft and warm, and the two of them spent a sensuously damp few hours alone among the dripping leaves. No man could keep Margaret from her main quarry, however, and despite the gentleman's pleas she was off to her next collecting base at Taormina the very next day.

She settled in quickly and engaged the hotel-keeper's son to show her the best hunting grounds. He, too, soon found it hard to concentrate on the business in hand. 'He told me how each time he had seen me, he had found that I was *encore plus jolie qu'il avait pensé*, and how he had become more and more *amoureux*. I said I was sure that in a few days he would begin to feel much better . . .' The transparent flattery of her companion was simply nowhere near as exciting as the beauty all around her. 'No wonder these southern natures are quick and passionate when every scene around them is such sensuous loveliness! A world of blue and tideless seas, and gleaming, sunny shores – blue the atmosphere, blue the glittering sea far below, blue the distant mountains on the shores of Italy, and I laughed from sheer delight at the scene beneath my feet.' The sensuality and beauty touched Margaret emotionally, too, of course, but she was not looking for love any more, and she was certainly not going to allow herself to be kissed by the son of a hotel-keeper, even if she did begin to feel sorry for him.

Margaret's final collecting base on Sicily was at Messina, where she arrived with every intention of cultivating a less obtrusive presence, but that soon proved impossible. She attracted men like mountain peaks obsess climbers, and the next contender appeared in no time at all. He was a suave French-speaking gentleman, who wined and dined her, took her to concerts and for romantic strolls by the marina, and she confessed in her diary she 'felt proud of the man on whose arm I leant, for he was tall and well favoured, with an audacity which in a man never fails to inveigle itself'. Yet she knew where all this was leading, and it was only a matter of time before they would be sparring.

Sure enough, her suitor wasted few days before boldly suggesting they consummate their friendship in the most natural way possible between a man and a woman. 'I felt subdued and rather unhappy as I answered that I didn't do that sort of thing. Had I never tried it, he asked, "Then you'll have to try tonight with me!" But I only repeated as before, *je ne fais pas ça*.' He let the subject go and took her to the water's edge for star-gazing instead. Her hand trembled in his as they studied a resplendent galaxy. His body brushed hers, as if by accident, and the heat between them sent quivers up her spine. It felt so natural, too. Waves lapped the shore in glittering surges, and a languid Mediterranean warmth embraced them. 'That night beneath the glittering stars, out there alone with this man, in the darkness, I stood on the very verge of what Society calls Ruin!' she confided to her diary. 'And he never knew how in my heart I did yield to him.'

How could she not respond? He evidently thought she would, and

Margaret froze in her nightgown when she heard the gentle knocking back at the hotel.

'Mademoiselle, are you going to open the door?' he whispered insistently.

'No,' she hissed and was hugely relieved when she heard retreating footsteps after what felt like an eternity. The lock on her door was barely functional. He could easily have gained entry.

Margaret's resolve is impressive, even over a century later. Irrespective of contraceptive danger and the social mores of the time, she was just as susceptible to physical desire as any woman today, and she admitted to herself in private, 'I might never have such a lover as he was again.' But she was sure he was not in love with her, and her pride could not stand for that. Undoubtedly Margaret's Church of England upbringing also exerted a constraining influence. Her Christian faith found it difficult to reconcile the animality of the sex instinct with being a decent human being, never mind a lady, and she wrote several times in her diary how tired she was of 'this strange, human nature that God has given to us'.

Fortunately she had her butterflies to take her mind off sexual distractions, and she was thrilled to find so many varieties of her sought-for *Melanargia*. *Melanargia galatea* looked as if it had been decorated by a child's hand, its black wings covered in irregular daubs of white. *Melanargia japygia*, on the other hand, was all leggy and elegant, its white wings veined by a delicate black mosaic scattered with eye shapes near its wing edges, the tenderest hue of dawn pink. Her heart missed a beat each time she spotted one fluttering in the mountain breeze, sending her slipping and falling as she gave chase. To have caught some good specimens and then to have lunch in the shade of a silvery olive tree was satisfaction indeed.

It was hard physical work hunting butterflies on mountainous terrain, however, and she was very grateful when Signor Amenta, another Sicilian entomologist, was introduced to her by a local professor. 'Many, many happy hours we spent together, roving over the hills around Messina, beneath a glorious sky, with the same pursuit in view, for he, like me, had *una vera passione per le farfalle*. Almost like two children together, I and this dark-eyed youth would chase the glorious *Charaxes jasius* (purple black, with dramatic orange and yellow edging on the wings) . . . quarrelling and disputing, sometimes in hot discussions.'

It was wonderful to be alive on days like that, and Margaret could almost forget the terrible damage Septimus had done. 'I soon began to find that a good long day out butterflying with Signor Amenta, making several good catches, went a good way towards healing the wound. A regular butterfly companion, ready to comply with my every whim and to give me all he caught, was not an advantage to be met with every day.'

Margaret was thrilled to discover a butterfly that neither she nor Signor Amenta could identify, and she could not resist the ultimate dream of any naturalist: to find and name a new specimen. It would be called *Argynnis hurleyae*, after her beloved nanny, she fancied. Signor Ragusa was unable to identify the butterfly either and sent it off to a German entomologist friend living in Aix-les-Bains. Of course it was vain to hope for glory so soon in her career as a collector, but it was only natural to get carried away with the excitement of this mystery.

She had returned to Palermo for the specific purpose of identifying her catch, but she also took time to step out with her gallant escort from the Hotel de France. He was a baron, she discovered, whose charm and cultivated manner made him an excellent companion for enjoying the urban delights of Palermo.

The sophisticated baron tackled Margaret far more elegantly than her other suitors. Instead of the usual banter and flattery, he appealed to her free spirit and intellect, challenging her with the idea of free love. She gave it serious consideration and came to the conclusion that perhaps the baron was right. 'He had brought me to feel that free love was better than that hallowed by the sanctity of marriage, that those bound in wedlock soon wearied and satiated of one another and then awoke to find themselves for ever bound together, to shiver for a life-time over the dead embers of an extinct passion, or to break their vows and bring shame and disgrace upon each other, and upon their children.'

She agreed with him but nevertheless refused the inevitable experience he offered her. 'You see that red light so far away,' she said rather pertly; 'imagine that little light ten thousand times farther off than we see it now and that is not so far as is the possibility of my allowing *you* to come and see me in my room tonight!'

Why she refused this intelligent, handsome and well-born lover she could not easily explain, even to herself. The simplest answer is likely to have been the truth of it: she was not in love with him, though she had become very fond of him and missed his company once he was gone. 'No, I should wait till one day a lover worthy of my acceptance should tempt me,' she wrote, 'and then I would no longer be ignorant of that great power which rules the world; the curse of some, the blessing of others. But the very thought of the Baron was repulsive to me . . .'

Poor Signor Amenta had no chance after the baron, though he tried hard when Margaret resumed her collecting expeditions with him. 'Look, *Signorina*, nature is all around us! And the birds, the butterflies and the flowers are all making love one with another. Why should we who are man and woman, and who come here day by day, why should we alone remain apart?' It was the tenderest approach, and Margaret allowed herself to sink on to the sunburnt grass to be held against a passionate young chest. His hands slipped hopefully along the buttons of her blouse. 'But, alas, my heart remained unmoved,' she wrote in her diary, as yet another lover failed to reach her; '. . . the cold heart of one that had received its death blow long ago, remained unkindled and unmoved,' she sighed to herself in a moment of private self-pity.

The attentions of all these men clearly went to her head, though, and her 'insatiable vanity' could not resist an invitation to dine with the professor, Amenta's associate. He was a beetle expert, with a patchy beard and cringing shoulders, who had about as much sex appeal as one of his creeping insects. But Margaret was still enjoying the power she could exert – the power to make men want her and to refuse them. The poor coleopterist was easy prey.

They, too, went for a stroll by the marina, and the professor was so excited he even suggested they both jump into the sea, clothes and all. 'Feel free,' she said, no doubt hoping it would dampen his ardour. Instead, he persuaded her to walk along some unlit side streets, where he spread half-a-dozen handkerchiefs on a stone wall for her to sit with him. Such forethought was endearing but hardly passion-rousing. Nevertheless, Margaret allowed him to kiss her, and she cringed as his trembling lips ventured to touch her brow, her cheeks and even her neck. Her repugnance was unable to allow kissing on the lips, and she records grimly in her diary: 'Well, if *this* is what it's like being kissed by a man one is indifferent to, the less I get of it the better pleased I shall be.'

Safely back in her hotel room, she scrubbed her face and neck to erase her shame. Next morning, when the professor arrived with flowers, she could not resist telling him she had washed all his kisses away with soap, but his crestfallen face quickly spoilt her heartless fun. For once she was not fending off improper suggestions. The poor man actually wanted to marry her. Marriage! She had quite forgotten about that, and it was not an idea she found attractive any more, least of all to this cringing little man with the 'grizzled head'.

The professor beat his retreat but not before telling Margaret she was the cruellest and most heartless woman he had ever met – a judgement she had already been given by several others on this trip. She knew they deserved her scorn. Nevertheless, she could not help thinking of herself as damaged goods. 'What I might have been, was indeed different to what I am,' she sighed to her diary, the ghost of her devotion for Septimus never far away.

Her final day with Signor Amenta was not without passionate appeals either, and he succeeded in getting her horizontal among the fragrant rock roses. Once more they lay in each other's arms, shaded by a wild fig tree, heavy with purple fruit, and Margaret's resolve temporarily drifted with the hot mountain air. Finally she resisted 'with all my might, and proved that a woman has the power, bodily as well as morally, to protect herself from dishonour, however near the edge of the precipice it may please her caprice to venture'. More to the point, she was disgusted by his admittance that he did not bother with taking precautions. 'I had no idea,' she wrote indignantly, 'that the passions of men were such a mixture of tenderness and brutality.'[9]

Amenta was ten years younger than Margaret and socially inferior, which probably helped her to keep him in his place, but she left him with a mixture of regret and guilt: regret for the passion unfulfilled, which she admits again she might have yielded to had she been in love; and guilt because she had rejected someone whose friendship and hard work on her behalf she genuinely valued.

Margaret's sense of guilt was tinged by a more complicated feeling, too, that she had somehow abused Amenta. She had been only too willing to use his youthful enthusiasm, his local knowledge and energetic butterfly-hunting to boost her own collection, without giving any thought to her companion's hopes or ambitions on his own account. He was as much a naturalist as she, yet his sphere did not and would never reach beyond his own parochial environment. He was tied to his native land as much by poverty as anything else and would never have the same opportunity as Margaret to widen his horizon, let alone become a recognized authority in his subject. Neither of them was a trained scientist, but Margaret had every reason to believe she would one day establish herself as a respected lepidopterist. Clearly Signor Ragusa believed that, too, for when he came to write his next article for the Sicilian entomological journal he mentioned her name but not Amenta's, who wrote a bitter letter to Margaret about it.

The unequal relationship between herself and those she encountered on her travels was to tackle Margaret's conscience many more times – just as it has every sensitive traveller since. She no more had solutions than the average tourist today, but she returned to England profoundly changed.

Butterflies were Margaret's key to freedom. Studying them gave her a socially acceptable way to exempt herself from a traditional domestic role in England. Collecting them, far beyond the constraining eyes of her own society, gave her the liberty to experiment with men. From now on she would be mistress of her own destiny, elegantly joining public and private pursuits in the name of science.

'Have I not the wide world before me?' she wrote eagerly back in England. Only her mother wished it were not so.

✸8✸
AMONG THE
AUSTRO-HUNGARIANS

ARGARET APPEARED IN the entomology world aged thirty-five, in 1897, fully formed and in perfect condition, just like one of her butterflies. What she lacked in experience and scientific training she made up with commitment and energy, and she was clearly a fast learner, because she quickly established herself as a serious collector. *The Entomologist* published her very first article on Sicilian butterflies that year, and the Natural History Museum in London was sufficiently impressed with forty-four of her specimens to send a Mr Heron to take possession of them. This was honour indeed. There were so many collectors in the 1890s that Margaret's butterflies must have been of outstanding quality and value, and thus began a close working relationship with the museum which lasted right up to her death over four decades later.

Margaret was ready to take her place in the world of butterflies and explore as much of it as she possibly could – and if she met some interesting people along the way so much the better. She particularly valued her friendships with men such as Mr Elwes and Bruno Galli-Valerio, so it was a pleasure to visit her Italian comrade *en route* from Sicily to England. They met at his father's house in Sondrio, north of Milan, which provided a refreshing break after the rigours of her Sicilian adventure.

No doubt her hosts were given a heavily edited version of events on the island, but there were other topics equally contentious which had nothing to do with Margaret's exploits, and they enjoyed spirited arguments. Both Bruno and his father were committed atheists, which distressed Margaret deeply, but there was no persuading them. One day she asked Bruno how he would feel if on death he discovered God existed after all and he found himself on the way to hell. 'In that case,' he answered confidently, 'I will find myself in the excellent company of other men of science, such as Voltaire and Darwin!' They would be much more interesting than the priests and nuns in heaven, he suggested, and Margaret could only laugh and agree, though privately she resolved to pray for her friend.

Back in England, her mother had decided to rent 7 Lansdown Place in Bath, so the family had a home once more, though the sisters found her more cantankerous than ever, especially Evelyn and Constance. Margaret resigned herself to her 'vegetable time', but at least this time there was a new challenge to take her mind off things. Bicycles were all the rage, and Rachel joined her for lessons with a 'fair youth' from Wallace's Cycle Depot. Soon they were off on a two-day jaunt from Bath to Bournemouth, and Margaret adored the heady rush of speed and freedom cycling offered.

She considered that the difficulties with her mother's moods were not that bad either, not least because she was 'so much occupied with her attachment to the Archdeacon that she seemed to have forgotten even to have rows'. Sadly, Evelyn's presence invariably resulted in a renewal of 'the frost', as the sisters called it, but her older sister was spared that year. Perhaps Margaret's chameleon skills of adapting to her company were sufficiently expert now to find ways of not provoking the likes of her mother, but it was never easy and always fraught with risk. 'It is like leading two lives,' she wrote in her diary, 'one Bohemian, the other Puritanical! It would never do to turn the underside up in either situation, or condition of life, the two sides would never do confronted one with the other.'

Margaret was always conscious that she had something to hide, especially in the company of women. Her adventures with men had cut her off from respectable Victorian values, which made drawing-room society almost impossible to endure. She had played other, more exciting games than draughts or bridge, and polite conversation was not only odious but dangerous, too. Margaret always feared she would betray her knowledge of the ways of men and find herself a social outcast. Much as she despised the confines of her class and background, she was in no way ready to give up membership. She wanted the best of both: respect and acceptance at home and freedom abroad. The former took all her mental energy, the latter all her courage and resourcefulness, yet travel abroad was her life blood now and she was incapable of staying out the winter in England.

She decided to explore Germany and Austria, though the chill winds buffeting the train in Holland made her wish she had chosen countries further south. She found the Dutch plain inexpressibly dull, and her introduction to Germany was no better. The porters in Dresden refused to release her luggage because she had forgotten to have it cleared with customs at the border with Holland, and Margaret cursed their dogged insistence on upholding the law. 'How I wished now I were in Italy. I could soon have got my own way then. The loose, unprincipled Italians would speedily have delivered me up my luggage,' she wrote indignantly. 'A little corruption in the form of a judiciously disposed lira would at once have brought matters to a close,' she insisted.

Driving sleet and piercing winds confirmed Margaret's antipathy to all things German, and only an introduction to the world-famous entomologist Dr Otto Staudinger persuaded her to stay. Mr Elwes had kindly written a letter for her, and she wasted no time in delivering it personally. She took an electric tram to his villa in the suburb of Blasewitz and was gratified to find Mr Elwes's letter had the desired effect, though not before the great man made it very clear he was extremely busy. No doubt he had little time for obscure lady amateurs, but Mr Elwes was a valued buyer of his specimens, and he graciously allowed Margaret to examine his splendid collection of European butterflies, the largest in the world at that time.[1] He also informed her the best hunting grounds for non-Alpine butterflies in Austria were in the immediate vicinity of Vienna, and Margaret needed no better excuse to leave Germany at once.

Armed with a further letter of introduction from Herr Staudinger, she arrived in Vienna at the beginning of May and found the city basking in warm sunshine. 'Of all the European capitals or towns of any importance that I have seen, never had one pleased me as did the fair city of Vienna,' she thrilled. She admired the great public buildings, the beautiful parks and the magnificent palace of Schönbrunn and found Vienna as elegant as she had found Dresden dull.

She set about looking up her next contact, Baron Adolf von Kalchberg, who was as warm and hospitable as Herr Staudinger was not, accompanying her on butterflying trips beyond the city and treating her to delicious meals at home with his wife. Margaret was charmed, but her joy was short-lived. A letter from Bath brought the news everyone had been dreading for years now: her sister Constance had died suddenly of yet another haemor-rhage in the lung. The whole family except Margaret had been by her bedside when she died, and Margaret felt her exclusion deeply. Both Geraldine and Uncle Lawes wrote to assure her she need not return to Eng-land, but of course that was out of the question. She left everything in her *pension* and took the next train back home.

The death of Constance was especially hard for Rachel, who had been very close to her younger sister, and Margaret tried to comfort her as best she could. They spent the month of June at Uncle Lawes's Rothamstead estate, playing croquet on the lawns of the great house and taking occasional trips out by carriage. It was the year of Queen Victoria's Diamond Jubilee, but the sisters were in no mood for celebrations and declined the chance to see their queen.

Rachel and Mother moved on to Aunt Anne's in Washingborough, but that was too melancholy for Margaret. Since her cousin Louie's death her aunt's house was a sad reminder of all the happy times they had spent there as children, and she chose to return to Vienna instead. There was nothing she could usefully do in England, and she would miss the butterfly season entirely if she did not leave soon.

It was hard to return to the place where she had received such awful news, but her entomology work soon took her mind off excessive grief. 'Any entomologist desirous of seeing the *Apatura* (Purple Emperors) reigning supreme must visit the Rohrwald, near Spillern, about twenty kilometres from Vienna, the first fortnight in July,' she wrote for her second published article. The iridescent wings of these lovely butterflies literally covered Margaret like so much giant confetti. They fluttered in her ears and settled on her hat, her blouse and even her net, and her spirit was irresistibly revived.

Sadly, this famous species of European butterfly is no longer found in Austria, long since exterminated by hordes of collectors, and even Mar-garet noted it was a miracle any survived in her day. 'Every peasant-boy was armed with a net of some sort, and I actually saw one lad with his hat decorated lavishly and wastefully with as many of those glorious insects as, with folded wings, he was able to cram together; that boy alone must at least have secured some thirty specimens,' she wrote in *The Entomologist*.[2]

Despite her joy of finding congenial company and beautiful insect prey, a chance conversation with the Baron about *Pararge roxelana* (a type of Lattice Brown butterfly) occurring in the Mehadia region of Hungary led Margaret to pack her bags almost at once. Only a few species of this butterfly occurred in the British Isles, so it was a great one for her collection, and she was also assured of finding another rare species – *Neptis aceris* (Hungarian Glider), which was entirely absent from Western Europe.

'Collecting should only be regarded as a means of procuring specimens for study and not as an end in itself,' the assistant keeper at the Entomological Department at the Natural History Museum had said, but Margaret was just setting out on her career as a collector and needed to impress. She wasted no time booking herself into lodgings at the famous spa resort of Herkulesbad, today known as Băile Herculane, in southwestern Romania. The town was on the main line of the Royal Hungarian Railways between Budapest and Orsova, so it was easy to reach, and Margaret could not help marvelling at the ease with which she could make her personal arrangements these days. Not so long ago she would have needed references from three clergymen before taking lodgings. Now she simply used the Cook's agent in Vienna to book her travel and accommodation according to her requirements. Most Continental trains had carriages reserved for the exclusive use of ladies – marked *Dames Seules* or *Damen-Coupé*, depending on the country concerned – and she did not have to worry about money either, since Cook's was already issuing an early form of traveller's cheque. Cook's Circular Notes to the value of £20 and up could be cashed in the local currency at any international Cook's office or participating bank.

She arrived in Herkulesbad past midnight, and her heart beat faster when she was met by a tall man with a dramatic mane of dark hair reaching down to his shoulders. She noted in her diary that her prospective landlord was past his prime, yet he was still 'the most artistic' figure of a man she had encountered in a long while. How thrilling to meet him in the dead of night and be swept off in his carriage, though she was glad his son-in-law was also present. He was a much smaller and less impressive figure, though a count for all that, and Margaret was grateful he spoke English. The father-in-law, Dr Popovich, sat in silence, an inescapable presence in his heavy mantle and immense felt hat, and Margaret found herself talking rather more than was ladylike.

The handsome doctor had three equally handsome daughters, who fascinated Margaret with their Bohemian lifestyle, though privately she disapproved of their untidy personal arrangements. Two of them were married but had dispensed with their husbands, and only the one married to Count Keglevich seemed to live by any respectable rules. But the women provided Margaret with welcome diversion from brooding on her sister's death, and she was soon a regular member of their daily tennis tournaments and occasional jaunts to the local casino.

Ever since her gambling in Monaco she had a horror of casinos and the people who frequented them, but she enjoyed the music and dancing, and it was the only time she met the doctor. 'Dr Popovich himself never appeared during the day time,' she marvelled, 'so that I only saw him on the evenings, when I accompanied them all to the Casino.' It was a shame she only collected butterflies during the day, the doctor commented on one of these occasions, for he was a *papillon de nuit*, and Margaret found herself inexorably attracted to him. He knew nothing about butterflies, but when he offered to accompany her one day she eagerly agreed.

Unfortunately, the morning in question turned out to be rainy and Margaret decided to lie in instead. But the doctor did not know butterflies only appear in sunshine, and Margaret was horrified when he let himself into her bedroom with her morning coffee. Worse, he made himself comfortable on her bed, and Margaret found herself making polite conversation in her nightdress. When at last he rose to leave, Margaret held out her hand, but instead of a handshake the doctor bent down to give her a long kiss on the cheek. 'Now I knew in Hungary it was the custom of the country for a gentleman to kiss a lady's hand, but I had never *heard* anything about the cheek,' she wrote, aghast. 'Still, as it might be a national custom, I overlooked the impertinence, and allowed him to go away under the impression that I would go for a walk with him that evening.'

But Margaret's instincts were right, and Dr Popovich was definitely not following normal customs, for he let himself into her bedroom a second time that morning, and this time he did not bother with a cup of coffee for an excuse. The thought of Madame Popovich in the very same house made Margaret burn with indignation – the attraction between them notwithstanding – and she resisted his kisses with all her vigour.

She should have moved out of the Popovich house straight away, but she was having far too much fun for that, and she also had her eye on someone else, a botanist she had met at tennis. He only spoke German, so romance did not progress very far there either, but at least he secured her the services of an excellent guide for the surrounding mountains who was so useful finding good butterfly grounds that she even recommended him to the readers of *The Entomologist*. Anyone visiting Herkulesbad should seek out the Romanian peasant Golopenza, she wrote, no doubt ensuring him work for years to come and perhaps atoning for Signor Ragusa's failure to mention Amenta in his writings on Sicily.

The ancient spa of Băile Herculane (Herkulesbad) nestles close to the Serbian border, in the south-western reaches of the Carpathian Mountains, and has been providing an irresistible combination of physical challenge and medicinal comfort for several centuries. Since it is located in a valley surrounded by towering peaks on all sides, there was very good reason for Margaret to hire a guide. The mountains claim lives every year, even now, from people attempting to climb without proper equipment or those straying from marked paths, and the butterflies Margaret was seeking were renowned for hovering in the most inaccessible ravines.

Perhaps to snub Dr Popovich Margaret invited his son-in-law Count Keglevich to join her in a day-long expedition up Mount Domoglet, over 1,000 metres high. She wrote gleefully, 'I don't think he quite knew what he was putting himself in for, indeed I think it was nothing short of cruelty the way I took this little drawing-room man over the very roughest ground . . . sometimes climbing on our hands and knees as we scrambled up the almost perpendicular side of the mountain, in some places so difficult, that I don't think even I, in my tennis shoes, could have managed to get up without the assistance of Golopenza.'[3]

She was terrifically excited to find *Parargue climene* (a type of Grayling) at the summit of Mount Domoglet, which was a great prize, since Lang's book on butterflies claimed it was only found in southern Russia. She must have been right, too, because *The Entomologist* allowed her to make her claim publicly. The Count was also pleased as the view from their perch was literally breathtaking. They could survey four different countries that day: to the north lay Hungary; to the south, beyond the snaking Danube River, Bulgaria stretched into a hazy blue horizon; west lay the Serbian plain of Vojvodina; and east was Romania. They smoked a celebratory cigarette and enjoyed their achievement.

'Yes, indeed,' Margaret wrote of that year, 'this was one of those rare days of which every summer brings me at least a few – a day of mountain panoramas, of climbing over rocks, of walking along the edge of precipices, of jumping and springing down the steep inclines of leaf-strewn forests, stopping perchance to drink some mountain spring, cold as ice, and throwing fresh vigour into my throbbing veins at every draught: a day never to be forgotten!'

Twelve hours of mountain hiking was nothing less than exhilarating to Margaret, whereas one hour among the 'false smiles of dressed out women and blasé men' made her feel weary beyond words. Much as she appreci-ated the company of her host's family, she felt their lack of common ground keenly. None of them had the slightest interest in natural history, and she could not share her pleasure with them. The doctor, meanwhile, tried his luck in her bedroom once more, only this time she was ready for him and dived under her bedclothes and refused to come out.

When it came time to leave Herkulesbad, the Count arranged for Margaret to be taken by carriage to the Danube at Orsova; she travelled the scenic route back by boat and train to Vienna, where the respectable welcome of the Baron von Kalchberg awaited. She was not quite ready to admit her collecting trip was over for that year and made one last visit to the forests of Mödling, outside the city, where she was rewarded with a freshly emerged autumn brood of *Colias chrysotheme* (Lesser Clouded Yellow). 'Such a bright, gay little butterfly,' she wrote enthusiastically, 'scudding over the rough ground on the heights above town, just the colour of the yellow flowers on which it loved to alight.'

After three days of hunting, she admitted to having wiped out that year's crop of butterflies at Mödling, and she hated herself for it, though her overriding feeling was one of a hunter's satisfaction, not least because she had caught a white female, which was unheard of in that species. She could not resist taking it to Dr Staudinger in Dresden on her way home, but he dismissed her find categorically, informing her that he had no such butterfly in his authoritative collection of European butterflies. It must be another species, he told her curtly, though he admitted that all *Colias* butterflies have white varieties of the female, so there was no reason to think the *chrysotheme* variety would be an exception. He brushed the tire-some English woman off, claiming important business elsewhere, but

Margaret was not cowed by greatness and took her find back to London, where she made a public appeal for information in *The Entomologist*.

Of course, the English climate was as 'detestable' as ever, but at least there was her entomology work and cycle touring to keep her busy and also the marriage to Dr Hill Leathes of her sister Geraldine, the first and last of the South Acre girls to get married. She did not envy her. 'No more life!' was her private view. 'No more adventures out in the world . . . no more exciting episodes.' But the wedding at St Marylebone Church in London was a joyful day, with all the surviving family attending and grand old Uncle Lawes giving away the bride.

Margaret was in an excellent frame of mind, not least because Mr Elwes was very interested in her white female *chrysotheme* butterfly, notwithstanding Herr Staudinger's views, and she could confidently look to a future where she might take her place among established entomologists. She wrote happily:

> I suppose some day I may be rather a distinguished person in the Entomological World, and though perhaps the distinction may not be the greatest I could have aspired to, every rung of the ladder of fame will have been pleasant, without one arduous or difficult step.
>
> For the way will have led me through flower-strewn meadows, over glorious mountains and sunny hill-sides, through the heart of dense forests, by the side of mountain streams, and on the shores of sunlit lakes. Does life present such varied scenes to everyone? I think not!

❀9❀

LADY ON A BIKE

'HE LIFE OF the spinster, odious as some may figure it in ideal, is as far as my experience of it has gone at present very delightful, and infinitely preferable to any other,' Margaret assured her diary.

Of course, it was less delightful in England than abroad, and the dreary weather and constant bickering in Bath were particularly depressing. But there were consolations to her 'vegetable period', too, such as an invitation to stay with her entomology mentor, Mr Elwes, at his estate in Colesbourne. To have this eminent man's undivided attention and spend happy working days studying his butterfly collection was a great privilege, and she was thrilled he shared his knowledge with her so willingly. It was yet another important step on the road to being taken seriously as a butterfly expert herself, and Mr Elwes was undoubtedly instrumental in her successful nomination for fellowship of the Royal Entomological Society in 1898.

Nevertheless, Margaret was always itching to leave England as soon as the Mediterranean spring beckoned, and this time she persuaded Rachel to accompany her to the French Riviera with their brand-new Coventry Humber bicycles.[1] She was a familiar customer at Thomas Cook's Head Office at Ludgate Circus in London by now, and its staff easily arranged for all of the sisters' possessions to be taken straight through to Cannes.

They booked into the Hotel St Barthelemy, having ensured against nasty surprises over bills by purchasing Cook's universally recognized Hotel Coupons. An early version of the all-inclusive deals of today, these coupons not only entitled the bearer to room and board at a fixed daily price but could also be used at any other participating establishment, so meals could be taken anywhere they pleased, not just at their own hotel restaurant.

Cousin Edith Curtois was to join them on their holiday, but Aunt Anne was taken gravely ill, and her daughter dutifully left just days after arrival. The sisters were sorry to see her go and sad about Aunt Anne, too. Margaret even pitied her mother, who was probably about to lose her favourite sister, but not enough to pack her bags herself. The rows had been vile of late, and Margaret wrote grimly in her diary that 'parents who imagine that their offspring will love them merely because they have brought them into the world will almost invariably live to find out, when it is too late, that they have failed to gain any filial affection and that in most cases the claims of duty being too frail to carry much weight, if any at all, a lonely old age will be in store for them'.[2]

It was only the beginning of February, but the sky was an azure blue and the sunshine was glorious. Who could bother with dreary old England? Not Margaret, who had brought along another toy, as well as the bicycle. She was the proud owner of a brand-new Bull's Eye Kodak camera, and she found it provided almost as much fun as her cycle. 'It was delightful skimming along on our bicycles,' she recorded, 'I with my Kodak attached to the weight carrier in front of me, so that whenever I saw any little group of peasants or animals that took my fancy, I had nothing to do but jump off and take a snap shot.'

Margaret and Rachel were happy tourists, flying along the coast road from Cannes to Menton, straight past the strutting crowds on the promenades. In Nice they saw Queen Victoria arrive in an open carriage – 'a little old lady dressed in black' – which provided excellent target practice for the camera, and there was endless fun to be had back at the hotel in Cannes, comparing shots with other guests. The sisters had tremendous energy, because even with taking the train back at the end of the day the distance from Cannes to Menton is the best part of eighty kilometres.

Losing 100 francs in the Casino at Monte Carlo persuaded Margaret she had better stick to cycling, and she persuaded her sister they should send their luggage ahead and try their luck with a more rewarding challenge: to cycle from Cannes to Venice via the Ligurian Alps. It was a journey of some five hundred kilometres that would take them along the French and Italian

Rivieras to the port of Genoa, over the mountains to Piacenza and across the sweeping plains of Lombardy and Veneto to Venice.

'Oh! Life is worth living to the touring cyclist, if it ever is,' Margaret wrote enthusiastically. With the spring sun on their faces and a good breeze behind them, the effort of cycling seemed nothing at all, and there was plenty of time for taking snap shots along the way, though not everyone was a willing subject. Some washerwomen in Alassio, across the Italian border, took great exception, and Margaret committed the cardinal tourist sin of snapping them anyway before beating a hasty retreat from swearing and stones. No doubt she was not the first to have presumed on those women, and she admits in her diary that 'it is a curious thing, when once a place becomes frequented by the foreign tourists, how the manners of its inhabitants deteriorate'. It was a problem set to get much worse with the advent of mass tourism over half a century later.

After Alassio the coast rose steeply, necessitating some walking, but the sight of coastal towns folded into the warm shade of sun-baked precipices was inspiration enough to push on. Beyond Albenza the coast smoothed out again, and the sisters set a flying pace through buttercup meadows and open country.

'Yes, it was a dream to feel so free,' wrote Margaret, as they crossed and recrossed the railway tracks heading east, feeling very superior to the carriages and mule carts that had to queue whenever a train was expected, while they simply slipped past the barriers via the pedestrian route. It was pleasant to pity the railway passengers, too, stuck in hot and dusty compartments.

They had lunch with a German lady cycling alone in the opposite direction, armed with a revolver to protect her virginity, which she claimed had been assaulted several times already. Margaret was not impressed. Her virginity had withstood many assaults without the use of firearms.

It was not all plain sailing, however. Rachel crashed her bike to avoid running over a dog, and, though she was unhurt, it was not the first time they had had trouble with animals. Wherever they went they attracted dogs that chased after them, and the donkeys were a menace, too, often panicking at the sight of billowing skirts on two wheels. Many a cart and carriage driver must have sworn at those foreigners on their fancy machines, but fortunately the sisters were never involved in a serious accident, though Margaret came close. Twice a dog got hold of her skirt and almost unseated her.

One of their overnight stops was in the coastal town of Savona, and Margaret was in her element laughing and flirting with the 'second rate commercial travellers' they encountered over dinner. Soon they reached the great port of Genoa, though neither sister thought it was at all '*superba*', as the city liked to call itself. It rained incessantly, and there were plenty of obstacles for cyclists in addition to the weather. The danger from horse, mule and dog was massively increased, and there were also treacherous tram lines and inconvenient waterways.

There was nothing for it but to sit out the weather at the Hotel Smith, where Margaret recorded that they were forced to pass the time with painfully boring guests. There was a multitude of heavily chaperoned English daughters and noisy Germans and Americans, and the sisters turned their backs on Genoa just as soon as the rain stopped. They were hardened cyclists by now, but they had not yet reached their greatest challenge, the Ligurian Alps, which rose up behind the city and blocked their path to Venice. The road north quickly began to snake its way into the mountains, and many hours of pushing the bikes on foot were necessary before reaching their first inn. It was a squalid hovel in the village of Tor-riglia, but they were grateful for food and a bed for the night and ignored the dirty cutlery and mottled sheets.

The weather was still very changeable, but the sisters preferred to press on rather than remain in their filthy hostel, resigning themselves to pedalling into the clouds, over 1,000 metres above sea level. Freezing rain almost blinded them on the downward slopes and the rain-slicked track was very dangerous indeed, forcing them to stop after just a few hours. Having no luggage, they had to retire to bed while their clothes dried over a fire, and Rachel decided to throw in the towel and carry on by diligence. But Margaret was determined to beat the mountains and the weather and was rewarded with a glorious day racing past bubbling cataracts and valleys just bursting into bloom.

At Bobbio the inn was so filthy Margaret chose to sit up all night rather than try her bed, but it did nothing to dampen her spirit. She had enough energy to write poetry until three in the morning and was ready and waiting when Rachel arrived in time for breakfast.

'How my heart responded to the gladness of earth and sky as I coasted along, ever descending from the bleak, cold mountains, down into the sunny plains of Italy,' she wrote.

The trees and bushes were already in full leaf, the nightingales sang all day long, and their hotel in Piacenza provided a welcome return to the comforts of civilization. They almost floated to their next stop at Cremona and stayed for four rest days, grateful to be reunited with their luggage and the opportunity of a change of clothes. They visited the home of Stradivarius – the world's most famous violin-maker – which was a café now, and Margaret delighted in the swallows flitting under the roof-tops and the grass growing on the streets.

It was a struggle for Rachel to keep up with her big sister, but she valiantly tried, cycling over seventy kilometres from Cremona to Mantua in one day. The landscape had flattened out by this stage, and the roads were excellent. On one occasion they went from one kilometre stone to the next in under three minutes, which was good going, especially without the help of modern gears.

By the time they reached Verona they felt they really had returned to the world again, which was not necessarily a good thing. In Vicenza they got caught up in a bread riot and were lucky to endure nothing worse than insulting gestures from the crowd. The increase in bread prices caused by the Spanish-American War had sparked serious riots across the country, and in Margaret's beloved Milan over 1,000 people were said to have lost their lives. In what was termed a revolution on the streets, the soldiers had shot demonstrators like so many fleeing rabbits.

But Margaret and Rachel were cushioned from the realities of life in Italy, only enjoying the best it had to offer without worrying about politics. The sensation of being an independent tourist was blissful, and it hardly mattered they had to take their final stretch by train. There were no roads across the salt marshes around Venice at the time, but arrival was sweet all the same. The fabled city of canals and gondolas was a magical place to end their adventure, and the sisters spent happy final days at the Hotel Metropôle, where their bedroom window soon became a popular spot for begging children.

Reluctantly Margaret bade farewell to her sister, who left to regale Bath with her adventures. But the butterfly season was only just beginning, so there was no question of Margaret returning home just yet. Uncle Lawes had given her an introduction in the Hungarian capital, and she fully intended to continue her successful collecting from the summer before. She had set her heart on a rare variety of her favourite *Melanargia* (Marbled White) butterfly, which she knew was only found in the forests near Budapest.

She took a boat from Venice to the great Austrian – as it was then – port of Trieste, and as the lights of the Grand Doge's Palace receded from view she tried not to feel the deep loneliness her sister's absence inevitably caused. Instead, she concentrated on the eternal marvel of travel and arrived in Trieste at dawn, its port bristling with a forest of mastheads and the quay jammed with noisy bullock-wagons. She stopped off long enough to have breakfast and buy a cycle touring guide to Austria-Hungary, before taking off under her own steam once more, this time braving steep wooded slopes alone. The land rises up dramatically above the city, a fore-taste of the Yugoslav mountains that wrap around its bay, and she was soon working hard as she climbed ever higher across the Istrian peninsula to Rijeka – in her day the Hungarian port of Fiume – where she could catch a train to Budapest.

It was terrifying at times, not because of the dark forests but because she came across a wicked-looking man as she took a walking rest who seemed ready to rob and murder her given the slightest chance. She was far from human habitation by now, and she knew there was no help near by, but happily she was able to escape before anything horrible happened, pedalling for her life – or so she thought. It took two days to cross what looks like a short distance on the map, and she was grateful to rest on the train journey north, where she would soon be making the delightful acquaintance of the gentlemen at the Budapest Entomological Society.

A jollier and happier group of men she had yet to encounter, she wrote approvingly after arrival, and was very pleased to join their weekly meetings at a local *Gasthaus*. It was the kind of gathering Margaret liked best: good food and wine in the company of men who shared her passion for butter-flies, unfazed by a female in their midst, yet gallant with it. They were a mixed bunch, too: the diminutive Herr Pavel did not appear to have made acquaintance with a bath yet was an excellent source of introductions. The young Herr Török charmed her with a rose at every occasion, while Herr

Aigner was an expert on the very butterfly she was seeking: the *suwarovius* variety of *Melanargia japygia*, 'a white, hovering butterfly, the very essence of elegance and purity – a gem'.

Each week she anxiously enquired after sightings of her quarry until, at last, she heard it was on the wing. 'On the 12th of June, beneath a brilliant sky, we started in the early morning from Buda-Pest,' she records in her second article for *The Entomologist*, 'a party of five in all, Herr Aigner acting as guide, as he alone had previously visited this wonderful spot.'[3]

They were heading for the forest of Peszér, several hours south of the capital by train and cart, and though the journey to Dabas was easy enough the cart ride was hell. At times the wheels of their hay wagon sank axle-deep in sand, and the poor horses had to work hard to pull them out. When they were not stuck in sand they were bumping excruciatingly over rutted tracks or sinking into the mire of flooded grassland, surrounded by immense herds of long-horned cattle. It was certainly no place for a bicycle, and Margaret was grateful she had heeded Herr Aigner's advice on that point.

It was over four hours before they reached the 'scene of action', but it was worth it in the end. All the hardships of reaching Peszér forest were forgotten at the first sight of swarming butterflies in sun-drenched clearings. The *suwarovius* was flying about by the hundreds, the white wings of the females suffused with a deep primrose tint which gave a lovely background to their delicate black markings. 'It is worth the long journey from England to Hungary, if only to pay a visit to Peszér in June,' wrote Margaret in her article on Hungarian butterflies, 'especially in the society of so many congenial companions and kindred spirits.' Sadly, modern enthusiasts would be wasting their time, because this particular Marbled White is no longer found anywhere in Europe.[4]

Margaret did not reach her hotel room until close to midnight that day, but she was so thrilled with her catches that she worked long into the night, setting her butterflies by the weak light of a single electric bulb. It was not only the butterflies that had fired her up, either. The dashing Herr Török had awakened a longing in her 'that all women must have sometimes', and she could still taste the wild strawberries he had gathered for her in the forest.

No man could compete with her commitment to butterflies, however, and she turned her back on potential suitors for a return to the rich hunting grounds of Karlsbad. Her trusted guide Golopenza was ready to take her wherever she pleased, and she spent happy days alternating between solitary cycling trips in the valley and strenuous mountain expeditions with him. She wrote, 'I often think how little my Mother's friends, who sometimes come to see my butterflies in the winter at Bath, realise the long hours of toil and heat and thirst those little insects represent, as beneath the scorching rays of a southern sun, after a hard day's collecting, I turn my steps homewards, with feet blistered and sore, sometimes with the insteps covered with mosquito bites and the irritating pricks of a thousand tiny spurs of dried up grass-seeds.' Yet she could imagine no better way of life, often spending ten or twelve hours out collecting, with nothing to sustain her but a few pieces of dried bread and sheep's milk bought from local shepherds. Physical hardships simply paled into insignificance compared to the pleasure of catching just one rare butterfly, and she learnt new tricks every season. In Karlsbad, for example, she discovered the best way to catch the rare Lattice Brown (*Pararge roxelana*) was to wait near an oak tree oozing the resin that the butterfly loved to feed on.

Tears ran down Golopenza's face when she announced her departure at last, and Margaret was deeply touched by his devotion. She never expected anyone to care about her and was always genuinely surprised by the affection she inspired, especially in those who worked for her. But Uncle Lawes's friend, the Baron Radossevich, had invited her to visit his estate in Karavan-Szakul, and there was little time left to take up his offer before the butterfly season was over. 'So it was that on a summer's evening, I found myself the sole inmate of a small low house, the windows of my room, which was on the ground floor, looking out on one side through leafy trellis work on to a courtyard at the back of a good-sized country house,' she records. Less romantic were the mice and ants infesting her room, but she coolly murdered the former in traps and the latter with benzene.

The local peasants struggled to make sense of the strange lady on a bike. Why did she need to come all the way to Hungary to catch butterflies? they wondered. Inevitably she also aroused suspicion, on one occasion even finding herself the target of violence when she inadvertently trespassed on the land of a neighbouring estate. The women and children working in the fields attacked her with their threshing poles, and she returned to the Baron covered in bruises.

It seemed a good time to leave, and though he was very kind about her ordeal she thanked him for his hospitality and took the train back to Budapest. At least there she was assured only friendly attentions from her colleagues at the Entomological Society, and it was good to see Herr Török one last time before returning to England. He wined and dined her, and together they enjoyed some very tentative romantic strolls along the shores of the Danube, where medieval Buda rises high above the river across from the imperial boulevards of modern Pest. The mighty Parliament lining the river looked a lot like Westminster, though it was much larger.

Margaret thought she could sense Török's growing love for her but was too insecure to let her guard down. Herr Aigner assured her his young friend was utterly besotted, that it was courage he lacked, not ardour. But he failed to declare his love, and Margaret left without admitting to more than friendship either. It was yet another missed opportunity, or perhaps it was simply self-preservation.

She took the train across Europe once more, stopping off in Milan to enjoy the 'peaceful intimacy of platonic friendship' with Bruno before facing the cool atmosphere of England, which quite literally arrived before she even reached her destination. On the train from Paris to Calais her underwear inexplicably refused to stay put, requiring a quick dash to the ladies, where she removed 'the articles in question, thereby being in a condition still more to feel the cold'.

Her return to England was even sadder than usual. Aunt Anne had died, and Washingborough Manor was to be sold. First Constance and Louie had been lost, then Aunt Anne, and now yet another familiar home was to go. It destroyed one more important link to England, turning Margaret's focus ever more clearly towards her new home, in the community of naturalists.

☙ 10 ☙
ROUGH RIDES IN GREECE

EATH STALKED THE winter season of 1898, and all thoughts of entomology were pushed aside. Rachel, Margaret's favourite sister and loyal cycling companion, developed pleurisy and then the early symptoms of tuberculosis, and the whole family feared for her life. Tempers flared and arguments over treatment opened a deep gulf between the sisters and mother. 'The old lady' – as she was now referred to – was determined to keep Rachel with her in Bath. But Margaret and her sisters hatched a plan with Uncle Lawes to get her as far away from the lung-rotting fogs of England as possible. He gave Margaret *carte blanche* with the expenses, and she set about hiring a doctor and nurse for the long journey south.

The theory was that Rachel would have a better chance of surviving the winter in the mellow climate of the south of France, and it would also help to keep her spirits up. She loved the Côte d'Azur above all places, and Margaret was given charge of getting her to Menton, where they had had such happy times so very recently. The strain of this responsibility weighed heavily on Margaret, but she used Cook's head office in London to best effect, and they not only booked all luggage through to Menton but also arranged for a private invalid carriage to be attached to the regular train from Bath to Dover and also from Calais to Menton.

It was amazing what you could do with unlimited funds, and Margaret was impressed enough to describe their travelling arrangements in her diary. Each train had a private van attached for their party which was 'fitted up with every convenience, lavatory communicating with two separate compartments . . . in one of which was slung a large basket bed, and there Rachel lay through the long hours of this tedious journey'.

After a night's rest at the Lord Warden Hotel in Dover, a bath chair conveyed Rachel down to the pier and awaiting boat, where she was installed in a private cabin. The crossing was thankfully calm, and, after another night's rest in Calais, Margaret, Rachel, a Dr Bannatyne and his nurse made the final twenty-three-hour journey to Menton. It was an arduous journey, even for a healthy person, but the thought of palm trees and orange blossom sustained them all, and Margaret made full use of Uncle Lawes's bounty in the dining carriage with Dr Bannatyne.

They booked into the Hotel d'Orient, which had served the sisters so well the year before, and the grim reason for their visit now was at least ameliorated by the luxurious apartments afforded to them by their kind uncle. But the prognosis for Rachel was not good. Her lungs were already badly affected, and there was little more to do than hope for the best. Margaret tried hard to stay positive, but it was a struggle. Only a visit from their cousins Edith and Lisle Curtois saved her from sinking into despair, and she was occasionally persuaded to leave her sister's bedside and go cycling for the day.

By May of the new year Rachel was recovered enough for Margaret to think of giving up her place to their younger sister Florence, and, though she left with a heavy heart, she was sufficiently reassured to allow herself to think of butterflies. Menton, that loveliest of places, had now become the saddest spot on earth. Her childhood companion and dearest friend was in the grip of an incurable disease – like Constance before her – and it was heart-breaking to think that Rachel would probably never again be strong enough to go cycle touring. Reluctantly she moved not far, to Hyères, at the western end of the Côte d'Azur, where she joined her old friend Mr Raine, who was no longer sharing life with Mrs Cooke but now had an official wife.

Margaret wondered how someone could be lucky enough to inspire the love of not one but two people, and she wished she were capable of inspiring devotion. But she had long ago convinced herself she was incapable of attracting honourable love, and she felt her essential loneliness more deeply than ever. She left the happy couple and moved north to Dignes-les-Bains, perched in the Provençal Alps, where the butterflying was said to be excellent and the company of fellow naturalists would distract her from the personal.

It proved an excellent choice, for the ebullient owner of the Hotel Boyer soon introduced Margaret to all the other entomologist guests, including Mr Henry Lang, no less, author of the only complete English reference book on European butterflies at the time. Margaret was thrilled to meet him, though not so thrilled with his wife, whose manners were 'most stand-off and repulsive', according to Margaret's diary. No doubt she was tired of ladies fawning around her husband.[1]

Margaret could bide her time, however, since she planned to spend a month pursuing her new project of hunting caterpillars with which to breed her own perfect butterfly specimens. There was almost more interest in this than hunting the insects themselves, as one had the added pleasure of seeing close up the extraordinary metamorphosis from caterpillar (larva) to chrysalis (pupa) to butterfly (imago). All she needed to do was to find caterpillars and their preferred food plant, take them home to her hotel room and then provide a safe enclosed area for the spectacle to unfold. It was surprising how simple it was. Any container would do, and Margaret's first breeding contraption was no more than a jar with a branch in it, closed over with perforated gauze at the top to prevent escape.

Each caterpillar would go through several stages of moulting – known as 'instars' – before attaching itself to a branch or leaf and then using special glands to create the hard casing necessary for pupation. It was a most tantalizing stage, because for up to ten days there would seem to be nothing going on at all. Yet one day – usually in the morning – the miracle of a perfect butterfly would emerge at last, pulling itself free of its pupal casing and hanging limply upside down to rest. The magic of this moment was a sight to treasure, and the highlight was yet to come, for it takes a butterfly up to an hour to get its blood pressure up to coursing through every last vein in its wings, inflating them sufficiently to spread and dry out. Until that final stage has been accomplished the butterfly is a crumpled, flightless creature, and the observer must patiently wait for the first flutter of iridescent wings.

Making friends with the Langs took a little longer than breeding a butterfly, but after a few weeks they warmed to Margaret sufficiently to go hunting with her, though even this was fraught with difficulty. Mr Lang was what Margaret called 'a dawdler', and it was a struggle just to get out of the hotel. When they did reach their hunting grounds at last, it became apparent that Mr Lang had forgotten his collecting box and had nowhere to put his catches.

'Every pocket was searched and patted, till at last it became extremely evident that no box was there!' Margaret wrote with astonishment.

'I've forgotten to bring one,' the poor man said, rather obviously.

'Never mind,' Margaret graciously replied and let him squirm for a while before offering to fetch him a suitable container from the nearest village.

The only thing Margaret could find was an old jam jar, which was hardly ideal, but her efforts were in vain anyway. By the time she returned, Mr Lang had headed off without her, into the gorge they had planned to explore, and Mrs Lang was busy reading a novel. It was as well to remember his true vocation was God, not butterflies, but Margaret could hardly believe this bumbling amateur was the author of one of her favourite reference books.

'So I saw no more of him and went back to Digne, leaving the worthy couple to follow their own devices,' she records tersely.

A Mr Kollmorgen from Berlin, on the other hand, told Margaret she was the most delightful collecting companion he had ever known, and she was sorry to see him go, notwithstanding he had a wife. But the butterfly season was almost over, and it was time to take care of Rachel once more. Temperatures were now commonly reaching 35 degrees centigrade in the shade – too hot for Rachel – and the doctor had dispatched her and Florence to the cooler climes of Switzerland, where Margaret returned to her sister's bedside.

She was in the village of Leysin, perched over 1,000 metres above the eastern shores of Lake Geneva, where English tuberculosis patients were a regular industry in those days. Their doctors' faith in the dry mountain air had resulted in several hotels being converted into large sanatoria, and the villagers were used to the sight of coughing foreigners on their deck-chairs. Every day they were tightly wrapped in blankets and lined up in neat rows to breathe the clean atmosphere and revive their spirits with the glorious sight of snow-crowned peaks. The other great occupation was gossip and intrigue, so Margaret had no hesitation in leaving Rachel for several hours each day to go cycling.

From Leysin a steep winding road snaked down to the vineyards around Aigle's medieval castle and, barely fifteen kilometres further, Margaret could cruise along the great lake to the café terraces of Montreux. 'There is a feeling about Switzerland quite peculiar to itself,' she wrote, 'the mountains of other lands somehow are not like the Swiss Alps – the very roar of their cataracts has another sound – and the scent of the Swiss hay fields is a thing apart.' Yet it was all a little too easy for Margaret, who always preferred a challenge. 'That very sense of safety in itself', she wrote, 'robs me of a charm for danger, risk and adventure which do possess a charm for some of us, and I own to being amongst the number.'

However, Margaret was there to take care of her sister, not have adventures, and she took her duty seriously in spite of being able to do very little. Death was coming to get Rachel, and it was pitiful to watch her decline. A painful hacking cough tore at her lungs, threatening her daily with yet another haemorrhage and causing great pain. Florence and Evelyn each took their turn in Leysin, and Margaret's only pleasure at this grim time was meeting Bruno in Lausanne on her way back to England. She travelled with her cousin, Florence Curtois, who caused great offence by saying she would not wish to be kissed by 'that little man'.

Bath brought no respite from sorrow. Hurley was also losing her grip on life, suffering from delirium and fever, and Margaret mourned her best friend, who had been her closest ally since childhood. Mother, on the other hand, was likened to 'a savage, ferocious lion', intolerable to live with and impossible to deny. Only a visit from the Langs gave respite from family rows, and Margaret was deeply grateful. Even better, the Reverend Lang offered the highest praises for the professional quality of her butterfly collection, and Margaret was delighted, conveniently forgetting her dim view of his collecting methods. 'Just now I seemed to be booming in the Entomological World,' she wrote happily.

Mr Elwes also honoured her with his presence and persuaded Margaret to lend him some of her finest specimens for a work he was about to publish. It hurt her to part with them, but she could hardly refuse the man who had given her so many of her best introductions and shared his expert knowledge with her.

Margaret saw in the new century back at Leysin, where the sanatorium did its best to entertain the guests with banquets and copious amounts of alcohol. But the inmates were dying at an alarming rate, and Margaret could not help noticing the almost daily arrival of silent horse-drawn hearses, whose visits were always timed to coincide with dinner, when everyone was occupied and safely out of the way. She was ashamed of minding so much about the intrigues and affairs that went on, but she did. 'Immorality is rife among the inmates of this cloud-world, and scandals are many,' she records. 'People eat, drink and make merry, and sometimes it is those who are nearest death that laugh the loudest.'

She knew she ought not to blame them, but it was a relief when spring came to Leysin at last and Margaret was free to set off once more. She needed to breathe more freely herself, only in her case that required Mediterranean sunshine, butterflies and the possibility of adventure.

Margaret chose the Greek Mediterranean for her first expedition in the twentieth century, renewing her acquaintance with several other entomologists during a visit to Corfu on the way and relishing the fact she was steadily gaining recognition as a collector. She also noted with satisfaction that her relations with men had 'advanced considerably, in spite of the great train of years' she now carried, and there was nothing she could not handle travelling alone. The terror of arriving at Limerick station without a clue was a distant memory. These days she knew just what to do, and arriving by boat in the busy port of Patras she calmly sipped a *café au lait* while hotel agents, porters and boatmen fought over her luggage. When at last she intervened to let them know her choice of hotel, the brawl instantly subsided, and she graciously allowed herself to be led away. But these were small pleasures compared to the joy of receiving a telegram that announced the imminent arrival of her great friend and mentor Henry Elwes.

They met in Athens, and Margaret was thrilled when he invited her to join him and his courier on his proposed hunting trip. What remnants of depression remained from her gloomy months in Switzerland evaporated in the busy days of preparation, and she even found time for a little romance, too, going for moonlit visits to the Acropolis with a young American called Mr Henderson. She admitted rather ruefully that the 'ground was getting just a little slippery beneath my feet', and she was not referring to the path. But Elwes's announcement that it was time to leave conveniently whisked her off to a more chaste environment, with no chance of sliding down the slippery slope of romance and disgrace.

Elwes and Margaret shared their common birthday – 16 May – in the Peloponnese mountains beyond Diakofto, and her spirit soared as she found herself riding a sturdy chestnut in the wake of Mr Elwes and his guide. They spent exhilarating days riding up the dramatic Vouraikos Gorge between Diakofto and Kalavrita, which rises almost 1,000 metres in the space of twenty kilometres, and Margaret felt liberated by Mr Elwes's suggestion of riding astride her saddle, rather than the old-fashioned ladies' way. She promised herself never to use any other method from now on. No doubt it was much safer, too, because there were no side-saddles to be found anywhere and the going was very tough.

'The Greek roads bore in many places a striking resemblance to the partially hardened surface of a ploughed field,' she was to write in her first article for *The Entomologists' Record*, 'and frequently there were no roads at all . . .'[2] Getting about on horseback was the only way to travel inland. As for the inns they encountered, 'the Greek innkeeper often seemed to think that to have two sheets on a bed was an unnecessary luxury, and sometimes they provided none at all'. But none of these hardships stopped Margaret enjoying herself, and she took bed-bugs and unfamiliar sanitary arrangements in her stride.

On one occasion Mr Elwes woke her at two in the morning, wondering if she could possibly be ready to catch a boat in quarter of an hour. 'Of course I could, and I did!' she wrote, delighted. 'And in the dark night with fitful gleams of moonlight, and now and then just a spitting of warm raindrops blowing on our faces, we found ourselves in a cockle-shell boat rocking over the waves of the Gulf of Corinth, Mr Elwes swearing loudly at the boatmen in English, while all I felt was that we were in imminent peril of being upset any minute . . .'[3]

At any rate, travel with Henry Elwes was never entirely without comfort, for he 'never took the trouble to do anything his courier could not do for him, and he never ate bad food where it was possible to procure better', she wrote fondly. He always included her in his purchases, whether it was a better horse or a finer meal. Best of all, he left her with his paid-for courier when it came time for him to leave, and she was happy enough to carry on her explorations alone.

Marcos was a good-looking young man, and, as usual, Margaret had to take care not to let things get too familiar, though luckily he did not speak a word of English. 'Often in the course of my life', she confided to her diary, 'had my words and actions kept pace with my thoughts, I don't quite know where I should have been, unless it were in Hell!' But it was difficult to keep the necessary distance while travelling rough in mainland Greece, where it was normal for a man to come into her bedroom at all hours of the day and night. If she wanted to be absolutely sure of privacy she had to rent an entire dormitory for herself, which seemed a bit excessive.

There was nothing for it but to concentrate hard on the butterflies, and she certainly made poor Marcos work for his wages. 'Marcos didn't appreciate the snakes at all,' she wrote of their hunting in the marshes around Messolongi, 'though he was never so vehement in his protestations that he was not afraid of them, as when he had just jumped half a foot off the ground at the sight of one, or possibly on no greater provocation than the rustle of a lizard in the grass!' But both Mr Elwes and Margaret had set their heart on the fiery copper butterfly known as *Chrysophanus ottomanus*, and the tall reeds and flowering grasses around Messolongi were its favourite haunt.

The richest hunting grounds, however, turned out to be in the vicinity of two remote monasteries in the Peloponnese Highlands, and Margaret spent the entire month of June 1900 there, riding out in temperatures well over 30 degrees centigrade. 'The monastery of Hagia Lavra is distinguished for having been the first place in Greece from whence waved the flag of freedom after the occupation of the Turks,' Margaret was to instruct her readers in *The Entomologists' Record*, 'and the monastery of Megaspelaeon is still more celebrated for having been the only place in Greece which, owing to its absolutely impregnable situation, never surrendered to the Turks at all.' Megalo Spilaio – in modern Greek – means 'built into the rock', and the monastery is literally tucked into the mountainside, a good 100 metres of sheer rock face above it, and only a steep winding path reaching up to the entrance. Sadly, where the Turks failed a powder keg left over from the War of Independence (1821–7) succeeded, and the original building was blown up, to be replaced by an ugly building in the 1930s. These days the monasteries do not welcome female guests, but in Margaret's time the monks were happy to share their simple but delicious meals with any respectful visitor.

On one occasion, when Margaret got drenched in a rare thunderstorm, the monks of Agia Lavra (modern spelling) even provided her with one of their own cassocks to wear while her clothes were dried over a stove. The local shepherds were equally hospitable, and very often she found herself sharing delicious fresh goat's milk and cream cheese, for which they invariably refused payment. '*Tipote! Tipote!*' they would cry, meaning 'nothing', whenever she offered them money, though the exceptions to this rule were always exorbitant in their price.

'To the butterfly collector in Greece *Colias heldreichi* is the one prize before all others,' Margaret wrote further, and the long thirsty hours in the blinding sun were all forgotten when she discovered this very butterfly swarming on the slopes of Mount Chelmos. Her entomologist's heart glowed as she jumped off her horse to skid and fall among the sun-baked crags, catching one magnificent male after another, and soon her collecting box was full of their deep-orange wings speckled with black scales and a wonderful shot of rich purple round the edges. Thus, yet another success-ful summer season was brought to an end, and Margaret took a steamer from Patras to Trieste and made her way back to Rachel.

The drawn-out tragedy of losing her sister was made worse by the arrival of 'the old lady' as well, and Margaret was disgusted to find herself cast in the role of spinster daughter. Geraldine had come, too, and it was the first time the Fountaine sisters were all in the same place for some time. If only the occasion had been a happy one, and worse was to come: a cable arrived announcing the death of their beloved Uncle Lawes from tropical dysentery. 'Since that day had dawned a great light had gone out, and we had lost the best and truest friend we have ever had,' she grieved in her diary.

She hurried back to England to attend her uncle's funeral without telling Rachel the reason for her sudden departure. They all agreed it would probably kill her, which might have been a mercy considering the slow, agonizing death she was already facing, but the decision was meant kindly. Margaret wrote of the funeral, 'I can recall it now. It is one of those scenes in life never to be forgotten, the coffin covered with flowers standing in the centre aisle, next the chancel, Cousin Charlie, the present baronet, as chief mourner, at the end of the pew in front of us, the crouching figures of Diane and Sylvia, the hymn spoke of loved ones far away, and made me think of Rachel . . .' It really was a tragic time. Within weeks of Uncle

Lawes's death, both his granddaughter Lilian's children died of the same disease.[4]

There was only one way to stay sane, and that was to keep busy. There was plenty to worry abut, too. Uncle Lawes's death meant the sisters no longer had a trustee for their money, and Margaret was charged with sorting out the bureaucracy. It was a daunting business, even though her uncle had left instructions for his accountant to help. The City was an even more strictly male preserve then than it is now, and just walking the streets there made Margaret feel out of place. But after many complications and a mountain of paperwork had been cleared it was established that the sisters' capital had increased to £35,000, which gave each of them an annual income of just over £300 a year – just as before. Uncle Lawes's son made no difficulties about separating the Fountaine money from his own, and thus the sisters' income was secured.

Margaret's only consolations for spending the autumn in London were the hospitality of her sister Geraldine in Richmond and her first public presentation at the October meeting of the Entomological Society of London. Jointly with Henry Elwes, she presented the findings of her Greek collecting trip in the presence of the President of the Society and many other distinguished Fellows, and the crowning moment was undoubtedly when Mr Elwes announced his opinion that she was the first British collector known to have caught *Colias heldreichi*, the lovely butterfly she had found in such profusion on Mount Chelmos.

'No matter what nationality, there's nothing like them,' Margaret wrote of her fellow naturalists on that day. 'They bring a whiff of the summer winds, a flash of the summer sunshine into their meetings', and no doubt the distinguished gentlemen enjoyed her company, too.

Rachel was to live for another three agonizing years, but her story fades from Margaret's diaries as the course of her own life sweeps her beyond Europe and into the arms of her partner for life. At thirty-nine, the most exciting and fulfilling decades were still to come, though Margaret herself had not the slightest inkling of it. By now she had given up on ever finding happiness with a man, and both her personal and her family life appeared dogged by a constant shadow of sorrow and death.

It was the end of the Victorian age, and Margaret experienced her queen's death, in the first month of 1901, on a very personal level. 'I am no lover or admirer of Kings and Queens as a rule,' she wrote, 'but Victoria was one whose memory the whole Earth must ever hold in reverence and veneration.' She was in London for her funeral, where she joined the huge crowds that came out to pay homage.

> So the same eight cream-coloured horses who had drawn her carriage on the day of her triumph at the Diamond Jubilee were now attached to the gun-carriage upon which the Royal coffin was placed . . .
>
> Immediately behind rode the King – now Edward VIII – in full military uniform, on his right the German Emperor on his white charger, and the Duke of Connaught on his left.
>
> The crowds were enormous, a great black moving mass, so silent except when Lord Roberts rode by, and then indeed even on this solemn occasion, a few subdued cheers were raised for 'Bobs' [who led the successful campaign against the Boers].

It was indeed the end of an era, both public and private. From now on Margaret would live most of her life far away from England, spending long periods of time in Africa, Australia, Asia and the Americas. It was going to be a time of great personal and professional success, and, though Margaret's path was never straight, even she would have been astonished to hear what fate had in store for her.

Margaret aged forty, from the frontispiece to her diary of 1903

LOVE
1901–1927

❋11❋

THE DRAGOMAN LOVER

ARGARET WAS ITCHING to experience the East – particularly the Holy Lands – and Thomas Cook's literature assured her that 'ladies, however helpless or nervous, need not fear to explore these lands of surpassing interest'. Margaret was neither helpless nor nervous and forewent the strictures of an escorted tour in favour of independent travel. All she had to do was choose between the mostly overland route via the Orient Express to Constantinople or the sea route via Marseilles, Alexandria and Beirut. She chose the sea route. A return ticket by Messageries Maritime liner cost in the region of £18 and was valid for 180 days, plenty of time for the butterfly expedition Mr Elwes had promised to join her on.

How thrilling to set off into the unknown! To leave the cold of Europe and embrace the heat of Egypt was bliss to Margaret, and she happily indulged a helpless Canadian missionary on his first trip abroad. He clung to her during their two-day stopover in Alexandria, and Margaret was glad for the confidence it gave her.

She spent ten days at the Hotel Allemand in Beirut by way of acclimatization and time for making arrangements for her journey into the interior, and she loved every minute of it. It was exhilarating to find herself in the cosmopolitan mix of Beirut in those days, where Turks and Greeks mixed with Arabs and Africans and the streets were a brawl of donkeys, camels and carts. Only the position of women marred her joy, and she felt great pity for the few she saw, who made their way without 'God's sunshine' on their faces, hidden behind their veils.

Travelling into the Syrian mountains, Margaret was appalled at the lives her female counterparts had to endure in this predominantly Muslim world. She saw them as prisoners who had committed no crime, slaves 'without the faintest hope of freedom'. She was particularly shocked by the fate of a thirteen-year-old girl living next door to some missionaries she visited a few hours' walk from Ain Sôfar. In this remote mountain village it was quite normal for the girl to have been married off to a man old enough to be her father, and that Margaret could reluctantly accept. But what she found intolerable was this girl's enclosure within the domestic walls of her husband's home, 'never to wander at liberty over the mountains and to behold the fair earth, which God made for her as much as for her husband'.

Finally she arrived in Damascus, where she was booked into the Orient Hotel under the proprietorship of the brothers Georges and Elias Kaouam. They came to collect her by horse-drawn carriage in the company of their dragoman (guide and interpreter), and Margaret recorded that her first impression of these three was not good. She was particularly unimpressed by the dragoman who 'instead of the sleek, well-fed appearance of the other two . . . had a crushed, almost cowed look'. She noted his boyish face and dark moustache which contrasted with his relatively fair hair, but his demeanour struck a pathetic note and she avoided eye contact.[1]

Damascus was already by 1901 a fairly large city, where a significant minority of Christians lived in an uncomfortable truce with the Muslim majority. It was a city renowned among Europeans for fanaticism because of the terrible slaughters of Christians that had taken place in living memory, and it took some courage for Margaret to travel alone here, not least because she was a woman. On the other hand, the excitement of being somewhere quite unlike any place she had seen so far was exhilarating, and she was thrilled to see streets so full of life and colour.

Once she had settled into her room, the dragoman came to introduce himself and quickly persuaded Margaret that exploring the city alone was out of the question, much less going butterfly-hunting in the countryside. His name was Khalil Neimy and, despite first impressions, he was extremely charming and attentive. Together they explored the tightly packed alleys of the bazaar, where you could buy anything from a turban to a shoe, and Margaret was so pleased with her guide that she hired him for the duration of her visit. He had been educated by American missionaries and spent four years living in Wisconsin, so his English was very good, even if it was with the 'wrong' accent, and his manners were almost impeccable. Only his insistence on greeting her with a kiss to the hand disturbed Margaret, but his charm allowed her to take it with good grace.

Privately she admitted she ought not to be so haughty with him, but she felt an undefined need to put him in his place. Perhaps it was the fresh flowers he brought her each morning, or his unceasing efforts to please, that brought out the worst. She slammed doors in his face in front of other hotel staff and was often severe with him. Nevertheless, he remained an excellent guide, not only talking them out of trouble whenever needed but also finding good hunting grounds for butterflies. She was thrilled to catch Syrian species she had never seen alive before, such as the extraordinarily delicate *Doritis apollinus*, with its translucent wings, and the lovely orange and yellow *Anthocharis damone* (Eastern Orange Tip), and she looked forward to finding many more with Mr Elwes.

But Mr Elwes failed to arrive. Instead, Margaret received a telegram informing her he had changed his mind owing to reports of cholera in Constantinople in the London press. How boring! Not least because Margaret knew perfectly well those reports were exaggerated, and she was unimpressed with her friend's lack of backbone. A veteran traveller such as Mr Elwes should not have been put off by mere press cuttings, she thought. She cabled a message informing him there was no quarantine locally but got no reply, and it became obvious that she was going to be spending the summer alone. 'Liberty is the dearest of all earthly joys, and after all I should have sacrificed my freedom the moment I had joined forces with Mr Elwes and Mrs Nicholl,'[2] she tried to reassure herself alone in Beirut, but it was disconcerting nevertheless.

Margaret spent a fortnight in Beirut debating what to do and evidently allowing herself to be drawn into some kind of amorous episode she felt so ashamed of that not even her diary could be told. 'I cannot immortalize the story of that fortnight!' she wrote, mortified, and took flight back to Damascus. She would hire Mr Neimy on a weekly wage to accompany her on a hunting trip north, to Baalbek in the Lebanese mountains, and concentrate on her butterfly collection.

Mr Neimy was thrilled, and even Margaret could no longer hide from the realization that he had fallen in love with her. 'Never had I seen any human face with a look more intensely of joy and gladness depicted upon it,' she wrote of their reacquaintance at the Orient Hotel. 'The tarboosh (cap) was thrown far back, as usual, and the tuft of fair hair waved above his forehead, his cheeks were glowing and his eyes were bright with happiness and excitement, and it was little more than the face of a boy.' He was twenty-four after all, fifteen years her junior, and Margaret had no intention of indulging him. She had only just escaped the arms of whoever had pursued her in Beirut. She was certainly not going to be wooed by her Turkish servant! Definitely not.[3]

They travelled by horse-drawn carriage to Baalbek, half a day's journey from Damascus, during which Margaret held fast to the thought she could never reciprocate her servant's feelings, while he took every opportunity to kiss her hands and arms. But they had not been in Baalbek more than a day before she regretted hiring this ardent young man. The endless combat with 'blind entreaties and mad infatuation' was exhausting, not to mention distracting. But when he presumed to hold her in a tight embrace to kiss her face she was furious and struggled fiercely to escape. This was intolerable behaviour. She threatened to sack him on the spot if he ever tried to kiss her face again.

Young Neimy's contrition and Margaret's temper lasted precisely one day, and then she was forced to record to her profoundest mortification that human nature was indeed weak, especially hers. '. . . only the very next day on the mountain side, under the shadow of some huge rocks in one of the quarries in the neighbourhood of Baalbek, I sank lower than I had ever sunk before; the very audacity of the man overcame my sense of all that was right and proper. Why are men such animals? Why are their actions so distressingly similar to those of beasts? I suppose because they *are* beasts.' She thereby conveniently excluded herself from any complicity. Nevertheless, she had every right to condemn the uncontrolled lustful nature of her guide, whom she accused of caring for nothing but his physical satisfaction, without any regard for love, much less for her.

She ignored him for an entire day after that episode and took time to regain her composure and self-respect by spending many hours in the company of some lady teachers at the local British Syrian School. The 'healthy atmosphere' was a welcome relief, even if Margaret did feel herself to be damaged goods among these proper ladies. She refers in her diary to 'acting the double part', which she was already so good at but which she now had to practise with even greater energy. 'It has been said that all women are born actresses,' she wrote, 'which is, I think, quite true. The circumstances of their lives from generation to generation have so compelled the necessity for it that the faculty has been sharpened and developed to perfection.'

The thought that she had almost allowed herself to become the lover of her own dragoman was swiftly banished sitting among the ladies at the English school, and Margaret felt sufficiently restored to take control of the situation. Mr Neimy would be kept firmly in his place by being set to work. They would make an expedition to see the famous cedar trees of Lebanon, which would require horses and much negotiating for provisions and shelter and leave no time for passion.

Travelling on horseback into the Lebanese mountains was Margaret's first taste of a very different kind of travelling, and she loved it. 'The grandeur of the distant mountains towards which we were riding, the little horses with their long sweeping tails . . . all these things were a joy never to be forgotten.'

The stony pathways and remote huts and villages they encountered also introduced Margaret to an unknown way of life she could only marvel at. Greece had been rough, but the Lebanon was astonishing. Never had she been asked to make her bed on the bare dirt floor of a windowless hut, nor to avail herself of the holes in the ground that counted for sanitary provisions. But since she had refused to take camping equipment she was forced to rely on Neimy's negotiating skills with the local sheiks to secure a bed for the night. It took some getting used to, and on the first day she turned a five-hour trek into a ten-hour one, just so they could reach a village with a guest-house.

It was not only the rusticity of the accommodation she had to get used to, either; she also had to accept the close proximity of Mr Neimy. There was rarely more than one room available, and, no matter how much British *sang-froid* she tried to muster, everyone always assumed they would be sharing that room. Yet even that was possible to get used to, she found, softening despite herself. Mr Neimy's unfailing devotion was hard to resist, and Margaret could not help thinking she was being offered 'the golden apples of youth'. A year from her fortieth birthday it was tempting to snatch a taste after all, even if she was weary of deception and the whole exhausting business of love. 'Nine years ago,' she recalled in her diary, 'I used to talk about "deceiving the public eye" in this respect, and now I was doing it still!'

It did seem very dreary not to have found a less complicated way of being, but it was ever so for Margaret. She understood that male desire was her adversary, but she was also honest enough to acknowledge her own. 'I saw now it would be one long continuous struggle often literally as well as figuratively to resist this man, and when the fight was hardest it would be because I was then contending with myself – an enemy which at present, thanks to the Grace of God, I had been able to subdue.'

For how long she would prevail she dared not consider, and Mr Neimy showed no sign of letting her off.

'You'll see,' he would promise her, 'if you be my wife, I'll kiss you all night!'

Nothing Margaret could say seemed to dissuade him, and he swore he would stay single for the rest of his life if she would not have him.

'Beat me, kill me if you like,' he would cry, 'I love you just the same, I can't help it', and no amount of bad temper from Margaret could stem the melodrama.

'I don't mind your temper,' he would say meekly; 'to me you are very sweet indeed.'

Slowly but surely he chipped away at Margaret's always crumbly defences, wearing her out with endless discussion about their sleeping arrangements. Why could they not spend just one night together in the same bed? he wanted to know.

'Only sleep in the same bed,' he would insist, 'not to do anything really!'

'Do you suppose in this hot weather I can have another person sleeping in my bed with me?' she replied indignantly.

But Margaret's deep desire for love, if not for sex, got the better of her at last.

The ruins of Baalbek on a balmy summer evening were the setting for Margaret finally to step over the precipice she had avoided for so long, and, having confessed her true age without ill effect, she gave herself over to the passionate embraces of her young dragoman. She kissed him delicately on his smooth pink cheek which was like a boy's and allowed herself to be adored from head to toe. Still she refused to make love, but it was bliss nevertheless. 'The sun set behind the purple outline of the Lebanon, the amber light faded from the sky and the shadows were no longer there, only the swallows singing on through the twilight,' she wrote of the magical night she agreed to become Mrs Neimy.

But it was all very well promising to become Mr Neimy's wife in a far-away land. How was she going to break the news to her mother and family back in England? It was the Septimus problem all over again. She felt her compromised position keenly, especially when they encountered an Englishman in the village of Blûdân, where she managed to avoid Neimy's kisses for at least half a day. 'But then, it was a summer morning in June, and the world was full of sunshine. What lover could be rejected long under such circumstances?' she wrote ruefully.

Of course, it was easy to snatch private moments among the remote cliffs and boulders of the Lebanese mountains, but back in Damascus Margaret could no longer hide from the fact she had got herself into an extremely difficult situation. She valued the status and privileges of a respectable Englishwoman very much and did not relish the idea of being shunned by polite society because of her choice of husband. 'Sometimes,' she wrote miserably, 'I would feel that I had a bright future before me, but far more frequently I was filled with apprehensions and misgivings.' It would take all her ingenuity, she confided to her diary, to make others see her choice in a positive light, but she knew in her heart they would not.

She felt a terrible fraud accepting the hospitality of Mrs Segall, the wife of the man who had hosted them in Blûdân, and even more so attending social gatherings at the local Consul's house. Her cheeks burnt when she remembered she had allowed herself to be carried off to her bed in the youthful arms of Mr Neimy just hours before taking tea in this respectable company. Surely she could never share her secret with these people, and yet she could not resist toying with them.

'Does he ever kiss your hand?' a matron asked of her dragoman.

'Oh yes,' Margaret replied brazenly, 'but then I am accustomed to it from having been so much in Hungary, where it is also the custom of the country, so I think nothing of it.'

Margaret and Neimy discussed getting married at the English church in

Damascus, but there were several obstacles. Despite being a Christian educated by Protestant missionaries, Neimy now belonged to the Greek Orthodox Church which meant that an English church wedding would not do.[4] For her part, Margaret absolutely refused to countenance the idea of becoming a Turkish subject. Losing her reputation was one thing, losing her rights and freedoms as an Englishwoman was another matter altogether. She would never do it – so they compromised with an agreement to go and live in America, where they could revisit the possibilities of marriage.

Whatever arrangement they came to, one thing was certain. Margaret would never assume the traditional role of a Syrian wife, be she Christian or Muslim, and Neimy needed to understand that in no uncertain terms. But this was not easy either. The more Margaret got to know Neimy, the clearer his traditional views became, and she was horrified to find that he expected a wife to do as she was told and bear as many children as possible. Thankfully the danger of the latter was unlikely, but she argued vehemently with him about the status of wives.

'A man may do what he likes with his wife,' he insisted bluntly.

The strain of the situation was almost too much to bear, for the truth was that Margaret was playing a double part on two fronts: one with her social equals and one with Neimy. She had let herself be swept away by his adoration and persistence, but the longer it went on the more she knew she was not in love with him. How could she be? They had absolutely nothing in common. Of course, the same had been true of herself and Septimus, and painful memories inevitably flooded back. She remembered how she would have done anything for that man – just as Neimy swore he would for her. Yet Septimus had forsaken her, and in some ways she felt she was now doing the same to Neimy. She was allowing herself to be loved without reciprocating the feeling, yet she did not have the honesty and courage to say so.

As so often when Margaret faced a dilemma she decided to take flight, and this time her solution to the problem was to hire Neimy for an extended trek on horseback to the holy city of Jerusalem. They would head south, far away from society and back to what she loved doing best: hunting butterflies.

The early morning air was cool as they rode out of Damascus and on to the plain stretching all the way to Mount Hermon, and Margaret breathed a deep sigh of relief to be free of convention once more. She was heading into unknown territory in every sense, but right now that felt wonderful. Neimy was riding by her side, and she was ready for whatever fate had in store for her. Most immediately, that meant getting used to the rustic travelling conditions, which included getting savaged by fleas on rank mattresses and being stoned by local women if she so much as tried to venture off with her net alone.

They rode along remote and dusty trails, passing villages of baked mud in searing heat. The light cut into their eyes like fire, but as they approached the valley of the Jordan river they also discovered rich and fertile enclaves, where it was a joy to sit quietly in the shade or hunt for insects. The Palestinian mountains beckoned on the horizon as they rode on towards the Sea of Galilee, and 'the ripple of the wavelets along its arid shores was like music that told of an infinitely wonderful story, which long centuries ago had been written on the blue waters of that same lake, now glistening and shimmering as its smooth surface reflected the torrid heat of the burning summer sky above'.

Many tourists had already ridden along those same tracks by the time Margaret and Neimy travelled that way, but thankfully there were no others mad enough to venture out in the summer season. When they reached Nazareth they visited the famous sites associated with Christ's life, but Margaret was not naïve enough to believe in the authenticity of any of it. Turning a profit from tourists is an ancient practice, and Margaret was perfectly capable of seeing through such charades.

They crossed the hot plain of Jenin and rode long, hard hours into the mountains to reach the monastery of Nâbulus, where Margaret was thankful to have a spotlessly clean room for a change. She and Neimy were used to snatching private moments wherever they could – even in a monastery – and he had progressed to her bed now. The weight of his body on hers was a sweet sensation and she longed to give him all he desired, though it was the last thing she could risk. Not only because of the obvious danger of pregnancy but also because she knew she would lose every last vestige of power over her lover if she gave him what he wanted most. 'So we lay together and yet apart, till I was weary of the burden of him, and the lust in his eyes almost frightened me . . . I longed to give him the delight he sought from me,' she recalled of those hot days and nights. 'Nature was crying aloud for me to obey her laws,' she admitted, and she felt with every fibre of her being that it was unnatural not to join her body with the man who wanted her so very much. But they would have to wait until they could reinvent themselves in America, and Margaret forced herself to push her lover away.

'If it was any other girl but you,' he said, 'I'd force her to let me do what I wish.'

'You would never be so mean as to force any woman to do a thing she didn't want to, just because being a man you would be much the stronger of the two?' Margaret replied, horrified, but his expression made his answer clear.

'Do you expect that I shall be your slave,' he asked angrily, 'and only do something when *you* wish it?'

Perhaps he was right, Margaret caught herself thinking. Perhaps she really did owe it to him to fulfil his desires whenever he wished. For the moment, though, she avoided the issue and fantasized about their new life in America, where she believed it would be easier to buck convention and raise Neimy to her own rank instead of sinking down to his.

They set off from the monastery at two in the morning to avoid the heat, and Margaret writes beautifully of those hours: 'We had three hours' riding in the white moonlight before the dawn came, and then the blazing sun rose up as usual into a perfectly cloudless sky, and the stars put out their lights one by one, and the face of the moon grew pale and wan, till soon it appeared but as a scar on the clear blue of the sky. And the butterflies began to wake and flutter out of their hiding places amongst the rocks, and we passed long strings of camels on their way to Jerusalem with corn.'

At last the domes and minarets of Jerusalem rose out of the shimmering horizon, glistening and tantalizingly close, yet still many hours' riding away. But when they arrived at last they found an English hotel to stay in, and Margaret was grateful their journey was over. It was deeply satisfying to have completed such a demanding journey, but she was physically and emotionally exhausted. She had no energy left for touring the sites of the Holy City, and she found the squabbling factions who claimed each shrine for their own religion deeply offensive. It seemed to her their main purpose was to make money, and it struck her as very wrong. The Wailing

Wall was one of the most piteous spectacles Margaret had ever seen, and she lost no time in leaving for the coast, where they could return to Beirut by steamer.

Much had changed during the seven weeks Margaret and Neimy had travelled together, and Margaret allowed herself a certain amount of pride that none of the other women on board their boat had such a handsome man in attendance. She had also succeeded in moulding his style and manners to her own taste, which was very pleasing in public, though his private views, especially on women, still left much to be desired.

'After the first time they get accustomed and it doesn't hurt them any,' he once tried to assure Margaret about childbirth, though she was not persuaded in the slightest. Nor did she agree that being accustomed to misery made it any more bearable or right that it should be so.

'I can tell you one thing,' she said indignantly to him one day, 'if, when I'm married to you, you even did raise your hand to strike me, I'd leave you that very day, and you would never see me again!'

❧12❧

DECEIT AND BETRAYAL

ARGARET LEFT BEIRUT by a French steamboat bound for Constantinople. She put Neimy's ring on the third finger of her left hand the minute they left port, and though she was determined never to set foot in Syria again she hoped against hope Neimy would come to join her in her world.

'It is said the approach to Constantinople from the sea is one of the sights of the world, and indeed I have never seen anything more beautiful,' she wrote of her first arrival in the city we now know as Istanbul. 'The Sea of Marmora was like one vast sheet of glass, where the Turkish ships that went past were reflected as in a mirror, the mountains of Asia Minor are on one side, and the shores of Europe on the other . . .'

'There was the Golden Horn,' she wrote in wonder, 'where ships of all nations lay at anchor, and the smiling Bosphorus, whose blue waters conceal the graves of so many murdered and innocent persons, for the secret of many a dark crime lies hidden beneath the sparkling surface,' she wrote, alluding to the many battles and assassinations provoked by this strategic waterway. 'And all along its sunny shores are palaces and pleasure gardens . . .'[1]

Many have found it is better not to land if they want to maintain the first glorious impression of this city, and so it was for Margaret. As soon as she disembarked she found herself fighting off thieves and a horde of porters, with only the butt end of her sunshade to protect her, and she was grateful for a kindly German who helped her to escape. Like so many other travellers before her, Margaret also discovered there was a limit to how much she could take in on one journey, and she had reached hers some time ago. She longed to be in a more familiar cultural landscape among her own kind, and so the sparkling domes and piercing minarets of Constantinople were brushed off with a 'glad to have seen it' in her diary and her bags gratefully loaded on to the Orient Express for Vienna.

How glorious to sip cool beer over a sumptuous dinner and enjoy the fleeting grandeur of the Bulgarian mountains. How calming to be rocked gently across the Hungarian plains and fall safely into crisp white sheets. It was what she needed after the months of physical and emotional strain during her Middle Eastern adventure. She planned to visit Herr Kollmorgen – he who had admired her collecting skills so much in the South of France years ago – but a severe case of head lice picked up in Palestine meant her first engagement was with a doctor who prescribed soaking her head in petroleum for several hours. Her scalp stung and the smell was overwhelming, but at least the treatment was relatively quick, and a long bath soon banished any remaining vapour.

Free of pests she was able to visit Kollmorgen and his wife, and she could not wait to share her news about Neimy with them. They would be her litmus test for later, in England, and perhaps also her advisers. She should have known better. Far from being pleased for her, the Kollmorgens were absolutely horrified to hear she was engaged to marry a Syrian dragoman many years her junior.

'He is only marrying you for your money, and you will lead a wretched life with him!' they cried.

But Margaret was more determined than ever to keep her promise to Neimy, though she realized with a shock that the Kollmorgens' reaction was just a foretaste of what she could expect in England, where such views would be much more difficult to repudiate. In fact, Mr Kollmorgen's objections were easy to disregard because, to her disgust, he made it perfectly plain he had been in love with her since their first meeting in Digne. Only the innocent trust of his wife had held him back, he claimed, adding that her Syrian would never be so faithful.

'But I have told him', she replied stubbornly, 'that if he is not faithful to me after we are married I will either amuse myself in like manner or else go away and leave him.'

Did she not realize, Kollmorgen put it to her, that a man with such a passionate nature as Neimy's could not possibly remain faithful, least of all, for example, were she to bear him a child? That shocked, and Kollmorgen pressed his argument even further by insisting that men were often unfaithful to their wives during the last months of pregnancy.

'You do not know what a man has to suffer, if he wants to do that and can't,' he claimed, no doubt speaking from personal experience, since his wife had just borne him a daughter.

'Nothing to what his wife is suffering for him,' Margaret replied tersely, liking her friend a lot less.

Her conversations with Kollmorgen were a stark eye-opener to the male psyche, and yet she remained determined to stick to her plan. Opposition always brought out the most stubborn and resourceful streak in her, though past experience had also left its mark, and she reluctantly agreed to let Kollmorgen contact the German Consul in Damascus to make secret enquiries about Neimy. It was an unhappy business, but she was the first to admit that if she was going to risk everything she needed to be absolutely sure of Neimy's legal status and good character.

In London, Geraldine's husband was predictably appalled to hear that Margaret intended to marry a foreigner fifteen years her junior. He was particularly offended by Neimy's youth, it seemed, but he also had no confidence at all that a marriage between an Englishwoman and an Ottoman could work. How different his attitude would have been if Margaret had been a man, she couldn't help thinking, though she knew perfectly well most Englishmen would have kept their foreign lovers as mistresses, not wives. It was not a good start, and Margaret balked at confronting Mother, especially since Rachel was much deteriorated. The moment did not seem right at all to bring further upset to the family, and so she kept her counsel, alone with her problems once again, just when guidance was most needed.

She desperately missed Neimy's embraces and loving words, but not one letter came from Damascus. How she wished to have at least one message to hold and read over and over – something to give her courage. Alone in England, removed from anything remotely connected with Neimy's world, it was so difficult to hold on to the reality of their relationship. Despite the ring on her finger she was tormented by the idea that her Syrian adventure had never really happened, that it was all a dream. Without a letter from Neimy she was also prey to thoughts of his disloyalty or, worse, his loneliness. All her mean and haughty words to him came back to haunt her, and she wished so very much she had been kinder and more loving.

It was several months before the much longed-for letter arrived from Damascus, but at least it momentarily dispelled Margaret's worst fears. He had not forgotten her at all. He had simply been away from Damascus, helping his parents care for his dying grandfather and then helping them again in the preparations for his sister's wedding.

'I wish for you to be with us,' he wrote enchantingly, and how Margaret wished it, too. She replayed every moment they had shared together over and over.

'If only I could find myself once more sitting on his knee, with his dear arms around me, and the sweet passion of his kisses on my mouth, if only I could look into his eyes and tell him everything, all the things that have been said against him, none of which I believed,' she wrote hotly.

The longer she was alone in England, however, the harder it was to keep her focus and remain steadfast in her intention to defy convention. Her grand relations were bound to turn their backs on her and perhaps even her mother and sisters. Geraldine had already sided with her husband's view, and Margaret's secret weighed very heavy indeed.

'The sorrow of being secretly engaged was almost more than I could bear, with my lover so many miles away,' she wrote despairingly. 'But I used to feel that even this separation I could endure for a time, if it were an acknowledged fact – an accepted position, instead of being unknown to those with whom I was compelled to mix and pass my time.'

It was yet another intolerable situation Margaret had got herself into, made so much worse by her profound regret at not having given in to Neimy's passionate entreaties. If at least she had known what it was to make love with a man who adored her, all her loneliness and suffering would have been worth while.

As autumn turned to winter Margaret sank into depression: 'So the dull, unlovely days of an English winter were creeping slowly by, and the grey clouds drifted across the dreary skies, and the cold, northern sea sobbed and moaned along the wet windy shore,' she wrote morosely.

The cruel hand of fate Margaret ever expected arrived on New Year's Eve, just as Margaret was going to join her family's celebrations in Bath. It was a letter from Neimy's cousin Elias Kaouam: 'Dear Lady,' it read and then explained Neimy had gone to Jerusalem with two people for about thirty-five days and not returned. His parents were very anxious to know what had become of him, even more so his wife, and they were all desperate for information. Did Margaret know anything that could help them?

'My first impulse when I had read this was to lie down full length on my bed, and remain quite still so as to allow one of the most awful moments I had ever lived through in my life, to pass quietly over me,' she wrote of her shock.

She slipped the ring on her finger off into her palm and then returned it. She was not twenty-nine but thirty-nine this time, and private grief was not going to get the better of her. She attended her sister Florence's New Year's Eve party just as she had planned, and no one guessed at the 'cold fingers' of disillusion which gripped her heart. No one knew her anguish as she tried to make sense of the letter in her pocket. Had everything between Neimy and herself been a lie? Surely not. But what she could believe was that Neimy's infatuation with her had led him to desert his wife and child – the one that had sat on her lap so prettily when she had visited Neimy's parents' house – and she pitied both the forsaken wife and the desperate husband, persuading herself she was the one who had got away 'almost uninjured'. How grateful she was, after all, to know she had not committed adultery with Neimy and that she had not yet made her engagement public.

She tried to persuade herself she could pick herself up and turn to other pleasures so long as she had money to buy them. But the thought of Neimy's wife would not let her go. She felt sincere pity for the woman she imagined trying to find her husband, wandering all over Damascus begging for information, even asking Elias to write a letter to London for her. It was a scenario that tugged at Margaret's romantic heart, and she found herself imagining a happy home wrecked by her arrival in Damascus. She could honestly say she had done her best to quench Neimy's infatuation, but she had found him irresistible at last, and he had given no sign that he had no right to love her, much less ask her to be his wife.

And yet, somewhere in her heart, Margaret could not bring herself to believe Elias Kaouam. She wracked her brain for any instance during her time in Syria and Palestine that could have hinted at Neimy's true status, but she could find none. It seemed too incredible that the same man who had sworn to love her to the end of his days was also a husband and father, and Margaret gradually persuaded herself that both Elias and Georges Kaouam were scheming liars. She had Neimy's and Elias's handwriting analysed by a Mrs Beelie, who conveniently confirmed her suspicion, suggesting the brothers were most likely intercepting her letters to Damascus and had their own reasons for undermining the relationship between their poor relation and Margaret. Perhaps they were jealous? There was no way of knowing, but Margaret was by no means ready to accept she had been deceived by Neimy. No man ever had a more loyal friend than Margaret, want it or not.

Ever resourceful, Margaret devised a plan whereby she would hire Neimy as guide for her next butterfly expedition to the desert lands – Algeria this time – which would give her an official reason for making enquiries about him and also ensure their reunion far away from Damascus. She wrote to her friend, Mrs Segall, asking her to find out if Neimy had any family ties that would prevent him from working extended periods away from home and was pleased with her wily tactics which gave nothing away yet served their purpose.

'And wherein does my power lie?' she asked herself rhetorically. 'In the chance game of Fate turning in my favour? In the solid background of a few thousands in gold, which are mine? In physical attractions, or mental affinities? No, in none of these things, but merely in my own identity.'

Power does not equal happiness, but that never stopped Margaret. She invited Mr Elwes's old friend Mrs Nicholl to join her on her hunting trip to Algeria and dreamt of Neimy running away – if there was anything to run from – to meet them there. But of course he did not come, and Margaret found it very hard to be in an Arab environment without her loyal dragoman to help her. The smart clientele of the Hotel Splendide in Algiers and the fussy company of Mrs Nicholl and her future daughter-in-law, Miss Gilbertson, made her pine for the wilds of the Syrian mountains and the simple onion salads she had shared with Neimy.

In Algeria there was no one to wash up her tea things in the afternoon and steal kisses from her, no one waiting patiently in the shade while she chased butterflies. Mrs Nicholl, who was in her early sixties, needed an ear trumpet to hear anything and was no longer the hardy fellow hunter of old. Margaret reflected sadly that companionship was much the most important thing. Life was so much more meaningful shared with a loved one, even if she could manage perfectly well on her own, and she felt sad and listless, reduced to playing patience with old ladies in a hotel stuffed with newly-weds. Even Mrs Nicholl seemed more interested in weddings than butterflies, preferring to make family plans with Miss Gilbertson rather than talk 'shop' with Margaret.

But at last she received a letter from Neimy which confirmed all her suspicions about the Kaouam brothers and cheered her up more than anything.

'My dear Margaret,' it began, 'it is with great pleasure I sent you this letter with my complement and my love and regards to you and to your family. I hope you be well and healthy all and for long time I did not hear from you. I cannot understand why you do not write me . . .'

So she had been right all along. Her letters to Neimy had probably been intercepted, and this one from him had been sent on from England. He clearly had no idea she was waiting for him in Algeria. But why had his cousins deceived him? Margaret could not figure it out. In the meantime, Neimy's letter told of his own miseries, including becoming ill during a guiding job to Jerusalem which resulted in spending over a month in hospital in Beirut. His parents had had no idea where he was and had assumed he had run away to America or England. Hence the idea of writing to Margaret, yet the cousins had taken care not to tell Neimy of Margaret's concern for him or the existence of any letters.

At least Margaret now knew who her enemy was, and she acted quickly to secure a new means of communication, sending her reply to Neimy in an envelope addressed by another's hand, via her friend Angelina in Milan, so Elias would not know it came from Margaret. In that letter she instructed Neimy not to reveal who the letter was from and promised him she would make arrangements for them to be reunited. She would send money to him via Mrs Segall so he could buy his passage to Marseilles, where they could meet, talk face to face and decide their future. Margaret was delighted with her strategy and prayed that Neimy would actually receive his post from now on.

With instant messaging around the world today, it is hard to appreciate the agony of waiting that communication involved in 1902, when Margaret was in Algeria. Letters carried by sea and overland could take weeks and months to reach their destination, and many got lost along the way. Far from home and without anyone to confide in, Margaret was utterly alone with her fears and worries, not least of which was not knowing if and when she would hear from Neimy again. Her nights were filled with hours of exhausting scenarios played out in her mind's eye, and she was haunted by what evil lies the Kaouams might come up with to thwart their young cousin.

At last she could stand it no longer and decided to set sail for Damascus. She had endured two months of loneliness and worry in Algeria, and it was already past Easter when she booked herself on to a boat for Beirut via Marseilles and Alexandria. She would find out for herself what was going on, but even this decision to act could only be realized in a painfully slow journey, prolonged even further by an outbreak of cholera in Egypt. It meant the boat's passengers were immediately quarantined on arrival in Beirut, adding an interminable five days in a hospital dormitory before Margaret was allowed to continue on her way. There was a small stroke of luck in this, however, because the delay meant she bumped into a friend of Neimy's in Beirut, and she immediately hired him to deliver a letter to Neimy in person.

'My dear Khalil,' she wrote from the Hotel Allemand in Beirut. 'You will be surprised to see that I am in Syria, and indeed I am very much surprised to find myself here! It is not at all what I wished to happen, but then things never do come as we wish them to in this world.' She went on to assure him that she had not forgotten him and had taken matters into her own hands because of the duplicitous actions of his cousins. He must come to Beirut at once, she begged, as well as offering to pay for everything. 'If you like I will pay you your expenses and give you 40 francs a week, the same as last year, till we have told each other our story, and rearranged together what we are going to do . . .'

It was now nine months since they had seen each other last, and the anticipation of reunion was very sweet. On the day of Neimy's expected arrival Margaret dressed to her best advantage and paced her hotel room in a state of high emotion. Soon she would be in the arms of her man. Soon they would tell each other everything and make a plan for the future.

Five o'clock had already passed, but at last the longed-for knock on the door was heard. She rushed to open it, but the person ushered into her room was not Neimy but Mr Segall. In an instant Margaret's temper rose to defend her honour, but Mr Segall's very first words took the wind out of her sails. 'Well, Miss Fountaine,' he declared without wasting time, 'I must congratulate you, for the man *is* married!'

Before Margaret could utter a single word he went on to inform her that not only was Mr Neimy married, he also had a son and a daughter who had died in infancy. No grim detail was spared, and Mr Segall assured her that the reason he had come in person was to protect her from public humiliation should Neimy have tried to leave the country with her before admitting anything.

'Mrs Segall wrote . . .' she protested weakly.

But her informant insisted his wife's enquiries had been adequate for the purpose of hiring a dragoman, and he had asked for an official investigation only when she had received Margaret's confessional letter admitting the true nature of the relationship with Neimy. Margaret had sent it in a fit of pious remorse to one she thought of as a friend – a grave mistake, as she could see now.

While Margaret had been languishing in quarantine, Mr Segall had discovered Neimy's true status with the help of the local Consul and by personally confronting him, whereupon he had soon admitted everything, though he denied proposing marriage. To the contrary, according to Mr Segall, he insisted that Margaret had proposed to him.

'Oh! Mr Segall,' Margaret cried, 'you didn't believe him?'

Margaret was caught between the humiliation of having this well-meaning gentleman trying to save her honour and the horror of finding out she had indeed been deceived by the man who had worked so hard to make her love him.

If there was anything more painful fate had in store for her, she was unable to conceive of it that awful evening. For this she had humbled herself in ardent prayers and put her faith in a man once more?

'I had said my last unanswered prayer!' she wrote in her diary.

The rector's daughter lost her faith in God at last and resolved on a future without him and without Neimy. If only she could have settled for the 'vegetable existence' of life in England; but it was no use, she knew she could not. At least if she remained abroad she could keep her social standing, and she acknowledged to herself there was no point going against destiny. She would continue to be the eternal wanderer, a stranger in strange lands.

As if to match her grim thoughts, Margaret witnessed one of the most grotesque religious ceremonies she had ever seen: a funeral procession for the Greek Orthodox Bishop of Beirut, whose corpse was paraded through the streets seated on a chair. Dressed in all his episcopal finery and a mitre on his head, he was followed by a long procession of chanting priests, a sight to make the blood run cold. Margaret was amazed how some people chose to practise the very same Christian religion she had just decided to give up. Meanwhile, Mr Segall insisted Margaret leave Syria without seeing Neimy again, and so she did.

Slowly she headed back towards northern Europe, paying extended visits to anyone she could think of along the way. She managed to spend two months in Cairo, staying with a woman she had met on the boat to Syria, followed by several weeks in Italy, catching up with Angelina in Milan and Bruno near Lake Como, but at last she could delay her return to England no more.

Seeing Rachel suffering so bravely helped put her own miseries in perspective, but the more time went by the less Margaret was able to admit defeat, and she ended the year with a promise to herself: 'No freaks of Fate should separate us, no intervention on the part of others' should stop them, she wrote of her determination to see Neimy again. His supposed wife was banished from Margaret's mind, and she chose instead to believe that if two people loved each other they must be allowed to be together. Thus, a letter was dispatched to Damascus once again, assuring Neimy of her friendship despite what had happened, and to prove it she offered to hire him as her guide on her first expedition to Asia Minor (Turkey). It was the kind of gamble Margaret loved, and it worked.

A reply from Damascus came far sooner than she could have dared to hope, and in it Neimy assured her he loved her still. He promised to tell her his side of the story just as soon as they were face to face and swore he had not meant to deceive her. He even offered to serve her all his life for no wages at all, just to be close to her. It was everything Margaret had wished for.

'Keep an account of all your expenses,' she insisted in her reply. There was no question of not paying him a wage and expenses, not least because it gave Margaret the happy illusion they were merely friends working together. As long as she was paying him, she persuaded herself, their relationship was beyond reproach.

Once again Margaret had engineered a future for herself it was impossible to gauge the outcome for, but she left England full of hope and anticipation. Even her dying sister had given her blessing, perhaps understanding better than anyone that life must be lived to the full.

'So I hurried on to meet my doom,' wrote Margaret, 'whatever it may be', the boat to Ostend taking her back to a seat on the Orient Express.

❧ 13 ❧

TURKISH DELIGHT

'EVERYBODY WAS DOWN upon me for going,' she wrote during her three days on the Orient Express. 'But Rachel herself understood, and the rest of the people I didn't care a straw about. Only Skye, when I went to see her in London, also seemed to know and understand, just as Rachel herself did.'[1]

Margaret was leaving England in the knowledge that while one sister blessed her another had turned against her. Geraldine had chosen to take her husband's side, and Margaret was sorry for the rift between them. But Geraldine's conventional choices elicited no respect from her wayward sister, and her regret was little more than sentimental. The ideal of family unity and love had never really existed anyway, and Margaret had long since made peace with that.

Telegrams went back and forth between Margaret and Neimy, and only the dreaded cholera quarantine could delay things now. Soon they would be reunited, and Margaret whiled away her time in Constantinople by visiting her distant relation Mr Harry Eyres, who was conveniently also the British Consul. His letters of introduction would prove vital in this part of the world, and she hoped very much he had had no contact with the gossipy Consul in Damascus, who she knew was entertaining dinner guests with her 'scandalous adventure'. All help would be denied if Harry Eyres found out the true relationship with her dragoman, of that there was no doubt. As it was, he disapproved of shipping in a guide from Damascus when there were plenty of local men for the job, but Margaret insisted that she could only trust Neimy. When she was not with the Eyres she visited the Gilbertsons, sisters to the Miss Gilbertson she had met travelling in Algeria the year before and a great deal more fun.

The strain of playing 'the double part' was agonizing, though, and it made Margaret ill to think how appalled all who met her would be to know what kind of a woman she really was – the mistress of a married Syrian and a liar, too. The waiting and anxiety took her to the brink of nervous breakdown, which was no time to be witnessing the bloody flagellation that took place during the Stamboul fête. But it was an event all tourists went to see, and thus she found herself pressed into a heaving crowd to watch scenes of biblical horror.

Flaring torches and huge bonfires lit an endlessly gory procession in honour of the Prophet Ali: youths beat their bare shoulders with chains, and a hundred shrieking men dressed in white robes brandished swords with which they continuously slashed their own scalps. Blood oozed down their faces and on to their clothes, an unearthly sound rose up from the musicians, and Margaret fainted to the ground. The self-inflicted torture and haunting music were too much for her overstretched brain, and she fought her way out of Stamboul just as soon as the kindly Persian by her side would let her go. Next morning a telegram announcing Rachel's death arrived – her dearest sister, dead at forty. Should she have stayed at her bedside? Rachel had not wished it, and yet she felt crushed by a terrible sense of doom and guilt.

It was in this mood of profound despondency that the news of Khalil's arrival finally came. It was what she had been waiting for, yet now he stood before her in the hotel lobby she could hardly find it in herself to respond. 'I half rose to meet him, and then recollected that it would be more dignified to remain seated,' she wrote dismally of that much longed-for moment. 'His face was buoyant and happy, much the same as he had looked that day on the platform,' she remembered.

It was impossible to be natural in public, but seeing Khalil's excited face only filled Margaret with dread, and she informed him in businesslike tone that he needed to get his papers in order straight away as she intended leaving for Broussa in just a few days.

Neimy must have wondered at the cold English woman who had been so passionate with him before. Was this the same Margaret who had lain with him in the distant Holy Land? But Margaret's consular friends and his lies had hardened her against Khalil for the moment, and he was not permitted one single kiss. She even insulted him by offering to pay for his gift of Turkish Delight, sending wildly mixed messages to her confused would-be lover. She was torn between her heart's desire and everything she believed in, and left him alone at the hotel until late that evening.

What should their relationship be now? she wondered. But the answer was not clear, and she brushed him off once more when he came to find her in her room that night. He wanted to tell her about his wife, how he had been separated for several years, but Margaret did not want to hear about it. After all the months and months of uncertainty and anguish she simply had no energy left to care if he was married or not. Only the tale of his daughter dying at eight months roused her pity, but for the rest she felt she really did not want to know. The feelings she might have had for Khalil had entirely evaporated – at least that is what she felt that first exhausting day in Constantinople.

Khalil did as he was told, and as soon as his papers were in order they took a boat south, across the Marmora Sea. The first collecting grounds Margaret wished to explore were near the great city of Bursa, at the foot of Mount Uluda (Mount Olympus), which rose up a mighty 2,543 metres, and it was not long before the pristine skies and mountain pastures calmed Margaret's nerves and allowed her to have faith in the future once more.

'The fire was growing fiercer, but the ice had not thawed very much,' Margaret wrote of her feelings during their first tentative days together. She wanted it to be clear between them they were no longer courting, considering his marital status. They could only be platonic friends from now on.

But Margaret's resolve soon collapsed under the weight of Khalil's determined romancing, and she confessed to her diary it was only a matter of a few days before his fire melted her ice. Far from the prying eyes of the 'outside world' she rediscovered her natural spirit, and though a certain sadness remained she allowed herself to believe her young dragoman really did love her, in spite of the fact he had no right to. In her own inadequate way she found she could love him, too, though all the world saw him as nothing but a penniless Syrian. At last she threw all caution to the wind.

'It was neither wrong, nor indecent, only natural,' she wrote, 'and nothing but the conventional laws of a deluded world, in opposition to the sweet laws of Nature, set a limit upon our intercourse . . .'

Aged forty-one, Margaret finally lost her virginity and discovered, like so many virgins before her, that dreaming about making love is nothing like the real thing. It was bound to be a disappointment. But it is also possible that Neimy's passion was not equalled by his love-making skills. He was a young man, after all, whose experience was limited to an unwilling wife and perhaps the odd prostitute, and he had made his views on women very clear. His idea of successful love-making was most likely limited to giving pleasure to himself, and so Margaret discovered that 'all the pleasure is for the man, for the woman remains only a heritage of pain'. She enjoyed the sensuous delights of lying in the open air on a sunny May morning infinitely more, especially if she was being kissed and held, and she loved Neimy so much more for agreeing to quench 'all the desires of passion' for her sake.

'Oh! That those summer days could have lasted for ever,' she wrote of that lovely Turkish spring.

The butterfly-hunting was not bad either, though she informed the readers of *The Entomologist* that April and May were too early in the season there. 'It was much too early to make the ascent of Mount Olympus, and much as I enjoyed the wonderful beauty of the country, and the eternal songs of the nightingales, about the 20th May I returned to Constantinople, intending to go on by the next steamer leaving for the Black Sea to Samsoun, *en route* for Amassia.'[2]

Ever since studying the wonderful butterfly collections housed at the Natural History Museum in Athens Margaret had dreamt of discovering Asia Minor for herself. Many of the finest butterflies seemed to come from this tantalizingly remote part of the world, and she was thrilled to be heading for the Anatolian mountains at last. Armed with letters of introduction and safe in the company of Khalil, she set sail for central Turkey full of confidence and delightful anticipation.

'Now there are so-called carriage-roads in most parts of Asia Minor,' she wrote authoritatively for the audience in London, 'but the advantages of this in practice I soon found to be somewhat dubious, for anything more appalling than the condition of these roads would be quite inconceivable.'

Travelling beyond the Black Sea port of Samsun was tougher than anything Margaret had yet encountered, and she was used to a lot by now. But heavy rains turned the dirt roads into quagmires and the local horse-drawn wagons – known as yileys – often sank axle-deep in sticky mud. The poor horses struggled to pull their legs out of sucking holes and there was no question of escaping the jolting yiley to continue on foot. Margaret and Khalil huddled under a blanket on the bare wooden floor of their wagon, crowded by their luggage and peasant hitch-hikers and lashed by rain through gaps in the canvas. Grim was not the word for it, and it went on for three days – three days of agonizingly slow treks up so-called mountain roads, crossing several dangerous swollen fords and sliding desperately close to fearful drops on the downhill parts. There were no inns or guest-houses in these mountains either, only *khans*, which were little more than shepherd huts, where Margaret's only comfort was her charcoal stove fired up on the bare mud floor.

At one point they got caught in the eye of a massive storm which provided a violent spectacle for them. 'It was a marvellous sight,' wrote Margaret for her article, 'as from time to time the thick atmosphere became one mass of lurid fire from the lightning, and the simultaneous roar of thunder was quite deafening.' It was utterly terrifying, and the impenetrable darkness of a rain-soaked night must have been deeply unsettling in this wild country. But Margaret assured her readers that the violent weather was the best protection against bandits and 'one must be prepared to encounter some inconveniences in order to reach such a butterfly paradise as Amassia was to prove afterwards to be'.

Nevertheless, after having her bones jolted a thousand times on the bare boards of the yiley, she chose to hire a horse for the final approach, lasting eight hours in a Turkish saddle before giving up and walking. Yet even this agony was as nothing in return for a first glimpse of Amassia (Amasya today). Never had she seen a place in such a beautiful setting.

'The town was, as it were, wedged into a huge cleft in the mountains, by which it was shut in on all sides, and the surrounding country in every direction presented an aspect which made me long to explore it at once,' she assured her fellow entomologists. Dr Staudinger had collected here almost thirty years before, and she could not wait to follow in his foot-steps. Guided by his book *Lepidoptera of Asia Minor*, and the local knowledge of a resident Armenian, she knew she would find good things.

Thus began an unforgettable summer, far from prying and judgemental eyes, where Margaret experienced fulfilment at last: each day brought a hundred attentions from her lover and a collecting box bursting with fresh discoveries. Each day she encountered a species new to her and sometimes even two or three. They were almost all from the Lycaenidae family which are generally small gregarious butterflies, and they presented delightful challenges to Margaret's net. Hour upon hour was spent chasing tantalizing glimpses of colour across remote mountain valleys and dangerous crags, and Margaret was delighted to discover that Khalil was a willing and very able assistant. Soon he was capable of distinguishing species, and he was also adept at the delicate art of setting. They made a great team, if not as lovers, and Margaret could think of no happier state. She had found a partner at last.

'We worked very hard and we were always underfed, but the days were not long enough to contain all the happiness which was ours in this wonderland in which we found ourselves,' she wrote happily. No honeymoon could have been sweeter than this.

In the balmy summer evenings, when the huge dome above was lit with diamond stars, they sat out in the barley field of their Armenian landlords and gazed out over the forbidding contours of Amassia's fortress, their eyes drawn towards the distant fires of shepherds' camps high up in the surrounding mountains. Cut into the cliffs above the town were ancient tombs of the Kings of Pontus, over two thousand years old, but they were of little interest to these two. They were only concerned with each other, and it was on one of those evenings that Khalil finally told Margaret the story of his life so far.

It was a sad story, of a father determined to keep his son in Damascus rather than lose him to America, where his missionary teacher had set him up in Oshkosh, Wisconsin. He had already become a naturalized American, but his parents insisted he return home where they forced him to marry a young girl of fifteen. His father had hired a professional match-maker, but he was deceived, and Khalil's young wife turned out to be the daughter of a prostitute. It was a shock for the whole family, yet the way Khalil told it he had been prepared to do his duty and be a good husband, work hard as a dragoman to keep his wife, even though he had not chosen her and did not love her. But instead of gratitude he got insults, and his wife turned to prostitution, just like her mother before her and her grandmother before that. She abandoned their first baby daughter, and Khalil was distraught at

Above left and left: South Acre church and rectory in the Nar valley, Norfolk, where, as a child, Margaret hunted for birds' nests and escaped lessons on her pony. Above: Margaret's beloved nanny, Hurley

One of Margaret's earliest butterfly passions was for the striking Marbled Whites (*Melanargias*), and she was the first English collector to hunt for them, on Sicily, in 1896. They are some of the earliest specimens in what was to become the Fountaine–Neimy Collection, left to Norwich Castle Museum after her death in 1940.

The sisters Fountaine (left to right, Constance, Geraldine, Margaret, Florence, Evelyn and Rachel) on the tennis ground at Eaton Grange, 4 April 1882

A photograph of Septimus Hewson, pasted into Margaret's diary in 1883

A page from Margaret's 1890 diary with a pressed honeysuckle picked for her by Septimus in Limerick

LIFE HISTORY OF CYMOTHOE ARANIS.

LIFE HISTORY OF SALAMIS TEMORA.

1. Young Larva 2. Full grown Larva 3. Pupa 4. Imago.

Above and top right: One of Margaret's most important achievements was illustrating the early life-cycles – from egg to pupa – of many tropical butterfly species. These previously unpublished illustrations are unique, because it is the only time she is known to have painted the butterfly stage as well. They were a gift from Margaret to Joe Eggeling, a colonial forestry official she met at the Budongo Forest Station in Uganda, in 1934.

Right: The twelve volumes of Margaret's memoirs contain over a million words, each page filled with a neat, cursive hand with decorative titles and borders to many of the photographs reproduced here. The diaries were locked away at Norwich Castle Museum until 1978, one hundred years after they were begun.

Right: Bruno Galli-Valerio on Lake Como, northern Italy, in 1895

Left: Fellow entomologists in Hungary

Below: Trieste dockyard pictured in a diary entry from 1898

amed across a mid ni

ring

Plau

ria w

dock.

llock wagons being

down on the quai, and

ies far away. I had

ore starting on my

as to have breakfast

of a câfe; the next

luggage registered

bird was to get a

Trieste Dockyard.
Austria.

, for the country I was about to pass through, which laste

MARGARET ELIZABETH FOUNTAINE, and NEEDLE.

Aged 37.— Aged 6.

Dec.1 1899.

The adventurous entomologist: Margaret, aged thirty-seven, with her bicycle – on which she cycled from the Côte d'Azur to Venice – and her dog, Needle; frontispiece from her diary of 1899

WHITE JESSAMINE.

These were the first flowers given to me by Khalil Neimy after we were engaged. Baalbek, Syria, June 1901

his arms around me & loved to see his eyes dilating and his chest heaving and to feel the intensity of his passion; but when he asked me if I cared for him as he cared for me, I turned away and did not hesitate to tell him that I did not, while in my heart I felt that I never would. But only two days off, we were engaged I struggled to free myself but it was only to draw the net more tightly round me. ... for how could I treat him thus? "I have not changed," he said very sadly "but if you wish it for your pleasure, I will say that I have." And I said there was but one way to extricate myself from the net into which I had fallen and that was to break through its meshes, but should I ever have the heart to do it? So the matter drifted on. I could often have wished he was not quite so coarse in his words and actions. One thing he would always say was: "I love very much your legs." Then another day he would encircle my knees with his arm and say, "How are the legs." Oh they

Top: Diary entry and the first flowers given to Margaret in Baalbek, Syria, in June 1901, by Khalil Neimy (above left, aged twenty-four, and, left, in Amasia, Turkey)

Above: Yileys in Anatolia provided very rough transport during Margaret's and Khalil's 'honeymoon' summer in Amasia in 1903.

Hunting butterflies near Broussa, Turkey, in 1903

Henry Elwes, whose collection at Colesbourne inspired Margaret's butterfly-collecting career

Margaret and Khalil riding through a cedar forest in Algeria

Top left: Khalil setting a butterfly in Tlemcem, Algeria

Above: Margaret, aged forty-four, from the frontispiece of her diary of 1907

Left: Arthur Henry Fountaine and Mollie Belle Williams at their wedding in Covington, Virginia, USA, 1910

Professional recognition: Margaret (circled) and Khalil two places to her left at the prestigious second International Congress of Entomology in Oxford, 1912. Inset: Margaret's delegate badge from the Fifth Congress in Paris in 1932

Left: Margaret in her West Hampstead studio, 1910

Left: *Papilio ulysses* found during Margaret's time in Queensland, Australia

Below: The ill-fated house at Myola in Queensland

Above left: Lee Fountaine, son of Authur and Mollie, aged five in 1917

Above right: *Papilio turnus,* caught during Margaret's visit to Hot Springs, Virginia, USA

Making bandages for the French Red Cross in Los Angeles, 1918

The Cunard liner *Aquitania* on which Margaret travelled from New York to Southampton in May 1921

Margaret riding a camel near Cairo in 1922

Margaret aged sixty in 1922; frontispiece from her diary of that year

Margaret in her Fellows Road studio, Hampstead, with butterfly cases in the foreground, 1925. Right inset: the house on Fellows Road today

Lee and Melville Fountaine in 1931 working on the Ford car given to them by Margaret

Lee and Frances Fountaine on the porch of their new home near Millboro, Virginia, bought for them by Margaret in 1936

Margaret's sketchbook, volume 2, p. 47, showing the Philippines butterflies she reared in 1924. Top row: *Nymphalis benguetana, Delias henningia, Euploea phaenarete althaea* Bottom row: *Troides rhadamantus* (*=nephereus*), *Atrophaneura semperi*

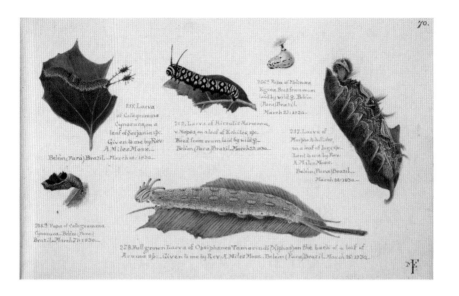

Margaret's sketchbook, volume 3, p. 70, showing the Brazilian butterflies she reared in 1930. Top row: *Callicore cynosura, Tithorea harmonia, Melinaea ludovica* (=*egina*)
Bottom row: *Opsiphanes tamarindi, Morpho achillaena*

Khalil and Margaret with a tray of butterflies, the only known portrait of them together, taken some time between 1925 and 1927, not long before Khalil died

the memory. 'She just crawled about the floor at home, crying all the time, and we could not feed her, and so she fell sick and died,' he told Margaret, with tears in his eyes.

Margaret's heart went out to Khalil, and she could not believe he had intentionally meant to cause her distress or harm by withholding the facts from her when they first met. As he explained to her, he had been so sure of getting a divorce it seemed unnecessary to tell Margaret the sordid truth about his life, though he had fully intended to come clean once he was free. But the Greek Orthodox Bishop of Damascus had refused to grant him a divorce, instead giving him permission to live as a free man, without responsibilities for his wife, who had deserted him. Perhaps money was the obstacle, Margaret surmised, but the result was that Khalil was officially not free to marry again, and this was not something he had wanted to confess to Margaret.

How well Margaret thought she understood. Had she not been equally duplicitous in her dealings with others? Being economical with the truth was second nature to her, and she could hardly blame Khalil for doing the same when it might otherwise have destroyed the very thing he craved most: the love of a good woman. There was no doubt in Margaret's mind that her man was honourable. No matter that he had fathered a child with his disreputable wife – she knew male nature well enough to accept it could be roused by any female, given close proximity. At least she could dispense with any last shreds of guilt on her part: she had not stolen a husband, only filled a vacant post.

For once Margaret was able to live for the moment, neither brooding about the past nor worrying about the future. Khalil was her husband in all but name, and they were as happy and contented as a couple could be. 'Yet the world would not recognise our ties,' she wrote, 'they would be considered neither legal nor sacred, so the world must never know, that is all; and children we could never have, even if my advanced years would not anyhow have precluded us from this greatest of human happiness.'

So there it was, resolution at last. According to Margaret, it was an arrangement Khalil was equally happy with, even the bit about loving nature and butterflies more than mere 'sexual intercourse'. Wishful think-ing it may have been, but she got her way, as she always did, and Khalil can hardly have been unhappy at the prospect of a guaranteed income for life.

Officially, he would be her courier from now on, referred to as 'Bersa' in all Margaret's future articles for *The Entomologist*. Margaret was happy to think, too, that an arrangement such as theirs was preferable to a conventional marriage because it saved them from 'that satiety which is so often the unwelcome guest to the soft downy pillow of the marriage bed'. We can never know what Khalil really thought about this, but at least they knew exactly where they stood with each other, and that was undoubtedly a great relief to both.

The air clear between them, Margaret and Khalil got down to the serious business of the butterflies: a daily routine which involved getting up by six and hunting until lunchtime, followed by setting and rest in the afternoons, and then leisurely evenings outside before a 'healthy sleepful night', she on her divan and Khalil on the floor in the next room.

It was indeed wonderful to be a 'free-born English woman, with the power, the means and the inclination' to travel in strange lands, but even Margaret was not so self-obsessed as not to notice the hard lives of those around her. She particularly noted the harsh treatment of the Armenian minority, who seemed to be prisoners in their own lands, prohibited to travel freely by the Ottoman authorities and obliged to put up with many humiliations wherever they lived. There had even been massacres, she heard, where Turkish soldiers had played betting games to see how many Armenian child heads lined up in a row could be severed with one stroke of the sabre. It was a shocking and pitiful image which haunted Margaret's susceptible imagination.

At last they continued their expedition to Tokat, a few days' travel south-east of Amassia. It required all Margaret's resources of British resolve to deal with blackmailing Circassians, reluctant *yiley* drivers and flea-ridden sleeping quarters. But she loved every bone-crunching minute of her summer in Turkey. Everything she could have wished for came together in this wild country, and there were always compensations for the hardships and dangers she endured. On one occasion, for example, she was mesmerized by the sight of a passing caravan made up of over one hundred camels led by drivers perched on bony little donkeys, accompanied by a great procession of lumbering buffalos harnessed to creaking wagons.

They returned to Constantinople with no less than nine hundred set butterflies, all safely stored in her purpose-built cases, and it was marvellous the way Khalil ensured that not one of them was damaged in transit. Inevitably it was a shock to return to the 'real world', however, not least because the news was full of horror stories that had never reached their Anatolian haven. The Pope had died and the King and Queen of Serbia had been assassinated, but most disturbing of all was polite society, where Margaret feared exposure at any minute. She was profoundly afraid of public humiliation, even while she was certain she had done no more than a man in her position and background might have done: travelled independently and experienced certain things that are 'better passed over in silence'. It was so hard, though, not to be able to claim the emotional support that any other wife could claim. Why did she always have to suffer in secret and alone, she wondered for the hundredth time in her diary. But it was her lot in life, and she could only hope she would not be exposed while staying with her generous cousin, the Consul and his wife in Constantinople.

Even worse than her imagined fears were the realities of the Ottoman Empire in 1903, which was suffering revolt and violence in many different regions, from Bulgaria to Beirut. Violent death threatened around every corner, it seemed to Margaret, and she hated leaving Khalil alone in the big city while she was safely installed with the Eyres. If only Khalil could return to England with her, but it was out of the question. Their relationship could not be carried out in the confines of English society, and she would not allow Khalil to visit her at the Consul's house, nor even to address letters to her in anything but the formal language she had taught him herself. He begged her to let him see her off, but she could find no way of inserting him into the busy social schedule the Eyres had tied her into. He must leave for Damascus.

So the lovers parted, reluctantly and without any idea when they would see each other again but certain in the knowledge they were committed to each other. How Margaret hated sending Khalil off to the dangerous climate of Damascus, where cholera stalked everyone and violence was endemic. Yet she had to face serious hardship herself, forced to change transport ten times on the long journey back to London because the Orient Express route was too dangerous.

'Finally arrived in London at 6 a.m.,' she recorded in her diary, exhausted and filthy. But instead of heading straight home, she washed and changed as best she could at Paddington Station and went straight off to instruct her lawyers. A codicil was added to her will ensuring that Khalil Neimy would receive an annuity of £104 per annum for life in the event of her death. It was as close as she could come to a formal tie between herself and Khalil.

❧14❧
MIDLIFE CRISIS

ETURNING TO ENGLAND was always depressing after the intense vitality of life abroad, but this time it was so much worse. With her surviving sisters dispersed, only Mother and a decrepit Hurley remained in Bath, and there was no one to share Margaret's real and imagined fears for Khalil's safety. The miseries of the past coloured her vision of the future, and she could not help but imagine the most awful scenarios in Damascus. It was not safe there, least of all for Christians.

'The story of my life always has been carried on by an undercurrent of events beneath the surface,' she wrote sadly of her lonely winter months in Bath, where her imagination was liable to run out of control whenever one of Khalil's letters failed to arrive.[1] Her butterfly work kept her busy to a certain extent, but that, too, was a solitary business, and not even her old friend Mr Elwes seemed interested any more. He had moved on to forestry, and Margaret noted sadly that their era together had come to an end.

Margaret saw in the New Year in London with her sister Florence, who had established herself as a sculptress at the Bolton Studios in South Kensington. It was a pleasantly creative place, if not too unconventional, and a welcome contrast to Bath. But soon Margaret was installed with her most respectable sister in Godalming, where Geraldine and her doctor husband had set up home. It was kind of them to have her, all things considered, but the months of loneliness and overwrought imaginings had taken their toll, and Margaret finally succumbed to a nervous breakdown. She made the mistake of attending some kind of spiritualist meeting which predicted Neimy's death in March, and she was incapable of distancing herself from the experience. Her susceptible imagination was far too sensitive for such things. She should have known better, but spiritualism was all the rage at that time. 'Never in all my life had such a terror come upon me, and – it is with me still,' she wrote almost a year later.

Only a supreme act of willpower saved her from psychosis, yet still she was tortured by sudden and unpredictable horrors and consumed by uncontrollable thoughts. At night her panic attacks were so severe that her sister had to sleep in the same room, and Hill was prevailed upon to drug her. A modern doctor would probably have diagnosed depression – something she had clearly suffered from most of her life – but in 1904 a person like Margaret, especially if they were female, could hope for nothing more than sedation and bed rest.

Of course, solitude and rest were the last things Margaret needed, and almost instinctively she found the energy to leave England and set off for Algeria, where she could safely reunite with Khalil. His care and companionship were what she needed to be well, and it was agonizing to arrive in Marseilles and find he was not there to meet her. The Hotel de Bordeaux was a desperately lonely place to wait for news from Beirut, but no telegram arrived. She had received no less than three letters from Khalil confirming he was ready to leave Damascus, yet he did not come, and at last she sent him a pre-paid reply coupon with a pitiful entreaty to follow her to El Kantara in Algeria. 'Anyone will be able to tell you how to go to El Kantara,' she ended. 'You first take the boat to Algiers and the train to El Kantara, which is about 20 hours' journey from the coast.'

Margaret expected a lot from her partner, but it was no more than she expected of herself. The journey across rough seas from Marseilles to Algiers took twenty-six gut-wrenching hours of uninterrupted suffering, and she stumbled ashore over heaving planks in the driving rain. The journey by train to El Kantara was only marginally less harrowing, and the best comfort Margaret could find on arrival was the fireplace in her room.

'Truly there seems to have been a peculiar curse upon all six daughters of the Rev. John Fountaine,' she wrote of those despairing first days, even wishing she could have been one of those who had died young of tuberculosis. Hope of ever seeing Khalil was fading by the day, and self-pity was added to despondency.

At last a letter from Khalil did arrive, however, which made it clear that her last three letters had gone missing, including the cheque she had sent for his travel expenses. He, too, had been in torment through not hearing from her for so long. 'Ah! There are no words to describe the reaction of happiness and relief,' she wrote ecstatically, reassured at last.

There was some welcome relief, too, when she met her Norfolk kinsman, Lord Walsingham, in Biskra. He was installed there with his mistress and their daughter, also waiting for the butterfly season to begin. He was co-editor of *The Entomologist*, and Margaret was delighted to see him, far too worldly to concern herself with his private arrangements and even rather pleased to meet another person of her class who chose to live life according to his own rules.

It was April before a reunion with Khalil was possible – two long and painful months after Margaret had crossed the Mediterranean. But at least she had the reassurance of knowing that the fatal prediction in Surrey had not come true, and the kisses among the wild asphodels and irises of the Anti-Atlas Mountains were all the sweeter. Algeria in those days was known as 'The Garden of Allah', and Margaret and Khalil spent months roaming its dramatic landscape of fragrant mountains and burning desert, usually on foot or on horseback but also by bicycle. Khalil took to cycling as quickly and enthusiastically as to butterfly work, and Margaret was delighted to have a cycling companion once more. She always shipped her own bicycle with her wherever she went, and from now on she would be shipping two.

The loveliest parts of Algeria were the mountains covered in cedars which still grew in plentiful splendour in the early part of the twentieth century. 'It was one of the grandest and most magnificent sights I have ever seen,' wrote Margaret in awe; 'some of the trees are enormous, and the steep inclines upon which they grow add much to the beauty of the scene as a whole.' One of the greatest cedar forests was near Theniet El Had, 3,500 feet above sea level south-west of Algiers, and they spent five happy and productive weeks there hunting butterflies and marvelling at the profusion of other insects. There were giant grasshoppers and sparkling dragonflies, scarlet bees and extraordinary beetles. Less welcome were the flying earwigs, which swarmed in their millions, and the snakes. 'I caught one in my net once, instead of the butterfly I was trying for,' she told her readers in *The Entomologist* of one unwelcome snake.[2]

Her articles were a jovial mix of travel writing and entomology, very much in keeping with the fashion of the day but also very specific on the location and number of species to be found. For example, she told her readers that the magnificent Greater Tortoiseshell, *Vanessa polychloros* var. *erythromelas*, was common at Theniet El Had in June but not out yet in May. Over sixty other butterflies are also listed and briefly described, proving just how rich Algeria's insect life once was.

An incessant wind which meant wing damage for butterflies sent Margaret and Khalil off the mountains at last, and they set off north on their bicycles down the valley from Teniet and on to the coastal plains, where a fifty-eight-kilometre ride took them to Affreville (Khemis Miliana after independence in 1962). Beyond Affreville they cycled south-west for several days, over high mountains and across a lonely plateau, before descending on to the vast undulating plain near the Moroccan border, where they were reunited with their luggage in the squalid little town of Sebdou. The heat was intense during the day in this semi-desert part of the country, yet at night the thermometer dropped close to freezing, and Margaret did not enjoy the cold or the 'hovel' they were forced to reside in.

Sebdou was disappointing for butterflies, too, but Margaret and Khalil were invited to dine with the local *kaid*, who treated them to sumptuous Arab food and hospitality. Margaret was even allowed to visit his harem, but her limited Arabic and the huge cultural gulf between herself and the women there meant nothing but 'vacant laughter' was possible. Nevertheless, the encounter made a deep impression, and Margaret found it tragic beyond words that these women were destined to live out their lives imprisoned in their windowless harem, never allowed to enjoy the sunshine beyond its walls. Her own choice to live in 'free love' could not have been more different. Yet when Margaret admitted she had no husband or children she found herself the object of pity. 'They showed me all their small offspring with great pride, and when I enquired conversationally as to the sex of each tiny creature . . . on each occasion in order to confirm the truth of their statements, an immediate upheaval of baby-linen was the result in order to show me beyond all doubt that the sex of the small individual was even as they said.'

Political trouble with neighbouring Morocco meant hordes of soldiers were roaming the desert, and Sebdou was no place for an English lady, not even one accompanied by a revolver-wearing Syrian. But the heat was oppressive and it was hard to think straight, and before Margaret could make a decision she and Khalil were both struck down by malaria. An epidemic was sweeping the land at that time, and though Khalil recovered after just a few days – no doubt hardened by his youth in Syria – Margaret was gripped by the disease. Her mouth, eyes, ears and nose became infested with sores, dark blood oozed from her nose and she was often delirious with fever. The military doctor insisted that they leave Sebdou despite the dangers of armed men, and Khalil manfully took charge of transporting Margaret over the mountains to Tlemcen. Her fever rose to over 40.5 degrees centigrade in the stifling heat, and all Khalil could do was to spend hour upon hour fanning her and wiping her brow. 'This man,' she wrote later, 'who I had been told to despise as unworthy of me, would spend hours changing the wet handkerchief of my forehead, the palms of my hands and the soles of my feet.' She would have died without his care, yet he succumbed to fever again himself. 'Water! Water!' she could hear him cry through the wall, too weak to reach him and give him the care he needed as much as she.

At last they were both strong enough to leave for the cooler climate of Milianah, which they were grateful to reach by first-class train, but it took many weeks before either of them was strong enough for the journey to Marseilles and the comforts of clean drinking water and reliable medical care. Margaret had lost so much weight that her skin sagged thinly over her bones and she looked much older than her forty-two years by the time she reached Europe once more. It had been so tough for them both that she booked them into the finest hotel in Hyères and did not even bother about what other guests might think, seeing her dine with her dragoman.

The relief of being safe and well was tempered by sadness, though, because soon it would be time for the inevitable goodbye. It was too painful, and they delayed for as long as Margaret's funds allowed. But once the money ran out they had no choice but to part, Khalil catching a boat to Beirut from Marseilles and Margaret heading north by train. Goodness only knew how many months of separation, delays and misunderstandings would occur before their reunion next summer, Margaret thought sadly on her way back to England, but she could have had no idea just how complicated her life was going to get.

The malaria fevers returned with Margaret to Bath, where the well-meaning spinsters and widows who made up her mother's friends were almost as intolerable as the Algerian heat.

'There is no loneliness like that of one who hangs aloof in a society which is utterly distasteful to him,' she wrote dismally in her diary. 'There is no solitude like the solitude of tired thoughts in the midst of happy talkers, whose minds, however small and contracted, are, at least, at rest.'

It was during this time of illness and loneliness that Margaret received possibly the most extraordinary letter of her life. It was from Edwin Gilbertson, Vice-Consul of Broussa in Turkey and brother to the Gilbertson sisters.

'My dear Miss Fountaine,' it began, and proceeded to explain that his sisters had decided he needed to settle down and, since they had all enjoyed Margaret's company so much the other year, would she not consider becoming his wife?

Margaret and Edwin Gilbertson had never met, and she was so stunned by the arrogance of this man (and of his sisters) that it took some time before she could take it all in. He even had the nerve to lecture her on the dangers of loneliness, though she had had plenty of conversations with his sisters about her decision to stay single which they must have shared with him.

'Of course,' he continued, 'having my sisters, I am not actually in such a position, but, nevertheless, the fact exists that they may not always be with me, for they are just as liable to marry as anyone, and that is why they desire that I should settle down.'

It was an outrageous presumption, made all the less attractive by his assurance that he could marry any number of other richer ladies but none that was English and only an English lady would do for him.

'I am perfectly aware that self praise is no good,' he wrote, 'but I can truly and honestly state that you may find my equal, but never a more true, loving and faithful husband, therefore you need not, even for a moment, hesitate placing your happiness in my hands.'

It was all too much for Margaret and, after discussing the letter with her mother, she replied with a respectful rejection of his proposal, assuring him she was not only safeguarding her own happiness but also his, because she was incapable of settling down at her stage in life. Never had she been more honest.

She was now receiving love letters from two men, neither of them suitable husband material – not that she was looking – but it did tickle her vanity to find herself in this situation approaching middle age. She was rather pleased with herself, boasting in her diary she had had 'immense experience amongst men of all descriptions – lovers and suitors of all nationalities', and in her opinion Khalil's love letters were by far the more appealing. At least she was certain of his devotion, and she reminded herself that a wandering life with a partner fifteen years her junior was much more enticing than a respectable marriage to a minor diplomat.

Yet the niggling voice of Victorian values whispered in her ear and made her unsure of herself. Mr Gilbertson's proposal made her question her choices, especially when he persisted with further letters. Fatally, she began to feel sorry for him, though she still resented his assumption that she would, as a matter of course, accept him in the end. Convention told her only a fool would turn down an offer like Mr Gilbertson's at her age, but then she would reply that she was a fool. All her natural self-doubt and the social expectations she had always sought to evade came back to haunt her during her malarial fevers, and it was no help at all having only her God-bothering mother to talk to.

Margaret was not too ill to realize, however, that Mr Gilbertson's attitude towards her would be very different if he knew even a fraction of her private life, not to mention her relationship with Khalil. She also sincerely believed she would be doing Khalil a terrible injustice after all he had done for her if she were to abandon him now. She could not help reflecting again that a man in her position would have had a much easier time of it: 'Yet how many men are quite satisfied to have led more or less wild lives, and yet will settle down in middle age, married to some woman, probably many years younger than themselves, without so much as a qualm of conscience or the slightest scruple, but on the contrary, probably greatly imbued with the thought of how virtuous it is of them to be settling down to a hum-drum married life at last; and why should not I feel the same?'

Margaret hedged her bets and sent a photograph of herself to Mr Gilbertson – hardly likely to encourage him, considering she took such a bad picture – but he promptly wrote back imploring her to visit him in Broussa, where she could convalesce among people who cared for her and one in particular who could make her happy. He can have had no idea he was touching on Margaret's most sensitive emotional wound by referring to himself as the one who could make her happy. The longing of her youth, buried deep under experience, was yet roused by Mr Gilbertson's appeals.

'Oh! But I could not possibly give up Khalil, my dear Khalil, who is so good to me,' she wrote in her diary, distraught.

Margaret was simply too enfeebled to see a clear path through her dilemma, and finding herself caught in a row between Mother and her sister Florence was the final straw. She took the only action she knew to resolve difficult situations and fled to the Continent. It was in no way a solution, not least because she was still unwell, but her Curtois and Lee-Warner cousins in Paris welcomed her with open arms, and it was almost like the good old days at Washingborough Manor. Margaret adored her cousin Annie Lee-Warner, who nursed her so kindly through yet another malaria attack, and then she moved on to Milan and another warm welcome from her dear friend Angelina.

Meanwhile, she was still receiving weekly letters from both Khalil and Mr Gilbertson – neither aware of the other – and Margaret continued to hedge her bets. In fact, she complicated matters a great deal more by sending Khalil money to meet her in Marseilles, while also allowing the Vice-Consul to believe she was considering his offer. Yet she knew what she was doing was deeply unfair to both men, and for two days she sat in the Milanese countryside pondering her future. Should she choose the man from her own culture and background, who would provide her with every comfort in life, as well as respectability? Or should she choose the companionship of her devoted Syrian, who would serve her faithfully on her travels around the world? The impossible but honest answer was that she wanted both, and both she would have, if only for a short time. She wrote to Mr Gilbertson, hedging her bets to the very last:

> I have not sent you a wire, for though I am going to say 'Yes', it is only on condition that you will allow me to have just this one last summer quite free as usual, for my life as it is now is a very, very happy one, and I have not that wish to be married, which some women have, but rather quite the reverse.
>
> However, if you will agree to these few months' delay, I will consent to be your wife, with, of course, always the right reserved for both of us . . . to change our mind.

She also instructed him to keep their engagement private until he could come to her in London in the autumn, no doubt to protect herself against recriminating letters from Mother for her decision to spend the summer with Khalil in northern Spain. It was the kind of gamble typical of Margaret and one that was bound to go wrong.

Nevertheless, it was liberating to have a plan of action, and Margaret wrote happily in her diary that her world was the 'burning, trackless deserts of torrid lands' where the nights were 'dark and lonely, but never sad'. It was as close as she could bring herself to admit that her idea of marriage to the fifty-five-year-old Edwin Gilbertson was as ridiculous as caging a wild bird, but at least the game would not be up until the autumn. 'Yes,' she wrote almost gleefully, 'I must give the Future to Edwin, but with the Future he must be satisfied. The Past could never be his, and the Present was mine.' She would spend the summer with her twenty-eight-year-old Khalil, and she had a brand new Beeston Humber bicycle sent over from England so that they could cycle from Marseilles to their hunting grounds in Spain.

Unwilling to live a lie with Khalil, she confessed her engagement to him once they were reunited and was surprised to find he was quite relaxed about it. Perhaps he knew Margaret better than she did herself and realized that she would never go through with it – certainly he stole kisses from her whenever he could – or perhaps he was simply being practical and determined to enjoy his last season with his favourite employer to date. Occasionally he could not help showing his feelings, but mostly they both ignored the subject of Margaret's engagement and carried on as before. She could not have hoped for better and confided to her diary that it was very pleasant to dance with the locals and get drunk on strong Spanish wine. Would Mr Gilbertson allow such things in future? Even Margaret could not doubt the answer to that question.

They settled into a rustic but comfortable *posada* in the Aragonese village of Albarracín, perched on the cliffs of the Guadalaviar Mountains, and no couple could have been more relaxed and happy than they, hunting butterflies and exploring on their bikes. Letters from Mr Gilbertson continued to arrive with irritating regularity, and their husbandly solicitations for her health and safety had precisely the opposite effect to the one intended. Instead of warmth Margaret felt irritation, and every question about her family and background made her feel constrained and put upon. Her answers became more and more businesslike just as her fiancé's became more and more familiar. He even took the liberty of addressing her as 'Maggie', but that was a step too far, and Margaret quickly informed him that no one had ever called her that and would not be doing so in future either.

As the weeks went by it dawned on her she was proposing to leave a man who could cope with her every whim and caprice, endure her many faults and serve her faithfully and with tender care, just because they could never be married. Edwin would never be capable or willing to play that role. Surely it was her duty to save both herself and Edwin from unhappiness by breaking off the engagement?

'Was I mad that I was about to close a chapter in my life the like of which I could never read again?' she admonished herself regarding her relationship with Khalil. How could she be so heartless? Tears came to Khalil's eyes on the rare occasions they did speak about their separate futures, but Edwin had insisted on making the engagement public and there seemed no way back. Mother had told all and sundry in England, and congratulations had begun to arrive from all over the world.

Each letter from Broussa heaped more discomfort on Margaret's reluctant conscience, but salvation came from the most unexpected quarter. A letter arrived from her cousin, the Consul of Constantinople, which was as damning of Mr Gilbertson as it was extraordinary. In it Harry Eyres informed her he had known the Gilbertson family for over thirty years and that they were in no way worthy of her. Edwin's father was 'not the sort of man' Harry would like to see any relative of his connected with. and, furthermore, though Edwin was not a bad sort, he was one of life's losers, not to mention far too old for any second chances. He ended his letter with a damning account of Edwin's financial status and prospects and assured Margaret that her life as the Vice-Consul's wife in Broussa would be full of privations. 'From all conventional points of view,' he wrote, 'I should say that you would be very ill advised to go through with this business and from the other side (the personal) which I personally lay more stress on, I cannot conceive its resulting in your happiness.'

Just when Margaret had been trying out the 'honourable part' in life, a man of the highest standing in conventional society was advising her to break off her engagement and retrieve the freedom she so dearly loved. It was a make or break moment in her life, and Margaret knew the minute she read the letter that her destiny was there for the taking. She immediately wrote to Edwin asking him to release her from their agreement. 'The sun shone brighter, and the sky was a deeper blue now, for I felt that a great weight was being lifted from my life,' she wrote of that day, and she felt happier than for many months. She was regaining her freedom and taking charge of her life once again. Soon she would recover her health as well, and two greater treasures she could not imagine.

But Edwin Gilbertson was not about to be brushed off so easily. As far as he knew, Margaret was simply having feminine nerves about her future. He knew nothing about the letter from Constantinople, and Margaret had hoped not to use it against him. She had simply written to say that she had changed her mind. There was too much at stake for Mr Gilbertson, however. He needed Margaret for many reasons, not least her income, and no doubt his sisters impressed on him the need to persevere. A pitiful letter arrived, recorded word for word in Margaret's diary, in which he reminded her of all their promises over the months and pleading for an explanation. He asked her to consider how ridiculous his position in Broussa would be, having to explain his situation in front of all the local officials, how publicly humiliated he would be.

But if his letter was intended to inspire pity and a sense of duty it had exactly the opposite effect, not least because he made the cardinal error of ending this pathetic letter with a threat to sue her for breach of promise. Nothing could have ensured his failure better than that, and Margaret instantly despised him and everything he stood for. Her reply was as brutal as it could be. She had never loved him and never would, she wrote, and she also reminded him that her very first letter regarding their engagement had included a claim to allow either party to change their minds. As to the threat of legal proceedings, she considered it on the level of barmaids and third-rate actresses and not an action anyone of *her* class would undertake, much less a gentleman against a lady. And that was that, though the strain of these exchanges was worse than 'twenty days of walking over the mountains of Losilla', and she immediately succumbed to another bout of malarial fever.

Khalil, her 'brother' as far as the villagers were concerned, nursed her with all the usual kindness, and even during her illness Margaret knew without a shadow of a doubt that leaving this man for anyone else would have been the real crime. A letter from Harry Eyres assured her Mr Gilbertson did not have the means to sue her, even if he really meant to, and she was happy to think she would never hear from that unfortunate man again.

Her season in the Aragonese Mountains came to a very appropriate end with a total eclipse of the sun. 'Darkness fell upon the plains and on the mountains, a darkness that was neither of twilight nor of moonlight, but rather as of the darkness of the earth before the sun was created. Two stars shone out clear in the skies of mid-day, birds were seen hurrying home to roost, and a faint red glow as of fading sunsets tinged the horizons on all sides, deepening towards the north-east.' A corona like a thousand rainbows shone around the darkened disc of the sun for a few brief moments, and then it emerged from the shadow of the moon to bathe the land in warm sunshine once again.

❦ 15 ❦

FREE TO ROAM

EADING BACK TO England after her butterfly season in Spain, Margaret received news that her mother was gravely ill, and she was filled with remorse. 'I had left her in anger,' she recorded in her diary, but now she was painfully reminded of the bond between them and that her mother had always tried to love her, despite their many differences. It was Margaret's turn to care for her mother, and she was determined to fulfil that duty.

So she settled into an even sadder routine than usual that autumn, caring not only for her dying mother but also for a decrepit Hurley, and it was almost inevitable that depression came back to stalk her. She was not equipped, mentally or physically, to cope with the strain of her position alone. In addition she was tormented by fears for Khalil's safety. The Ottoman Empire was in violent decline and political unrest was rife in many of its disparate parts. A power struggle for control of Macedonia was raging, and the English papers were full of articles predicting more massacres of Christians.

The political crisis blew over, however, and Margaret was delighted when her mother revived sufficiently to allow for a short trip to Corsica the following spring. It was close enough to get back to England quickly, if she needed to, and it was wonderful to return to that beautiful island with Khalil. Much had changed in the thirteen years since her last visit, and Margaret was pleased to note a great improvement in the standard of hotels. They spent the summer based at Evisa, close to the wild tracks of the Valdoniello forest.

Margaret and Khalil had known each other almost five years now, and the physical passion between them had already died – at least it had for

Margaret – though she admits to her diary that the 'laws of nature' had to be obeyed occasionally. But much more important was the profound bond of loving companionship, and Margaret knew without a shadow of a doubt that Khalil's devoted care of her was not just for the money. They slept in separate rooms, yet they were as close as any traditional couple could be, and there was a great deal more respect and care in their relationship than in many a marriage.

When the news of Mother's death reached Margaret it was a shock, not least because she had only recently received a letter from her claiming she was well but it also forcefully reminded Margaret of her own selfishness. She had left her mother to seek her own pleasure knowing perfectly well in her heart she was probably not going to live much longer. Failing to be a respectable wife was one thing, failing to be a dutiful daughter was another, and the guilt she felt over her mother's passing was profound. She locked herself in her room to grieve and give herself over to self-hatred and remorse. The weather added to her punishment by making it impossible to leave the island. Summer storms whipped up the sea, and Margaret was even forced to miss her mother's funeral.

Nevertheless, as soon as the weather allowed Margaret decided to part company with Khalil and return to England. She and Geraldine were her mother's executors, and there was much to do, not least the disposal of the remaining family effects in Bath. It was a distressing task, made worse by the discovery of boxes and boxes full of items once belonging to Constance and Rachel. Thankfully, the sisters had no cause for fighting. Florence had refused to have anything to do with her mother for years and was excluded from the will, Geraldine already had a furnished home and only wished for trinkets, and Margaret and Evelyn had no desire to set up home together, so most of their mother's things were sold.

Only three graves in Bathwick Cemetery recall the Fountaine family's era in Bath, one of the saddest, as far as Margaret was concerned, and she turned her back on the city without hesitation, determined never to set foot in it again or be constrained by any member of her family. From now on, Margaret decided, her home would be wherever her butterfly cabinets were housed, and for the time being that would be West Hampstead.

She was pleased with her new base and surprised to find that this obscure suburb of the capital was not 'a slum, peopled with 'Arries and

'Arriets' but very decent and only twelve minutes from the centre by the Metropolitan Line. She rented a studio to work in on Sherriff Road and lived at Quex Lodge, on West End Lane.

In the autumn Hurley followed her old mistress to the grave, and Margaret's deepest bond was gone. To lose her nanny in the same year as her mother was hard, even aged forty-four, and Margaret felt very small and insignificant in London on her own. 'Should I ever be able to get up to Watkins and Doncaster's and effect the crossing of the Strand twice,' she asked herself, uncharacteristically timid.[1]

Nor did she feel very confident among the smart set at her cousin Skye's home on Park Lane. She preferred the company of entomological friends, with whom she could forget her insecurities and be the vivacious butterfly collector she was. Fashionable people made her feel like a dowdy spinster, but serious entomologists did not care about her lack of elegance and even less about her private life. They admired only her butterflies, and she was very pleased to find herself much praised on that account. The high quality of her specimens and meticulous setting meant that the Natural History Museum was a very willing recipient for some of her rarer finds and in years to come would even pay good money for them. In the meantime she welcomed visits to her butterfly cabinets in West Hampstead, where the neighbours had much to speculate about, not least when Skye turned up by hugely glamorous Motor Hansom with a pair of footmen in attendance.

Most of all, however, Margaret yearned to be alone with her man, alone and far away on some wind-swept mountain; and, in time, she realized the two profoundly important deaths that had occurred gave her the freedom to do just that, whenever she wished. Never again would she be duty bound to spend damp and lonely winters in England. Freedom was truly hers at last, and she felt deep empathy for all women who yearned for the same, even if she did not always approve of their methods.

Hyde Park, in the spring of 1907, was full of Suffragettes agitating under banners claiming 'Votes for Women'. It was a just cause, of that Margaret had no doubt, and she was sincerely shocked by the brutality used against demonstrators by the authorities. On one occasion armed and mounted police charged defenceless crowds of women, and many injuries resulted. 'It is curious,' Margaret noted in her diary, 'how all over the world the strong feeling there is in men to trample down and crush the weaker sex, not only in the East, where the tyranny in this respect is carried to horrible extreme, but in Europe, too, and now in England.'

Margaret was one of many fired up by the violence, and Quex Lodge was regularly enlivened by fierce debates among the residents. Margaret was certain that women were on the cusp of throwing off their yoke as 'favoured playthings' and ready to take on the responsibilities of equal rights. Yet she was by no means a man-hater. It was not equality she believed in but equal rights, and men were not to be despised but enjoyed. 'Personally, I have not a word to say against the opposite sex,' she wrote in her diary, 'men are always my friends – indeed they exalt me far higher than I deserve to be exalted in one way, and they do not at the same time seem to despise me in other ways.'

'Signora, una lettera espresso!'

It was a letter announcing Khalil's arrival in Italy, where Margaret had once again been suffering the torment of waiting for him, and they were reunited at Brindisi in time for Easter. Margaret could live again, forget the terror in her mind and the grief in her spirit and look forward to a future exploring the world with her dragoman. She decided to cross the Adriatic where the Dalmatian coast and Montenegrin Mountains beckoned, and it was not long before Margaret and Khalil were sweating up mountain passes and hurtling down winding roads on their bicycles. This was life, as far as Margaret was concerned, and it was even better shared with her 'brother' Karl, as Khalil became known. It meant they could reasonably share hotel rooms and stretch Margaret's money a lot further, and Khalil seems to have behaved himself sufficiently to make this possible.

By summer the butterfly season was well under way, and Bosnia-Herzegovina's streams and meadows were rich hunting grounds. They spent happy and productive times in Mostar, Jablaniça and Sarajevo, but then illness intervened once again, and this time it was Khalil who needed urgent hospital care. He developed a serious case of pleurisy after getting caught in a rainstorm, and Margaret had to spend several weeks visiting him in the local hospital in Sarajevo. It was traumatic for both of them, with Margaret unable to argue against a raft of horrible treatments and Khalil condemned to endure them. Wet sheets were regularly tied around his body, but that was nothing compared to the needles inserted into his chest to remove the water on his lung.

Every day Margaret cycled from the centre of Sarajevo to the *Landesspital*, in the hills above the city, to spend wearisome hours at Khalil's bedside, her only comfort that the doctors confided in her fully, believing she was the patient's sister. It was a huge relief to be entitled to the fullest information and comforting sympathy from the nurses, and Margaret and Khalil were amused to find he had become known as *der Engländer*, though it was not amusing at all when the British Consul and his wife decided to visit the so-called Englishman. Luckily, Margaret was present on their arrival and quickly ensured her brother was far too ill to speak.[2]

An invitation for tea with the Consul was politely avoided, and Margaret and Khalil left Sarajevo just as soon as he was fit enough to travel. But it was mid-summer by now, and time and money were running out. The doctors had convinced Margaret the South African climate would be ideal for Khalil's lung troubles, and, since she was determined not to lose another loved one to lung disease or part with him for another lonely winter in England, she needed to head home to see her bank and make their travel arrangements. A brief separation was necessary while they both put their affairs in order, and thus Margaret returned to London to cram setting her summer catches into six weeks rather than six months and prepare for her first journey south of the equator. She could not wait to get going, and for once she was too busy to worry about Khalil back in Damascus.

There was much to do: she commissioned purpose-built butterfly boxes that could withstand the ravages of white ants and other tropical vermin from J.J. Hill's in Willesden, she went to see Cook's at Ludgate Circus to book her berth on the German East African liner *Prinzessin* to Durban, and she reluctantly went to see a variety of garment shops for tropical wear. She hated shopping for clothes – it was all much too fussy and she had no interest in fashion whatsoever. What she wanted were loose blouses and skirts suitable for riding bikes and horses, which could be adapted to her entomology work by having large pockets sewn all over them.

Meanwhile, Khalil was instructed to meet her at Port Said, where he could join her on the journey through the Suez Canal and down the East African coast. Geraldine saw Margaret off, and she felt a brief pang of guilt for leaving her sister to the English winter while she chased the summer weather south, but not for long. Every fibre of her being yearned to be reunited with Khalil, and not even four grumpy German ladies sharing her cabin could spoil the happy anticipation of her months ahead. It was her first journey in one of the large ocean-going liners of the day, and she soon discovered that travel in one of these was very different to the journeys she was used to on small steamships. These big liners were more like floating hotels, where passengers played tennis on spacious decks and ample dining-rooms beckoned for sumptuous meals. There were plenty of English passengers, too, mostly heading for Mombassa, and she soon made friends, even finding a few butterfly people.

For once the reunion with Khalil went smoothly, and Margaret's fears dissolved into unutterable happiness at the sight of her beloved dragoman approaching in a small boat from the harbour at Port Said. There would be no separation now for the longest time, and she could hardly contain her relief, much less disguise her love. Together they marvelled at the extra-ordinary experience of being transported through the desert on a narrow strip of water and thrilled at the tantalizing horizons of the Red Sea.

It took six days to reach Mombassa from the port of Aden, and though Margaret and Khalil were continuing to Durban they were allowed to disembark for twenty-four hours. Margaret recalled excitedly: 'And what a day it was, directly after breakfast I landed with Khalil to have my first experience of tropical butterflies, and never shall I forget it! A big *Papilio demoleus* (lime butterfly) flying hurriedly from flower to flower almost took my breath away, and of course I was much too excited to effect his capture.'

Margaret quickly discovered that chasing butterflies in tropical heat was quite a challenge. The intense humidity and heat soon brought on exhaustion, yet the thrill of discovering an entirely new face of nature was intoxicating. The glittering weaver birds, the dripping foliage, everything was wonderful to Margaret – even the heat was bearable when there were such magnificent butterflies to be caught. It was love at first sight and, though she did not know it then, from now on Margaret was destined to spend most of her life working and travelling in the tropics. From Africa to China, from Cuba to Brazil, her happiest and most productive years were going to be in the lands of dry and wet seasons, where the sun is never far away and skies are never grey.

❊16❊
A NATURALIST IN AFRICA

'THAT NIGHT IN Mombassa has left a lasting impression upon me,' Margaret wrote of her first day in the tropics, and it was quickly joined by many others.[1] They passed Dar es Salaam and then the island of Zanzibar, where they saw the extraordinary sight of a preserved 'mermaid'. Margaret assumed it was some kind of seal, though it was probably a manatee. According to the locals it had cried tears in so human a fashion that they almost felt they were committing murder when they killed it.

At last they arrived in Durban on the morning of 9 November 1907, and it seemed to Margaret it was the loveliest summer morning she had ever known. Soon they were installed in a guest-house in the lush hills above the city, and Margaret's heart missed a beat when she spotted outsized butterflies flitting about right in front of the house. A child in the proverbial sweetshop could not have felt more excited, and Margaret was out with her butterfly net just as soon as her luggage arrived. In no time at all she was chasing giant African swallowtails and the golden wings of *Eronia leda* (Autumn Leaf Vagrants).

'That first week or two in Durban was almost the happiest time I have ever known,' she wrote breathlessly; 'everything was so fresh and new to me . . .' It was not only the kaleidoscope of butterflies that thrilled Margaret, either; she also found colonial English society was much looser than at home, and no one was particularly concerned about her so-called courier, Neimy. People were more relaxed and informal with each other, though there was plenty of scandal, too. The daughter of the former English Consul was having an affair with the Zulu king, Dinizulu, though it was not the affair that bothered people as much as the suspicion she was encouraging him to foment rebellion. Some even suggested she should be tried for treason, along with her lover, who was charged the following year.

Except for a problem with ticks, Durban was just about the most perfect place Margaret had ever encountered, and it made her impatient to explore further. But travel in Zululand was out of the question, given the tense political situation, so they hopped on a liner going further down the coast instead, to East London in the Cape Colony. Why Margaret chose this place is not recorded, but she took an instant dislike to it, in spite of the lovely beach, and returned to Durban within a week. She had hit the entomological jackpot first time, and she quickly realized there was much work to be done. The stunning variety of tropical butterflies was not the only challenge, either. She decided to have a go at breeding them, and, for the first time in a decade, she took up her sketch book to record their unique life-cycles.

It had been a long time since she had sat down to paint and draw, but she had lost none of her artistic flair, and she began an entomological record which is still consulted by experts today. The beauty of her artwork is matched by scientific precision – each egg and caterpillar shown on its relevant food plant – providing a precious source of information for modern conservationists.[2] In fact, Margaret's time in South Africa produced some of her most important entomological work, leading to the discovery of life-cycles previously unknown to science for eight butterflies. It was a significant achievement which has been unduly forgotten, despite publication of her work in the *Transactions of the Entomological Society of London* in 1911. No doubt the momentous political developments at the time and the approaching world war had something to do with it. But at least as important was Margaret's absence from the all-important establishment circles in London. She simply did not network and promote herself in the way ambitious people must if they want public fame. The only recognition she craved was that of other entomologists. Her achievement was substantial nevertheless and can be gauged by the fact there are still around two hundred European and North American butterflies – so much more accessible than African ones – for which the larval food plants are unknown. In the tropics food plants for entire taxonomic groups of butterflies are still a mystery, with the result that many extinctions are occurring before their life-cycles have even been recorded.[3]

At first Margaret's ignorance of local plants resulted in the death of all her larvae, but gradually she became more successful. Butterflies lay their eggs in an extraordinary variety of places, from inside seed pods to the underside of leaves and even on lichen. It all depends on the food plant the emerging caterpillars are going to need. Some butterflies even drop their eggs in mid-flight, scattering them in the grass their caterpillars love to eat. Margaret's challenge was therefore to spend many hot and sweaty hours tramping through tangled undergrowth, scanning everything from trees and prickly shrubs to flowers and grasslands for eggs and caterpillars. The eggs themselves come in a surprising variety of shapes and colours, too, but over the months Margaret and Khalil learnt to distinguish them all, knowing just by the appearance of an egg which species of butterfly would eventually result.

The challenge was to find not only the correct food plant for each type of caterpillar but also the right conditions. Caterpillars will not move on to the next stage of development, to pupation unless the climate is right, which could be very inconvenient when travelling all over southern Africa, from highland frost to coastal heat. Despite relevant food plants, Margaret's breeding cages could not always reproduce the correct environment, and she records one failed breeding attempt, where she spent six months with the caterpillars of the *Dingana angusta* butterfly (as it is known today) only to have them all die because they had cotton wool instead of cool earth to hibernate on. In fact, not even modern scientists have ever succeeded in breeding any of the seven species of *Dingana* butterfly through to adulthood, so Margaret's failure is in good company. But success was more frequent for her, and Margaret's long hours of observation of caterpillars led to all sorts of interesting behavioural observations as well. Caterpillars are by no means just dumb eating machines. They have clever strategies and instincts, such as gnawing off branches where all the leaves have gone, so as not to waste time crawling along them twice; or securing a chosen leaf for pupation by fortifying its stalk with an additional silk web, to make sure it does not drop off while the chrysalis is hanging from it.[4]

At last the Dinizulu affair was settled with his surrender, in 1908, and Margaret was free to travel into fertile Zululand, where pockets of forest and African bush were hidden treasure troves beyond the endless cane fields near the coast. The Zulu capital of Eshowe was an ideal base for hunting expeditions, and Margaret and Khalil spent many happy weeks living and working there. The wife of their hotel proprietor was carrying on with two men right under his nose, but Margaret did not concern herself with that, rather enjoying her company. Khalil, meanwhile, caused a sensation by telling terrifyingly accurate fortunes. It was a sideline he would profitably use wherever they went, and one can just imagine the queue of swooning ladies ready to pay good money to have this charming Arab stroke their palm and gaze into their eyes. Margaret thought it harm-less fun, and she enjoyed learning the secrets Khalil's 'customers' shared with him.

Margaret had little time left over for scandal and secrets, however; she was far too busy with her breeding programme, which was very labour intensive. Finding eggs or caterpillars in the wild was just the beginning of a process that could take many weeks, and often months, and required daily attention. Each aspect of breeding butterflies in captivity takes many hours of every day. For example, fresh food plants have to be found and every cage replenished, which is not just a matter of sticking new branches in with the old but means carefully picking all the caterpillars off the old branches and encouraging them on to fresh leaves. Since Margaret's cages held up to a hundred caterpillars each, just this one task was a huge under-taking. Cleaning was another daily essential, as caterpillars eat a great deal of indigestible cellulose and quickly fill a cage with vast amounts of drop-pings. And all the time careful record-keeping and observation were needed to note the amazing natural process from egg to butterfly which can be so different from one family to the next. It was a subject Margaret never tired of and, the more expert she became the more she became fascinated by the extraordinary lives of the caterpillars. Each one shed its skin several times, eating all except the head casings which scattered on the bottom of the cages like so many dropped beads.

Unfortunately there are almost no scientific observations in her private diaries. Occasionally, a particularly interesting feature got a men-tion in her writing – such as the fact that if a caterpillar loses an antenna the future butterfly emerges with one missing – but these are only snippets. All that remains of her unique learning is the artwork, represented in the life-cycles recorded in her art books. It is for this reason, too, that latter-day scientists have found it easy to forget her work. The modern prejudice against taxonomy, which regards it as a poor relation to theoretical science, combines with the view that results without scientific notes are not valid. There is truth in this, of course, and it remains the greatest obstacle to her reputation ever rising above that of a respected amateur. Bizarrely, however, in her own time an amateur naturalist enjoyed the higher standing, since professional men were only one step up from tradesmen – a position a member of the Victorian upper class would never have considered for themselves. Gentlemen and ladies were amateurs in the best sense, untainted by the need to earn a living and free to study their subject in the greatest depth. Such were Charles Darwin and the Rothschild brothers, as well as many others.

Dedicated as she was, Margaret's butterfly work never smothered her wanderlust, and after successfully breeding ninety-seven Pearl Charaxes (*Charaxes varanes*) she decided it was time to visit Victoria Falls and see the stupendous waterfall Livingstone had first set eyes on barely fifty years earlier. They travelled by train across the endless African veld, from Durban to Ladysmith, from Ladysmith to Bloemfontein, from Bloemfontain to Kimberly's diamond mines, and on to Mafeking – famous battle site of the Boer War. The biting cold of South Africa's central plateau froze them to the core at night, but after one of Khalil's campfires spread fire into the bush they thought better of trying to keep warm that way. At least the days were mild, and at last they passed into Zimbabwe – Rhodesia then – changing trains for the last time in Bulawayo for the final leg of their journey to the falls. They arrived at dawn to see a tantalizing white cloud in the distance which they knew to be spray rising from the giant waterfall.

'To attempt to describe the magnificent beauty of these marvellous Falls would be in vain,' Margaret confessed to her diary. 'I can only say to have lived and died and never to have beheld them is to have lived and died without seeing the greatest glory this earth has to show us.'

Margaret and Khalil were covered in a moist film of droplets, their ears filled with the roar of millions of gallons of water falling, and their hearts beat faster as the great arc came into view at last: an immense curtain of water with myriads of diamond rainbows hovering in the spray. The earth beneath their feet seemed to tremble, and the lovers stood speechless in amazement.

The famous doctor had stood in their place just a generation ago, yet compared to nature's creations 'civilization's' efforts were really very puny, especially in Rhodesia at the time, whose capital Margaret dismissed as 'a small collection of low roofed houses covered with red dust'. Harare (Salisbury then) had only been founded fifteen years previously, so perhaps she was being a little unfair, but Victoria Falls is hard to beat in any era. They moved on to Mutare, in Mashonaland, where the tropical winter season provided exhilaratingly crisp blue skies under which to hunt more lovely butterflies. Fiery *Acraea acrita* fluttered up from the mountain grass like stray hibiscus petals, and only the occasional lion footprint stopped Margaret in her tracks. The locals told them several bullocks had been taken lately and advised taking a black boy with them. Apparently lions preferred African flesh to that of Europeans, but neither Margaret nor Khalil thought it fair to take someone along for the express purpose of being eaten instead of themselves.

In the end it was not predators that chased them away but bush fires. The local tradition of setting fire to the winter grasses destroyed every last inch of butterfly habitat for miles around, and Margaret fled to the Portuguese African settlement of Macequece instead. Goodwin's Hotel was a well-known expatriate watering hole there, and Margaret and Khalil were assured a warm welcome since they had already made friends with Mr Goodwin's mistress, Mrs Gilmore, during their stay in Mutare. They were greeted like long-lost friends and installed in a spacious hut on the grounds of the hotel, where Khalil was delighted to find that blossoming trees meant hunting trips into the surrounding bush were no longer necessary. They could find all the butterflies they could wish for right outside their window, encountering nothing more dangerous than the occasional baboon.

At last the rainy season arrived, but Margaret loved the hot rain almost as much as the sun for the way it made everything so verdant and lush. 'Ah! I can hear it now on the iron roof of the little shanty, where we had put up during our stay at Macequece,' she remembered.

Quite often she would also hear Khalil thrashing around in his adjacent room, trying to discourage the ever-present crickets from their endless cacophony and the crab-sized poisonous spiders from creeping into his bed. There were all manner of creepy-crawlies, from huge beetles to stinging insects, but worst of all was the incessant gnawing of white ants which fed on anything made of wood. A gentle drizzle of sawdust fell from the rafters at all times but especially at night.

In Pretoria, later in the year, Margaret was invited to visit a Dutch farm, where she was intrigued to hear the Boer perspective on the recent war, but interest turned to outrage when her host suggested British officers had sent African soldiers to loot Boer farms and rape and murder their women. 'It is interesting to hear the Boer side of the War,' she wrote, 'but I could not help rising in indignation when he said that the British officers systematically sent Kaffirs to raid their farms, not only to loot cattle but also to seduce and murder the women and children.' Margaret was sincerely sure that if such things had happened the African soldiers were entirely to blame and not their British officers, who would never have sanctioned such behaviour. Such were the certainties then, when the myth of wartime honour and glory was still alive.

By the time they returned to Durban six months had passed, and they had been in southern Africa for almost two years. Margaret's funds could go a long way in this part of the world, and Durban was simply too wonderful to leave. Flowering trees and shrubs grew in every garden in flamboyant profusion and colour, and the hillside suburbs of the city looked down on to the purple sea of the Indian Ocean. Durban's natural harbour curved in a generous arc to form a sweeping bay, and Margaret could think of no lovelier place to live with her dragoman, who was by now not only her best friend and companion but also her equal in the entomological work she pursued. He had a sharp eye and as much energy and enthusiasm as she, and he was also a meticulous setter of insects, at least as professional as she when it came to preserving specimens.

Unfortunately, Margaret's fellow entomologists were not all as expert as they seemed, and she paid a heavy price for trusting a certain Mr Clark, who advised her to pour bisulphate of carbon into each of her collection boxes to protect them against infestation. The result, she discovered with horror, was that all the fine hues and colours of her butterflies faded. It was a devastating blow. Over a year's work was lost because of this mistake, and Margaret wished she had trusted her own methods. Naphthalene had never failed her before, yet she had allowed herself to be persuaded to try something else.

Determined to replace as much of her lost work as possible, Margaret and Khalil set out to breed as many species of local butterflies as they could, and Durban remained their home for yet another season. It was a key year for Margaret's butterfly work, but it was also a key year for the southern African colonies. Union under the Cape Dutch or not was the issue of the day, and even someone as disinterested in politics as Margaret could not help being drawn into the vigorous discussions going on all over Anglophone Durban.

On the day Natal's fate was to be decided by public vote, Margaret and Khalil went down into the city centre to observe the historic event first hand. The square in front of the old town hall heaved with a noisy crowd, and Margaret could not help thinking the silent bush was so much better than any man-made spectacle. The result was not good either, at least not if you believed in the British Empire, for the result of that referendum was that Natal came under Dutch control.

Durban's English society did not let political upheavals get in the way of their lifestyle, however, and Margaret and Khalil were invited to as many dinners and bridge parties as before. By now she was known throughout the city as 'the Butterfly Lady', but Margaret was by no means a regular on Durban's social circuit. She was far too busy with her breeding programme, and in any event nothing could compete with her entomological work for the pleasure it gave her.

'Only out there in the Bush alone with Khalil I would feel young again,' she wrote, 'as with light, noiseless tread I bounded through the sunlit glades or moved along the shady tracks, often singing too as I went along . . .'

Margaret noted the beginning and end of her elysian time in Africa with romantic precision. They had shared two years and two months together: from 11 October 1907 to 11 December 1909. Never had she been so happy and content, nor produced so much important entomological work, and she could hardly bear to think it was already in the past. Khalil clearly had equally strong feelings and sent intensely passionate letters from Damascus.

'My Dearest Margaret,' he wrote in April 1910, 'when I get it before I open the letter I kiss it many times and you see me here I am writing and watching the postman every minute to see him and get my sweet hart letter . . .'

❧17❧

AMERICAN ODYSSEY

L ONDON IN COLD December fogs was hard to bear after living in Africa for two years, but Margaret threw herself into her entomology work, and the weekly letters from Damascus were enough to sustain her for the moment. Her African collection needed meticulous cataloguing: over one thousand set butterflies each required a small tag indicating date and location of capture or breeding. All the Satyridae went into one box, the Acraea into another, and Margaret was relieved to note that most of her butterflies had not faded as she had feared they would.

When she was not in her studio she made visits to the Natural History Museum in South Kensington for advice on naming some of her more unusual African specimens. It was one of the few occasions when she made an effort with her appearance, but it did her no good apparently. A certain Mr Frank Heron was unaccountably rude, as was his boss, Sir George Hampson, and Margaret could not help feeling it was due to her age. 'I wish he did not resent my middle-aged appearance quite as much as he certainly appears to,' she wrote with disappointment; 'he was so affable and friendly some fourteen years ago, and indeed the change in me is no greater than in himself.' She made up her mind to discover the names of her butterflies at source whenever possible to avoid future brush-offs at the museum.[1]

Margaret was discovering the extraordinary process by which women of a certain age become invisible to men, but the thought of her devoted Khalil was more than enough to revive her self-esteem. How many women pushing fifty had such a passionate and devoted partner in life? She had nothing to be ashamed of, and Mr Heron's fading hairline was not exactly a picture either. But private concerns were very trivial in the face of the momentous political events occurring at this time.

King Edward VII died suddenly, and everyone agreed it was the burden of the European crisis that had killed him. The Great War was looming, yet in the spring of 1910 it was still possible for the German Kaiser to accompany King George V during the funeral cortège through London. Margaret and Geraldine watched from the window of their cousin Skye's Park Lane home, deeply moved by the pathetic sight of the riderless charger accompanied by the dead king's terrier.

A more uplifting, though equally moving, procession was provided by the Suffragettes that year. More than 10,000 of them marched silently up Piccadilly on their way from the Embankment to Hyde Park, and Margaret sincerely wished them well. She was particularly impressed by their dignity in the face of incessant jeers from onlookers. 'They are certainly fighting a just and noble cause,' she wrote, 'that of liberating their fellow women.'

She knew very well how privileged her own position was compared to most women of her era, and even those married to kind and wealthy husbands were not as free as she was. Yet Margaret was perfectly aware that it was the vast majority of poor women who really needed help. To be a working-class woman 'getting less than half the pay a man earns for exactly the same amount of labour' and to be legally obliged to hand that over to her husband, who could spend it all in the pub if he wished – that was an injustice worth fighting. How shocked Margaret would have been to know that over a century later women are still asking for equal pay.

Margaret's plan for 1910 was to visit Arthur in America. He had been sent away as a young man 'to learn farming', and Margaret had not seen her only surviving brother in over twenty-one years. He had left England with youth on his side, but Margaret knew from her sisters that he had not thrived. The word was that he had become a wretched alcoholic. Still, visiting Arthur was a good excuse for a trip to the New World with Khalil, where they could expect to travel as unencumbered by European convention as in Africa.

In the meantime, she could not wait to introduce Khalil to London, and she arrived at Victoria for the Dover train long before it was due to arrive. Her heart pounded as she searched the crowd for Khalil's face, and when she spotted him at last they fell into each other's arms.

'*Habibi*' – 'Love' – he whispered in her ear, as an army of bodies swept them along the platform.

'I will not even attempt to describe what it was like going up to Cook's in Ludgate Circus and knocking about London with Khalil,' Margaret wrote happily.

He was a hit with the ladies at Quex Lodge, too, which greatly pleased Margaret, and she could not help noting that a certain Mrs Williamson took to wearing her most 'juvenile hat' for visiting the sights with them.

They sailed for America on the *Adriatic*, which left from Southampton packed with returning tourists. Margaret found she did not care for the heaving mass of holiday-makers, and her antipathy towards Americans was only increased by the humiliations of the American Custom House. She hated the endless formalities they had to endure before they could even enter the country, but the warm welcome they received from Mrs Kollmorgen quickly banished ill feeling. Despite everything Mr Kollmorgen had said against Khalil all those years back in Vienna, he and his wife were the perfect hosts, introducing their old friends to the wonders of New York, which was now their home.

But Margaret felt duty-bound to set off for Virginia as soon as possible. During the long train journey south she tried to prepare Khalil for the wrecked man she had been told to expect, but nothing could have prepared her for the shock of actually setting eyes on Arthur. Seeing her young brother with his lovely blue eyes reduced to a slow, stooping figure who did not even recognize her was awful. Realizing he was already drunk, first thing in the morning, was appalling. 'And the saddest part of all,' she wrote, 'was that the same kind, affectionate nature of the boy of so many years ago was still there. Indeed the poor thing wept with joy more than once when he talked of my having come at last . . .'

Arthur was reduced to living in a boarding-house, desperate for money. He was living the squalid life of a destitute drunk, and Margaret and Khalil would have thought nothing of leaving him to it had he not been her brother. He was by turns maudlin and emotional or violent and aggressive, a grotesque man who had let himself go completely, and it was only his pathetic neediness that kept Margaret from leaving Covington immediately. But she did wish she had not brought Khalil with her, especially when it became patently obvious that her brother had homosexual tendencies.

'It was after a Fancy Dress Ball we had all been to at the International Hotel, and the poor thing [Arthur] was so awfully drunk he really did not know what he was doing,' she wrote of one particularly offensive night. For some unaccountable reason Margaret failed to persuade Khalil to lock his bedroom door, which meant she had to spend much of the night turning Arthur out of her lover's hotel room, dressed in nothing but her night-gown. 'This is what I had feared all along, and this was why I knew it was against my own better judgement, that I had brought Khalil with me to this country,' she wrote unhappily. Perhaps it was also the true reason for Arthur being sent away as a young man. It was the standard method used by the English upper class to get rid of troublesome offspring.

It was a delicate business explaining to Khalil why he must make absolutely sure that Arthur 'respects him', but her darling got the message in the end and dealt with it admirably. In Syria he would have been entitled to shoot him.

Covington was nothing but a 'sewer of drunkenness', according to Margaret, in spite of the fact that it was officially a dry town. But the Virginian scenery all around, with its rivers and creeks and rolling wood-lands, was beautiful, and not bad for butterflies either. Margaret, Khalil and Arthur used to go out by horse-drawn buggy to explore, and Arthur introduced them to several farming friends, including the Williams family, who had a pretty twenty-seven-year-old daughter called Mollie. She was uneducated and backward in her manners, but Margaret and Khalil both agreed she might be the perfect solution for Arthur. Margaret got the distinct impression she had a soft spot for her brother, which is hard to credit, considering he was forty-two and gone to ruin, but Khalil predicted she would be married before the year was out, and Margaret sincerely hoped it would be to her brother.

Mollie may or may not have fancied Arthur, but she made it very obvious she liked the exotic Arab in their midst, and Margaret wished even more fervently she had not brought him with her. Mollie swooned over Khalil until everyone got quite cross about it, including Khalil, who ordered her to marry Arthur. But Arthur was too inebriated to know a good thing when he saw it and had not even thought of proposing.

There was a lot of groundwork to be done to save Arthur from himself, and Margaret did her best to work on her brother while Khalil tried to turn

Mollie's fancy away from himself and towards Arthur. It was an uphill struggle persuading her to accept a broken relic for a husband – despite the financial incentives she doubtless offered – and Margaret and Khalil left without obvious results. But when they had done all they could, Margaret could not wait to get away. The combination of Mollie's infatuation with Khalil and Arthur's drinking was more than Margaret could stand for long.

They took off south by train, through the cotton fields of South Carolina and across the swamps of Georgia, heading for Florida and a boat for Havana. A terrifying hurricane blew up in the Gulf of Mexico while they were at sea, between Tampa and the Florida Keys, and they spent ten fearful hours being tossed and rolled on mountainous waves. They were not safe even moored at Key West, where the locals sank to their knees and prayed when another cyclone followed the first. Margaret and Khalil were trapped in their cabin on board while many houses were completely flattened by the terrible winds sweeping rain and sea on to the streets and into people's living-rooms.

The following day the weather had calmed down, but Margaret's innate fear of the sea was at fever pitch, and she was beside herself when the captain said they would risk putting out to sea. She tried to comfort herself with the thought that, if they were all going to drown, at least she would die in the arms of her love, and she clung to him for the entire journey before arriving in Havana exhausted and traumatized. The intense heat and the recent horror at sea meant Margaret did not take to Havana at first, though in retrospect in her diary she seemed to think it was a fine city after all. But after a few days in the Cuban capital they moved west to the more peaceful environs of the small village of Marianao, where they spent a happy month hunting butterflies in the Caribbean bush and sharing a room as 'brother and sister'. Margaret was very impressed with the huge variety of products being made from the local woods and commented presciently in her diary that it would not be long before Uncle Sam would take possession of this undeveloped wealth.[2]

Several hundred miles south-east of Havana, the old colonial town of Santiago de Cuba, set on a lovely inlet facing Jamaica, was an ideal base for butterfly-hunting. The former capital was rather dilapidated and the hotel rooms were infested with scorpions, but its location, embraced by tropical mountain forest and emerald sea, was spectacular. The only serious problem was that Margaret could not get her London cheques cashed there, so they were forced to leave for Kingston, where the British colonial authorities controlled the banking services. Margaret's heart sank at the thought of going out to sea again, especially since she could only afford the cheapest tickets in the bowels of the ship. But her nerves were spared as the *Alleghany* floated across a waveless Caribbean sea, and the captain was kind enough to let them set their camp beds on the lower deck. They travelled in the open air under a balmy starlit sky.

The biggest shock in Kingston was the relaxed relationship between the races. Unlike in South Africa, where Africans also far outnumbered whites, in Jamaica black people inhabited every hotel, theatre and tram car she cared to use, and she quickly had to get used to their close physical proximity. A product of her times, she was not happy about this, and she blamed the British very much for importing slaves and blamed them even more for leaving them there and fathering children with them. She cursed English men for their failure to 'curb their filthy passions, even with negresses'. Her attitude is shocking now, but in the early part of the twentieth century it was the prevailing view of Margaret's peers.

Margaret's disgust at miscegenation did not stop her enjoying the physical beauty of Jamaica, however, and she was entranced by the loveliness of the island's Blue Mountains. The tropical forest and sapphire sky made her naturalist's heart sing for joy, and she was even persuaded to present a talk to the Kingston Naturalists' Club.

'Whatever you do, don't make it too long,' advised Khalil; 'just please remember what we suffer in church on Sunday, when the clergyman gives us a tremendous long sermon!'

It was sound advice, and Margaret's fifteen minutes on 'The Sagacity of Caterpillars' was met with enthusiastic applause. Her audience had come in their finest evening wear, and she had only found the courage to step forward by treating the whole thing like one of her singing engagements from the distant past.

It was while they were based in Kingston that Margaret and Khalil received the welcome news that Arthur and Mollie had got married. Khalil was thrilled his prophecy had come true, and Margaret quickly sent off the most generous cheque she could afford. She hoped against hope that it was the beginning of her brother's salvation. Arthur and Mollie had bought a seventeen-acre farm near Hot Springs, Virginia, and one just had to have faith that Mollie's farming background would set Arthur on the right track. He had been meant for farming in the first place, after all.

A friend suggested that the butterflying might be even better in Costa Rica and Panama. Margaret had never heard of Costa Rica, but she did want to see how the Americans were getting on with building the notorious Panama Canal, and so they set off for the port of Colón on the local mail steamer. She was impressed to note how American engineers had succeeded where the French had failed, their rusting machinery still visible along the jungle railway tracks. And there were indeed some spectacular butterflies to be caught. The giant blue Morpho butterfly (*Morpho peleides*) was Margaret's most exciting catch, its iridescent wings the size of a child's hand. But butterfly-hunting was extremely exhausting in the humid heat of Panama, where the only access to open space was along the claustrophobic railway lines. On Costa Rica's swampy eastern coast it was the same. Penetration of the forest was impossible. It was too dense, too swampy and too full of poisonous insects and snakes.

'It was a never-ceasing mortification to me that there were no tracks leading through those prolific forest swamps of the lowlands,' Margaret informed her readers in *The Entomologist*, 'or even if there was a small path, it soon came to an end, and, moreover, more often than not was rendered useless and impassable by the constant and heavy rainfall.'[3]

The river banks of the Banana River, near Puerto Limón, were teeming with tropical species, but trying to catch butterflies from a boat was impossible, and Margaret began to feel despondent. She loved the tropical environment, but somehow she had not found the right place on this journey. Each location had presented them with different problems, and each they had left without the slightest hesitation. Margaret began to feel her expedition to the Americas was a failure, and she was plagued by undefined feelings of foreboding. Perhaps it was the incessant rain and damp atmosphere of the jungle. Instead of feeling carefree and happy, Margaret and Khalil began to feel trapped in each other's company and cut off from the outside world. For once Margaret wished she was back in the cool solitude of her Hampstead studio, though she could not explain why. 'What more could I want?' she wrote disconsolately in the spring of 1911. 'And yet I do want something though I know not what it is, and as I lay inside my mosquito curtain and heard the rain again falling outside, the same steady, ceaseless down-pour, I still felt my soul was very weary and my heart was sorrowful . . . and yet I know not why.'

The fact was there was no purpose to the hardships they were enduring. The physical constraints of their environment meant they could do no meaningful entomological work, and there was nothing else to divert them. No sex life, no social life, no decent food and no children. It was enough to make anyone gloomy. And yet there was a very tender love between Margaret and Khalil. They were warm and affectionate with each other, reaching out to hold hands from their separate beds each morning. Khalil liked to hook his little finger with hers before greeting her with 'Good morning, ya habibi' (Good morning, my love).

They tried to escape their low spirits by changing location yet again, eventually hauling up in the Costa Rican capital, San José, and here at last they had found their ideal base. Set in a highland valley of the Central American mountains, the climate was less oppressively humid and the open landscape was ideal for butterfly-hunting. Their guest-house, just outside town, gave spectacular views across the city and towards distant volcanoes, and it was a relief to find somewhere 'civilized' to stay at last. A flowering shrub, called lantana, with brick-red blooms, was a great favourite with the butterflies, and Margaret gloried in the huge number of unfamiliar species so easy to catch. They spent two months in San José, and by the end of their time in Costa Rica Margaret had no less than 157 species to add to her collection.

It had been a successful trip after all. But the undefined foreboding Margaret felt that year found reason in letters from England. Both Geraldine and Evelyn had undergone serious operations, and there was bad news about Septimus, too. How Geraldine had found out about him Margaret does not say, but she was deeply saddened to hear what had become of the man who had cast such a dark shadow over her youth more than twenty years earlier. According to her sister, he had died a drunk, reviled by his own family and in and out of the workhouse infirmary. When well enough he had played the piano in low public houses to earn enough for the next drink, but he had died unmourned, an outcast in his own community. Even now, and despite Khalil's best efforts, Margaret could not shake off the private grief she had carried with her all these years. She was deeply sad to think the man who still came to her in her dreams and who had made her feel like no other man ever could had wasted his life so tragically. What might she have felt had she known that her lowly Septimus was in fact related to wealthy Anglo-Irish gentry? Perhaps Septimus himself had not known, as his rich relations belonged to a separate branch of the family. Nevertheless, there is a Castle Hewson at Ballyengland, Askeaton, about twenty miles west of Limerick.[4]

The news from England was not good, and Turkey was at war with its European neighbours, but it was time to head home. The best route to London was via Trinidad, and thus they had to descend to steaming Puerto Limón once more to catch a boat for Port of Spain. It was the penultimate leg of a journey that had taken them from London to New York, down the Atlantic seaboard and across the Caribbean Sea to Central America: an exhausting year and a half by anyone's standards, and the best was yet to come.

'I don't think I have ever seen any place quite so lovely before,' Margaret wrote of the St Anne Valley beyond Port of Spain, 'ultra tropical and therefore to me intoxicating to a degree in its luscious loveliness, where *Morphos* flew down in the dark shades in the depths of the forest, floating and soaring along the devious course of the stream like blue spirits of light . . .'

Of course, Margaret was not so other-worldly as not to notice the large number of German gunboats in Caribbean waters and to ponder the dangers ahead. 'Heaven grant such insanity as a War between these two great nations [England and Germany] will never come to pass,' she wrote in her diary in early 1912.

But the *Trent* took them safely back to Southampton docks, and Margaret was grateful that the lady sharing her cabin made no fuss about the pupating larvae and emerging butterflies crowding their already cramped living quarters.

Khalil moved into a bedroom on the ground floor of Margaret's Hampstead studio, and they settled down to spend the chilly winter months working on their butterfly collection. At last she could introduce Khalil to her sisters as well, but, if she thought Geraldine and Hill's attitude might have softened, she was mistaken. Her sister disappointed her by sticking with her husband's disapproving attitude, and Margaret was forced to acknowledge there was never going to be a warm, much less familiar, relationship between themselves and the Hills. Margaret took it in her stride, though. There were worse things to worry about, and a letter announcing her sister Florence's sudden death from appendicitis put all other matters in the shade.

How she wished she had asked Geraldine for her troubled sister's address. Had she known she was ill she would have gone to her at once, despite their differences. Her youngest sister had been a talented sculptress, but her life was blighted by drug addiction, and it broke Margaret's heart to think she had died without any family at her side. She chose a quiet spot in Norwood Cemetery for Florence where she was buried on a beautiful crisp afternoon in March. Only Evelyn and Hill joined Margaret and Khalil at the graveside – Geraldine being too ill with newly diagnosed heart disease – and Margaret could not help brooding on what a miserable lot her family were. It seemed extraordinary how the South Acre children had either died young or faded so soon after middle age. Margaret's theory was that it was due to having elderly parents, yet she herself was in rude health, as ever.

Margaret was still nervous about admitting her true relationship with Khalil in public and often made him go out if she was receiving visitors at her studio. Yet, when she was invited to attend the second International Congress of Entomology in Oxford that summer, she insisted on taking Khalil with her. They were partners in work, after all, and he must be acknowledged. To her delight he was welcomed by everyone, and they both received very cordial attention. They were even pressed to be in the photograph of assembled dignitaries – no surer sign of being respected members of the entomological establishment – and Margaret was quietly pleased. It came as a very unwelcome surprise, therefore, when the sister of one of her best entomological friends told her everybody had been talking about them. Was she married to 'Bersa', as he was known in entomological circles, they all wanted to know!

Margaret was mortified but had the good sense to cut her gossipy informant – who had always been very keen on self-promotion – and deal only with serious people. The President of the International Congress, Professor Poulton, was encouraging regarding both Khalil and her membership of Congress and even pressed her to join the famous Linnean Society. She declined for the present but was enormously gratified. What did it matter if she was married or not or what small-minded people thought, as long as the Fountaine–Neimy body of work was acknowledged around the world.

News arrived of the birth of Arthur's and Mollie's first child, a boy, and it was very comforting to think the American journey had not been a wasted effort. Perhaps Arthur would bring honour to the Fountaine name after all.

❀18❀

AUSTRALIAN EXILE

MARGARET SPENT MUCH of 1912 and all of 1913 on the Indian subcontinent, from the remote kingdoms of Tibet and Sikkim in the north, to the island of Sri Lanka in the south, which resulted in eight store boxes with 1,329 specimens being sent back to London. She was fêted in the local press, most notably by *The Times of Ceylon*, but it was not a particularly happy time for Margaret personally. She had been forced to endure a long separation from Khalil owing to the political strife in the Middle East and Balkans, and she had found India profoundly unsettling on her own. She hated the Anglo-Indians, 'with their brains and bodies soaked in Whiskey', and she abhorred the 'dark flood of human cruelty and foul deeds' she perceived throughout the Asian subcontinent. At one point she had been so lonely that she even took to attending other Europeans' funerals, just to hear familiar Christian music. India left a 'deep scar' on her mind, and she felt old for the first time.

Khalil and Margaret wept tears of joy at their reunion when he reached India at last, and yet there was discontent as well. He had failed to get his divorce papers because all the Greek Orthodox priests had fled Damascus in the face of the Balkan Wars in 1912 and 1913, and Margaret had to accept that marriage remained impossible. The prospect of their wedding was rather faded by now anyway, and there were other, more pressing things to worry about. The roller-coaster of events preceding the First World War meant they could not easily return to Europe, and Khalil got a little too used to the colonial habit of drinking. She made him swear not to touch whisky again, and he seemed to comply, but it was another burden on Margaret's already overwrought state of mind.

She decided that they would make a new life in Australia. Europe was out of reach, and she saw her chance to have it all. A self-governing colony of the British Empire, Australia was the ideal place to make a home without losing the protection and convenience of British institutions. Even better, the tropical north-east promised many undiscovered species of butterflies, and Margaret imagined that she might even indulge her childhood fantasy of breeding horses as well. She would buy a farm, and they could become ranchers in Queensland!

They travelled to Singapore, where Margaret wrote gloomily about the endless rubber plantations of Malaya – a disaster for entomology and 'all that is beautiful and soul-inspiring' in the name of profit. It made her glad to leave Asia behind, and her next letter of credit reached them at Cairns – a small coastal town then – where Margaret set about looking for a suitable property in the interior. Conveniently there was a brand-new railway snaking into the highland rainforest beyond the coastal plain, and she decided to make the little village of Kuranda her base for searching out a suitable property. Set on the banks of the mighty Barron River, it was a lovely spot surrounded by jungle-covered highlands, and a couple of hotels made for comfortable living.

She and Khalil were 'cousins' now, Khalil having become 'Karl', which seemed to work for everyone, and, what with the huge Papilio butterflies hovering in the sunshine and the wild cockatoos screeching in the verdant canopies, it was impossible not to believe in success. Today the railway from Cairns to Kuranda and the spectacular gorge that hides the Barron Falls beyond are a major tourist attraction. In 1914 the valley and the rainforest were almost entirely uninhabited. Silent tracks led into the dappled light of primeval vegetation, and Margaret and Khalil spent happy days exploring on foot and on horseback. Where hordes of tourists now jostle for the best photo opportunity Margaret and Khalil used to wander alone.

A high strip of land overlooking dense rainforest caught their imagination, and Margaret decided to buy it, despite the fact there was no house there. It was simply love at first sight, and the daunting task of building a farm was tempered by the thrill of embarking on something completely their own. She hired an architect to design a house in the familiar local style: a wood construction supported on high poles to avoid the poisonous snakes and insects, with a spacious covered veranda running around the entire exterior. The shaded area below the house would make an ideal workshop and provide an escape from the sun for their planned flock of chickens and sundry farm animals. Margaret could indulge her love of dogs again. It would be South Acre in the tropics, with endless countryside to explore and animals to love, far from the misery caused by man. Most importantly of all, it would be her first proper home with Khalil.

Margaret knew there was probably little or no money to be made with their venture and she also knew her finances might not cover the cost of building a home and paying for their hotel at the same time, but her Australian dream had got hold of her. 'Ah! But it is sad to have to think of such sordid matters as these,' she remembered about her dealings with land agents and local bankers, 'when life might be a dream lived in a sunny garden, full of flowers and gorgeous with butterflies . . .'[1]

A great deal of property was for sale, which Margaret was worldly enough to find suspicious. But the terms were good and their local advisers knew nothing of Margaret and Khalil's other motive for settling in Australia, which was to enable him to become a naturalized British citizen. It was the condition Margaret had set for marriage, should it ever become possible, and if it could be achieved without ever living in dreary old England, so much the better. Why Khalil's American naturalization was not acceptable is not recorded, but it is possible he never admitted that fact to her.

They set about the heavy work of clearing their 160 acres at Myola, on the edge of Kuranda, but the grim slaughter commencing on the other side of the world intruded even in this remote spot. Young 'back-country boys' from the mining districts were signing up to fight for the British flag by the train load, and everyone cheered as they passed on their way to ships waiting at Cairns. Margaret did not presume to recite the history of the First World War in her diary. She knew others would be far better equipped to do that, but she and Khalil kept a keen eye on the news, and her heart went out to everyone trapped in Europe.

A generous host and friend in Kuranda was a fellow butterfly collector called Frederick Dodd (1861–1937), who had settled his family in Kuranda almost a decade earlier. In future years he was to become known as 'the Butterfly Man of Kuranda' for his famous display boxes which tourists flocked to see. He ran a boarding-house, too, but his main business was the sale of exotic insects to rich patrons in Europe. Lords Rothschild and Walsingham were both regular customers, and their purchases from Dodd have since found their way to the Natural History Museum in London, to make up the most important collection of antipodean insects outside Australia.

'I cannot understand, Miss Fountaine, why *you* wish to come and settle out here in Australia,' Dodd said, and Margaret worried what he might have heard about her on the entomological grapevine.

It would not have been unreasonable for Dodd to consider Margaret a threat to his business, but he was already well established in Kuranda, and Margaret's main focus was on ranching and horse-breeding at this time. He advised her against it, as did several others, owing to the tick fevers warm-blooded animals were prone to there. But Margaret never let well-meant advice get in her way, and so their course was set. As soon as fences were up Margaret bought a couple of fine young horses.

The hot Australian sun beat down on them as they cut and chopped and burnt their land to make paddocks and chicken runs. The wattle trees were in blossom, and the creek near their house was a riot of colour and wildlife noises. Jackasses shrieked in the forest, cockatoos busied them-selves with their nests and a kaleidoscope of butterflies flitted among the fragrant shrubs and trees. If Margaret had not known that her countrymen were being hacked to pieces on the other side of the world she could have been blissfully happy. The war had more concrete effects as well, which caused very real problems in Kuranda: Margaret had planned to pay for the house by cashing in some investments, but the London Stock Exchange was closed and her shares plummeted in value. With only her periodic letters of credit to pay all the bills, Margaret suddenly faced serious financial prob-lems. How to pay for her dream weighed heavily on her mind. and she was appalled to find herself the object of malicious gossip, stirring up trouble. Rumour had it she could never pay her bills, which led to unpleasant scenes with the builders, and there was very little Margaret could do to allay their fears. Cables to her solicitors in London went unanswered. Khalil had already lost all his savings after his bank had collapsed in Damascus, and they had virtually nothing to fall back on. It made her physically sick to think about it.

The hardship of grubbing out tree stumps and preparing their farm combined with the stress of money worries substantially weakened Margaret's physical and mental capacity, and it was not long before she succumbed to a dangerous fever. Perhaps it was a recurrence of her malaria, or it might have been one of the many local 'bush fevers', but the result was eternal sleepless nights. When she did manage to sleep she was tormented by disturbing dreams. In one of them she was on her way to getting married, riding in a horse-drawn carriage through the streets of Cairo with her mother and sister Rachel, when a woman rushed forward and tried to stop the carriage. 'Stop,' she shouted. 'He is my husband!' It made Margaret think the dream was a bad omen, and she resolved to tell Khalil that they should never attempt marriage.

The weeks of fever left Margaret so weak she was barely strong enough to walk and needed Khalil's arm and the aid of a stick just to get around the house. She rarely left her bed for more than a few minutes, and the best she could manage was to sit on the veranda. It must have been deeply worrying for Khalil to see Margaret failing to revive, week after week, while he toiled away in the dreadful heat.

At least their money worries were settled. Margaret's lawyers succeeded in getting a loan from the Bank of England which allowed her to pay off her Australian debts, but the dream seemed fatally wounded. A time that should have been the happiest in their lives was instead turning into a daily torment, and Margaret struggled to revive her will to live. She was so exhausted, mentally and physically, it was tempting to allow herself to become a permanent invalid, but she made a supreme effort to return to life. Her indomitable spirit was not completely cowed, and slowly but surely she regained enough strength to go beyond survival and back to living life to the full. Every day was a burden, but it was not Margaret's style to merely exist, and where others would have admitted defeat she was determined to go riding in the bush with 'Karl' once more. She hired a housekeeper and her young son to live with them and help around the house, but it still took the best part of half a year for Margaret's health to return.

Mrs Miles and her son were meant to make life easier, but in the long term they turned out to be a big mistake. Margaret had been so grateful to have someone to care for her during her illness that she had allowed her housekeeper to make herself very much at home, even to the extent of encouraging her to feel on equal terms with her employers. It was a condescension Margaret should have known better to avoid, but by the time she was fully recovered she found Mrs Miles had virtually taken over their home. She acted as if she owned the place and embarrassed Margaret by behaving very uncouthly towards their occasional guests. Worse still, she tried to start something with Khalil, who begged Margaret to get rid of her. 'Send this woman out of the house,' he told her. 'She will ruin our lives and give our house a bad name.'

Margaret did not listen to him at first, mostly because she had a soft spot for young Sonny, the housekeeper's son. But eventually Mrs Miles behaved so badly, forcing a row with them in front of guests, that Margaret sacked her on the spot. Getting rid of her was not so easy, though. Not even her own brother wanted to take her in, and they had to endure some very uncomfortable days stuck with this woman, who continued to make all kinds of accusations against Khalil. In fact, Margaret and Khalil had already had plenty of rows over his handling of their housekeeper, and the atmosphere in the house was not much improved by her eventual departure. Margaret was certain she would spread malicious gossip about them in Kuranda.

It was hard and lonely out there on their ranch. Clearing the land was much tougher than they had anticipated, and their closest link with civilization was the railway track which passed close to Myola. As often as not, the train did not even stop at the rickety tin hut of a station. Instead, the guard would just throw the mail bag – if there was any mail – out of the moving train to be picked up later. Similarly, if anyone wanted to post something they had to tie a bag to a bamboo hoop and hand it to the guard as the train passed by. If they needed to post something larger than a letter, such as hen boxes, Khalil had to step out in front of the train and wave his arms and hope the driver would stop in time.

News from the outside world reached them only intermittently, and the occasional visits from bullock drivers and farmers were not Margaret's idea of good company. It was a lonely and boring life at Myola for much of the time, filled with the drudgery of daily farming life. The only relief from the monotony was riding out on her horse, but the land was suffering one of the worst droughts in living memory and the Barron River was almost dry. The creeks had shrivelled, and the cattle were beginning to die. The putrid corpse of a horse lay near the track at Myola station for weeks, and no one cleared it away. One of the dogs died of tick poisoning, and then it was Khalil's turn to get ill. A long-term genito-urinary problem recurred, which meant that he could no longer join Margaret on their riding expeditions, and life became even duller than it was before.

Without long rides into the bush to divert them they had very little to enjoy, and they both sank into a slough of despondency. Ranch life became deathly quiet as the animals either became diseased and died or were moved to better pastures on lower ground. Only the hum of insects never ceased, and Margaret and Khalil found themselves with far too much time to brood on the most unspeakable horror the 'civilized' world had ever known. Margaret felt so useless in her tropical trap. If only she could have done something to help the war effort, like those brave French women riding motorbikes to the front with vital messages. Instead, she was stuck in Queensland fighting nature.

One day Khalil returned from a trip to Cairns completely drunk and raved at Margaret. He accused her of all sorts of cruelties and betrayals, and it was a good two hours before she could persuade him to come home from the train station. But the row lingered on into the next day, and he left without a word. 'Why in the midst of all his fierce protestations of undying love for me will he never now believe that I love him too?' she wrote in anguish. It crossed her mind that he might have gone mad and would do something terrible, and she dressed quickly to ride out and look for him. Had someone turned him against her or was he just raving mad from the alcohol? she wondered. She rode to a neighbouring farm where she could telephone Kuranda to ask about Khalil, and she discovered he was indeed there, moping at one of the guest-houses. She left a message to say she would wait for him at Myola station.

But it was a cold and bitter man who stepped off the train, who would not even smile, much less embrace her. Margaret was beside herself. What had happened? She hardly knew him. A deep gulf seemed to have opened up between them, and she had no idea how or why it had happened. Certainly she knew herself to be completely innocent of his accusations against her, which seemed to centre around some kind of perceived infidelity. She tried to reassure him in a hundred different ways, but she could see he did not believe her in his heart. His jealousy and rage frightened her. He ranted and raved, accusing her of betrayal and humiliation. Nothing she said could persuade him otherwise.

At last Margaret could endure his hateful looks no more, and she ran off towards the river crying that she would rather drown herself than listen to any more of his horrible accusations. She had endured enough in life. She did not deserve the vicious insults Khalil was shouting after her.

'I don't care whether you drown yourself or not,' he called. 'I will drown myself, too. We will die together.'

'I love you! I love you!' he cried as Margaret fled.

Nothing could ever be the same between them now. She felt her innermost soul had been violated by his viciousness, and all for what? For nothing! She was innocent of all charges.

Khalil chased her down to the river, still raving, and Margaret ran across the hot sand where water should have been. At last she sank down on her knees, and he collapsed beside her in utter weariness and misery. They talked and even kissed, seeming to have reached a quiet understanding. But then his anger and mistrust flared up again, and Margaret felt her heart was crushed and broken on that riverbed. One minute he was all over her, insisting they must be married as soon as possible, the next he was shouting disgusting accusations. She did not even know who she was supposed to have had an affair with, but it hardly mattered. He could kill her, as far as she was concerned, but she would never marry him now, British citizen or not.

At last they walked back to Myola, but it was not a happy homecoming. Margaret was mortified to find that Khalil had asked to lodge with Mr Dodd while he was in Kuranda, and she hated the thought that everyone there might be discussing their private business.

What happened to Neimy? Perhaps if one considers he was a man of not yet forty it is possible to find a reason for his frustration. He was a man in his prime trapped in an alien environment, cut off from his own culture and language, without real friends and without the solace of physical love with the woman whose life he was sharing. They did not even have children to care for, and what was life without a family to love? He seemed to have no meaningful purpose at all. The thought that he had abandoned his loved ones in Syria to live alone with an ageing Margaret was bad enough. To believe that she had betrayed him with someone else was unbearable.

No wonder he had begun drinking again, and he was undoubtedly easy prey for any manipulative gossips in Kuranda. Tropical heat can do strange things to the mind, especially in isolation, magnifying every fear and imagined scenario until it is impossible to know truth from phantom.

The loneliness Margaret and Khalil felt on their farm was beyond endurance, and yet neither could find a way back to the other. Both felt utterly abandoned and yet trapped together. They hardly noticed as one miserable year followed the next. Their misunderstanding was profound, and Margaret began to think their house must be haunted by evil spirits. It was the only explanation for their misfortune, she felt. Yet it was a wonderful house, standing tall on its raised platform of telegraph poles and views over the rainforest as far as the eye could see. Many decades later, contemporaries in Kuranda remembered the little village as a happy place, with a great community spirit. Today Kuranda is full of market stalls selling crystals and healing potions from the jungle. Yoga, meditation and alternative therapies are offered in what is believed to be a place with great positive energy, but for Margaret and Khalil this Queensland haven was their undoing.

'The poor thing was on the verge of insanity, though it took me some time to realise it,' Margaret wrote about her darling. But one night she was woken by singing and raving coming from his room, and when she went to him he did not know her. She crouched beside him on the floor, trying to hold him and calm him down, but he was out of control. Another housekeeper had come to replace the foul-mouthed Mrs Miles, and she did her best to help Margaret during these night-time horrors, but mostly Mrs Fowler was no improvement. According to Margaret, she 'added mischief and lies to the rest of what he used to say he had heard', and she hated anyone witnessing their misery. The doctor had actually advised Khalil to use whisky to calm his nerves, but the constant 'medicinal' tipples had very negative side-effects.

The war of attrition was briefly interrupted when something happened to lift his spirits. His naturalization papers arrived, and he came bounding into Margaret's room with the good news. She thought she could see his old happiness returning, and they hugged and kissed and cried tears of joy. It was almost fifteen years since Margaret had first promised to become his wife among the ruins of Baalbek, and now, after all this time and everything they had been through, there was something to celebrate at last. For a brief moment their future together seemed assured. But their tears were as much for what they had lost as for what they hoped for.

Margaret quickly discovered Khalil was much less eager to get married now his papers had arrived than when there had been obstacles. Suddenly he came up with all kinds of excuses to delay, even dreams. He claimed that his wife and father had come to him, chastising him and insisting that he could only have one wife. In an act of almost absurd generosity Margaret made the entire Queensland property over to Khalil, but it did her no good. They agreed it was probably best to give up all idea of marriage, and Margaret was too exhausted to argue about it. She had never really believed his first wife was truly out of the picture anyway, though she did hope their agreement not to marry would somehow improve relations between them.

It did not. His drinking and violent mood swings continued unabated. The housekeeper left, and for the first time in their relationship Margaret began to fear Khalil. His nocturnal raving was terrifying. She lay awake in her bed, night after night, listening to him crashing around the house, wondering if her locked door would hold out. It was not much better during the day. Khalil's mistrust was total, and he put her under constant surveillance. His antics would have been funny if they had not been so painful to Margaret. She had been found guilty of playing the double part by the one who mattered most, on possibly the only occasion in her life when it was untrue. If she went to collect wood, he spied on her in case she was meeting her lover. If she went to the hen house to feed the chickens, he followed her every move from behind the shed, but he never caught her at anything – just as the wicked housekeeper had warned him he would not. Once, when she was returning from a night-time visit to the closet, he confronted her with murder in his eyes, and she realized she really was no longer safe.

They agreed it was probably best to move out of their haunted house and lodge in Kuranda instead, only staying at the farm in daylight hours. But the result of this was that thieves began stalking the property. All of Margaret's remaining jewellery was stolen, including rings given by Khalil, which hurt very much, and their best laying hens and tools were also stolen. It was soul-destroying after all the hard work they had put into making their home, and the dream of their Australian life faded by degrees. The death of their first-born foal was the final straw, as far as Margaret was concerned, and they put their farm on the market. The poor thing died in agony from the strychnine she herself had given him to treat his tick disease, and she wished she could have lain down and died with him.

As if to add insult to injury, their neighbours were very happy to snap up bargains and buy the contents of their home, but no one wanted to buy the farm itself. At last, however, they managed to find a tenant, which was better than nothing. They had lost much more than money during their years at Myola.

'So our home was quite broken up,' Margaret wrote bitterly, 'and this was the end of our North Queensland venture, a pitiable and hopeless failure . . .' She blamed the 'vileness of the people' they had come to live among, which was no doubt unfair. Whether she was afflicted with the same paranoia as Khalil is hard to say, but she insisted in her diary that their neighbours and people in Kuranda did everything to undermine them, from spreading malicious gossip to turning their animals loose at night and threatening to feed ground glass to their dogs.[2]

They moved to lodgings in Freshwater, on the Mulgrave River, with their remaining four horses, and the relief of getting away from Kuranda was great. For the first time in what seemed like an eternity, Margaret and Khalil enjoyed each other's company again. They went for long rides into the bush and swimming in the sea, but the gulf between them was still there. Margaret got a taste of the poison Khalil had been infected with when an anonymous letter arrived from Kuranda.

It has come to our knowledge that you are carrying on your old games now at Freshwater that you did in our little hamlet up here among our young lads . . .

We do not intend to let you rest anywhere in the district . . . We know now what you are and how you cloak it.

Margaret was aghast. The viciousness was unbelievable, and if Khalil had only believed a fraction of this malice it was clear to her how deeply his trust had been damaged. No wonder he cried for his 'wrecked life' and accused her of not caring any more. He was sick with drink and poisoned by lies. He should have known better, but he did not.

Finally they pawned their horses, since no one would buy them, and left Queensland for good. They had been there for almost three years – the longest Margaret spent anywhere in her adult life – and their home-making had come to nothing.

'It was indeed with a heart full of the saddest memories that I watched the harbour lights grow dim as the steamer slowly left the dock at Cairns,' she wrote of their departure for Sydney. They were heading back into the world, but the world they had known was gone. The First World War was still raging in Europe, and even their boat was full of soldiers, either setting off or returning, many of them maimed and disabled.

Khalil was not allowed to leave Australia for another twelve months if he wished to make his British naturalization permanent, which meant he had to stay in Sydney until May 1918 at least. But Margaret was not about to prolong the agony of her Australian nightmare – especially since they were no closer to resolving their differences. It was truce between them rather than peace, and the desire to part for a while was mutual. They tried to find him a job, but, like all their joint efforts, this came to nothing, and finally Margaret set him up with a small grocery shop on Alfred Street in northern Sydney. She found him a decent boarding-house, at number 38 Alfred Street, and left him to fend for himself. She had failed to persuade him of her innocence, failed to get him off the whisky and failed to make a home on her Queensland farm. Saying goodbye was the loneliest, most desolate experience of her life. She still worried about his mental health, but there was nothing more she could do for him.

Margaret set off for San Francisco on the *Ventura* with only a ring to remember her love. Everything was uncertain – her future with Khalil, the future of the world even – but she wore her ring with pride, despite their rift. It had three blue sapphires set in gold.

✤19✤

PAINFUL SEPARATION

MARGARET ARRIVED IN San Francisco shortly after Christmas 1916, grateful for the modern convenience of steam central heating at the Stewart Hotel but otherwise deeply depressed. She was desperately worried about Khalil's mental state, and it hurt her very much when two letters arrived, written in someone else's hand and only signed by him. They were very formal and businesslike, revealing nothing beyond the fact that he had already fallen out with the people at his grocery store and planned to move back to Cairns. It struck Margaret as a very bad idea indeed, but there was nothing more she could do for him at present. She must let him go his own way.

She spent three months in a Los Angeles boarding-house on Bonnie Brae Street and recovered at least some of her own spirit in the company of friendly, easy-going people. She came to love Los Angeles. Its climate was wonderful after the oppressive heat of Australia. Here there was warmth and sun, but with the magical ingredient of a sea breeze. There were also plenty of flowers growing wild and in immaculate gardens, and Margaret felt the entomologist in her revive. Despite its promising environment, she had done no butterfly-collecting in Queensland, but now she began to roam the Californian canyons and to rediscover her joy of nature.

For the first time in years she felt free and unencumbered. California brought back happy memories of exploring the mountains of southern Europe. She had been a young woman in her prime then, still full of hope. But the knowledge that thousands of people were dying every day in the European trenches overshadowed all thoughts of the personal. America had not yet entered the war, but Margaret did her bit for the soldiers back home by volunteering for the French Red Cross in Los Angeles. It was a relief to have found something useful to do, and she spent many days winding bandages. Margaret even enjoyed the camaraderie of the other women, though it embarrassed her that her bandage technique was so poor compared to the others. Khalil wrote to say that he had taken a shop on Kent Street, in downtown Sydney, instead of moving away, and Margaret was hugely relieved.

The summer of 1917 saw Margaret visiting Arthur and Mollie on their farm in Covington, Virginia, where there were now two Fountaine children to admire. Lee was already five years old, while his brother Melville was just fifteen months. 'Thank God that in this case at least, the sins of the father have *not* descended on the children,' Margaret wrote with relief.[1]

Mollie told her that Arthur really had given up drinking completely, as the whole State of Virginia had been 'dry' for three years owing to the new Prohibition Laws on the sale and manufacture of alcohol. His decades of self-abuse had left their mark, though. Very feeble physically, he was also prey to unexplained headaches and depressions which made him very bad-tempered, especially with the children. Margaret reminded him of how naughty they had been at South Acre when he was too severe with Lee and especially counselled against beatings. She was sure it caused nothing but stubbornness and emotional damage, and she adored Lee's cheeky spirit. His bright blue eyes lit up with enthusiasm when she introduced him to the thrill of butterfly-catching, and she forgave him everything, even running off with her setting tools.

She spent four peaceful months in Covington, though she was always aware of the injustice of it. It did not seem right that they should be enjoying even a brief moment of family happiness when so many countless others were having theirs destroyed. America had joined the Great War by now, and many young Virginians were being sent off to fight for a cause they did not understand, and Margaret wished so very much she could return to Europe with them. But it was impossible. Not only were enemy submarines stalking the Atlantic but one needed a passport to travel now, and none was being issued at this time. In any event, women were barred from entering England or France unless on military business, and the best she could do was to have her latest butterflies shipped to London. 'I was now practically an exile from my own country,' she wrote despondently.

But she was also deeply grateful for the opportunity to live out the war in the 'summer-land of California, where the sun always shines, and where the roses ever bloom'. America would always hold a special place in her affections for its generosity of spirit.

Margaret moved to a boarding-house on Whitley Avenue in Hollywood, where the gardens were full of flowers and she could meet fellow entomologists at the Lorquin Club.[2] She felt the burden of her Australian disaster lifting at last, especially since it appeared Neimy was managing in Sydney, and she thought their correspondence showed signs of trust returning. She dared to hope they would be reunited, just as soon as he could get permission to travel, though her ability to look on the bright side was always fragile. After the battering experience of Queensland she could never quite shake off her tendency towards feelings of foreboding and sadness, but the balmy Californian climate was a great help.

She really felt her age. She had packed into her life several lifetimes of hardship and emotional drama which weighed heavily on the downhill slope to sixty. Yet there were advantages to being 'middle aged'. She had always hated being fussed over and crowded by unwanted chaperones just because she was a woman, but male attention was no longer a problem. When she travelled to Arizona, for example, not a single man bothered about her mounting a horse and riding off on her own, much less did any help her saddle up or return the horse to its corral. No one molested her during her excursions into the Yuma Desert, and she adored the sense of freedom and peace she got from long canters along the Colorado River. She had come to Arizona in search of an extremely rare species of desert white butterfly, and while men did not notice her she was rather pleased when the *Arizona Republican* did, reporting her expedition on 23 February 1918. A reporter had woken her in the middle of the night for his interview, and she had shouted her answers down the telephone.[3] But news of the German offensive in Flanders sent her guiltily back to Los Angeles and work for the French Red Cross. She could breed butterflies and roll bandages at the same time and not feel too irrelevant.

It did not feel good, though, living in peace and sunshine when millions of others were being sucked into the vortex of death and destruction in Europe. Preparing abdominal bandages was all very well, but Margaret would have preferred a more active role in the war effort. It annoyed her when the ladies at the Red Cross preferred to discuss their latest love affairs, and it grated even more if anyone dared to say it would have been better for America to stay out of the war. It was a natural sentiment on the other side of the world, but Margaret found such views intolerable and regularly absented herself to get away from the chattering and hunt food plants for her caterpillars in the Holly Springs Canyon instead.

Her breeding programme had new significance, too, because for the first time in her life she needed to earn a living. The British government had substantially raised taxes to pay for its war needs, and Margaret's trust earnings no longer covered her expenses. Her entomological expertise was no longer just her life's passion but also her key to financial survival. She was sufficiently well known as an entomologist for a variety of American institutions – such as Ward's Natural Science Establishment on the East Coast – to hire her as a professional collector. Commissions came in for everything from spiders and moths to butterflies, and she soon learnt to adapt her skills to trussing and stuffing spiders. She could earn up to seven dollars a day with her collecting – the price of a good hat in those days – and, though it was mechanical work filling orders, it was very satisfying as well.

In the autumn of 1918 Margaret even got herself a proper job, working for private collectors in Pasadena. Mr and Mrs Newcomb paid her 25 cents an hour for doing everything from washing glasses and fixing up specimen cases to actual collecting and setting. She was conscientious and efficient in her work and rather proud of herself, though she was also profoundly grateful that she was not like those women in the factories who had no choice but to spend their whole lives toiling away for a pittance. She could stop any time she pleased, and playing the humble assistant was almost fun, especially when rich customers arrived at the Newcombs' in their fancy automobiles. They treated her with the condescension her lowly position invited, but privately she laughed to think how differently some of those stuck-up people would have treated her had they known she was related to half-a-dozen aristocratic families in England. Americans, she found, for all their democratic ideas, were just as snobbish as Europeans. They were always impressed by royalty and the like.

In spite of her good fortune, and regular letters from Sydney, Margaret was desperately lonely. She had been on her own for almost two years now, and she longed for a reunion with Khalil. The dear man had been so shocked to hear she was short of money that he had sent her a cheque for £25 from his own savings, but she was earning enough not to use her trust money and had the comforting knowledge that it was accumulating steadily while they sat out the war.

'Then came the most wonderful Day: the 11th day, of the 11th month, when at 11 o'clock in the morning on those war-torn fields, far away in France, the Armistice was signed.'

She sat in the warm sunshine in Pasadena reading all about it in the newspapers and could hardly believe the world's most dreadful war was over at last. Her next thought was that Khalil would be able to apply for a passport now. But joy was short-lived. The influenza epidemic that gripped the world immediately after the First World War was killing millions, and there was no question of travel, except for troops. One hundred and ninety-five thousand Americans died of influenza in October 1918 alone, and coffins were stacked high on the streets in almost every major city. Schools, theatres and churches were closed, and still people were dying every day, especially children and the elderly. Margaret went about with a gauze face mask and managed to avoid the illness, but Christmas 1918 was a dismal affair with all the churches closed and frosty weather in Pasadena.[4]

She moved to San Diego in the new year, no longer able to find cheap lodgings in Hollywood, and the disheartening news from Sydney was that Khalil was not only ill with the dreaded flu but was also suffering a recurrence of the chronic genito-urinary problem that had afflicted him in Queensland. Margaret never spelt out what his problem was exactly. If it was syphilis it might explain his mental decline, but it could just as well have been any number of other afflictions. He had mutated from 'Karl' to 'Charles' by now, and this was the name that was to stick. Khalil was always Charles in Margaret's later diaries.

Margaret was almost happy travelling around California, from Mount Shasta to Sisson. The people she met were warm and friendly, but this made her feel the long separation from Charles even more. She was just killing time now, but the Australian authorities would not give him the necessary medical all-clear to travel, and Margaret found herself moping around San Francisco on the off-chance that Charles might arrive on the next boat from Sydney. She had saved $1,000 – a huge amount – and she was determined not to spend another winter in America. She would travel to the Fiji Islands or New Zealand. At least she would be a few thousand miles closer to Charles, and perhaps he could come to join her there. She had sworn never to set foot in Australia again.

Arranging international travel was no longer an easy matter, however. The First World War had changed many things, including the conditions under which one could move from one country to the next. Official passports and unheard-of paperwork were now required, but Cook's agent in San Francisco managed to get Margaret a berth at last. All the boats were booked solid for months because everyone who could wanted to travel now, but Margaret finally boarded the *Tofua* for New Zealand in December 1919, almost three years to the day that she had first stepped off the boat from Australia. The world Margaret was re-emerging into was nothing like the one she had left before the war, nor was she the same woman. The disappointment and sorrow of the past six years were etched on to her face in deep worry lines, and it was a lonely old lady who arrived in Wellington in hopes of meeting her 'husband' there.

She headed north by train for Auckland, but the New Zealand landscape failed to lift her gloom. She found its green meadows and damp weather far too reminiscent of the Old Country. Only the snow-capped peak of Mount Egmont proved she was not in England, and Margaret tried to focus on a reunion with Charles instead of brooding. But the weather was cold and windy, and Margaret did not like Auckland any better than Wellington. She found that being a few thousand miles closer to Charles, yet not reunited, was worse than being on the other side of the Pacific, and she desperately wished he could get well enough to pass the medical examination required for travelling. But Charles was still unwell, and a major strike by marine engineers in Sydney made a reunion soon very unlikely.

Without butterflies to hunt or introductions to local people to divert her, Margaret spent many hours in her hotel room, 'prey to every horrible imaginary evil' her brain could concoct. The strike in Sydney meant no comforting letters, which was awful, though Charles did manage to cable her eventually. Reassured, Margaret decided there was no point being miserable in Auckland, wasting valuable savings, and booked herself on to the next boat for Suva in the Fiji Islands. At least she could earn good money from collecting insects there. But a mild recurrence of the flu in

Auckland meant that all passengers from New Zealand had to submit to a five-day quarantine, and Margaret found herself dumped on an isolated island, where men and women were obliged to sleep in large barns on camp beds, sharing wash-stands and all other 'facilities'. Some Pacific island groups, such as neighbouring Samoa, had lost 80 per cent of their population in the influenza epidemic. Fiji's officials were right to be cautious, and Margaret did not blame them. Her only objection was on account of the inflated price she had paid for her ticket, but at least she had the consolation of wading out to mesmerizing coral reefs where she could marvel at beautiful shells and amazing coral formations. Shoals of brightly coloured fish flitted past her legs as she stood in the aquamarine water, just knee-deep, even a mile from the beach.

When she was allowed to set foot on Suva at last, she found the island was as lovely as the surrounding sea, with rich tropical vegetation that seemed to promise many exotic butterflies. But mankind's destructive influence on nature had already caused much harm in the Fiji Islands: Minah birds had been introduced to keep down the locust population, but unfortunately they also enjoyed the fat caterpillars of butterfly and moth species. Even worse, large orange hornets had accidentally been imported from India, and they were eating larvae and eggs at such a rate that almost no butterflies were hatching at all. Older residents on the island told Margaret that moths and butterflies had indeed once been plentiful on the island but no more. The only solution was to go out hunting for eggs herself, and in this she was successful. She managed to breed some rare species of *Hypolimnas* (Blue Moon butterflies), which would fetch good money in Europe and America.

But the strain of worrying about Charles, who was still failing to travel, was too much for Margaret. She became ill with fever and was also plagued by a chronic leg infection brought on by too much exposure to poison oak in California. A huge abscess developed on her right calf which refused to heal in the tropical humidity, and she was reduced to a hobbling cripple confined to the hotel veranda. There seemed no end in sight to Margaret's many worries, and only the kindness of others at the hotel kept her from losing the will to live. She was so weary, though. How she would have loved to go to sleep and never wake up. But the pain in her leg often kept her awake.

'This is how I spend my days now,' she wrote disconsolately, 'reading novels and swatting flies, of which there is a considerable abundance . . .'

❧20❧
THE LONELY LEPIDOPTERIST

I

T WAS APRIL 1920, and Margaret and Charles had been apart for almost four years now. Was it too much to ask to be reunited? Margaret wondered, stuck under her mosquito net on Suva. But the eternal waiting continued for the rest of the year: waiting for her septic leg to heal, waiting for Charles. The pain and disfigurement caused by her abscess were very distressing, but the tropical climate made healing a slow process, and Margaret was forced into a period of inaction, which was very bad for her mental health. Alone and sick, her imagination constructed all kinds of torments for her.

There were worse places to be trapped than the Fiji Islands, of course, and Margaret was not without friends either. A Mrs Walsh, who lived across the street from her boarding-house, provided maternal affection that was very comforting. She always knew how to make Margaret feel more hopeful about the future, and then it was lovely, after all, to look out over the jungle-clad mountains and listen to the gentle lapping of an iridescent sea. When she was well enough to walk without too much pain, Margaret enjoyed hitching lifts on the sugarcane train, whose driver would drop her anywhere along the track and pick her up again at the end of the day. Best of all, use of the train was free, and Margaret made good use of it. A hoard of onlookers from the native villages inevitably gathered around her as soon as she was spotted with her butterfly net, but she found a coughing fit always brought instant relief. Fear of the dreaded influenza was still very powerful.

Months went by, and Margaret worried incessantly about Charles's health. He had had to endure several painful operations that year, including circumcision, but at last he was passed fit to travel. He was due in to

Wellington on the SS *Moeraki* in the second half of November, and Margaret caught the next boat back to New Zealand, full of hope.

She stood shivering among the heaving multitude waiting for loved ones at the wharf, but the ship's deck was so busy with passengers that Margaret found it impossible to spot Charles at first. When she did, she was strangely disappointed. He was standing alone at the railings, apparently not driven by any urgency to scan the crowd or even to get off the boat. 'No, it was not possible after such sufferings as that, that we could either of us ever be quite the same again,' she wrote regretfully, but it hurt to see how little emotion he showed after so many years apart.[1]

More disappointment followed when Charles failed once again to arrange things for their marriage – a formality they had agreed to complete in New Zealand, if only because it had been the plan for so long. This time he made the mistake of admitting to his previous marriage and lack of divorce papers, and the authorities duly refused permission to marry. Neither Margaret's nor Charles's heart was in it anyway, but, since neither felt able to say so, the charade had to go on, and Margaret was left with the embarrassing task of uninviting their wedding guests while Charles sulked. Then, as if to add insult to injury, he announced that he intended to leave for Damascus as soon as possible. He wanted to see his ageing mother, and Margaret was left with the hollow consolation that he might also, finally, get his divorce papers at the same time.

'Surely I felt hurt,' she admitted to her diary; 'we had hardly met before he was planning to leave me again, and I raised a strong protest against it.' He would not be persuaded, though, and it was no good pining for the devoted young man she had once known. She tried hard to hide her disappointment by being as loving as possible, but she could not help feeling they were a blighted couple, destined never to enjoy peace of mind again. 'It seemed as though, to a slight degree, even after all these years, his mentality was still clouded at times,' she wrote sadly, 'and he would intimate suggestions and throw out hints, of which I was often absolutely unable to grasp the meaning.' Traces of the old suspicions still lingered, which hurt Margaret even more than Charles's failure to show more pleasure in her company.

Their parting in Wellington was deeply passionate, though. Charles accompanied Margaret on board the *Marama*, bound for San Francisco, and they hugged and kissed and held each other tight to the very last moment until all visitors were asked to leave. Each waved to the other with tears in their eyes, and Margaret tried hard to believe they would see each other again before long. The idea was to meet in London once they had sorted out their respective affairs in Damascus and America, but Margaret had very little reason to think Charles would hurry back to her. She prayed for his safe journey across the Indian Ocean, to Suez and Beirut beyond. And she prayed even harder for the return of her darling, the man she had once known and staked her life on.

By the time Margaret arrived in London on the *Aquitania* from New York she had not set foot in England for nearly nine years, and she was shocked by the begging ex-servicemen she encountered on the streets of London. It was appalling to think that they had risked their lives for their country only to be left destitute, and she determined to use her newly acquired right to vote to turn out the government of Lloyd George at the next opportunity.

Her studio was at 126 Lexham Gardens now, just around the corner from the Natural History Museum and the Entomological Society in Kensington, but she hated the noise and bustle of London. The new place held no happy memories of Charles calling to her from his room, as he had done in West Hampstead, and it was a lonely business setting the several thousand butterflies she had sent back from Asia, Australia and the Americas. Her only consolation was her friendship with Mr Riley at the Natural History Museum, who helped her to identify many of her specimens and treated her with far greater respect than his predecessor.

As 1921 passed into 1922 Margaret's hopes of seeing Charles again were raised several times, but something always happened to frustrate their plans. Either he got sick or his mother got sick, or local malaria outbreaks restricted travel. At one point Margaret even spent a small fortune travelling to Beirut, imagining she was coming to his rescue. But it had been a false alarm, and she was mortified when an emaciated but otherwise radiant Charles informed her he only had a week to spare before he needed to return to the care of his mother!

From that day on, Margaret swore she would never again allow herself to be emotionally dependent on him. He clearly did not need her as much as she needed him, and that imbalance had to be corrected. 'For I had reached the limit,' she wrote. 'I could not and would not suffer any more for the sake of this man who preferred his mother every time; not that I could blame him for this.'

She still loved him, no matter how hard she tried to deny it, and he still loved her. But the bond they had shared before their Australian disaster was gone.

Almost a year after their failed reunion in Beirut, however, Margaret did succeed in prising Charles out of Damascus with an offer to explore the Far East together. Perhaps he needed the money, but their meeting at Port Said was one of the happiest they ever had, unblemished by mishaps or delays, and Margaret even dared to hope it was the beginning of a new chapter in their life together. 'I simply felt intoxicated with happiness and contentment,' she wrote of that time, 'and now the rest of the voyage was indeed a continual joy to me.'

Other passengers warned them they were heading for all kinds of danger, from being crushed by boa constrictors to being eaten by tigers, but nothing could diminish their joy at being at large in the world again. The risk of being eaten by a tiger was not nearly as terrible as the thought of never seeing one at all.

They watched for whales in the ocean beyond Sri Lanka and tracked flying fish as they passed the mysterious Andaman Islands, until at last they reached the steaming banks of the Irrawaddy River and the Burmese city of Rangoon.[2] It was a 'huge, dirty, straggling place', according to Margaret, but the Buddhist golden pagodas were entrancing. They travelled hundreds of kilometres north on the Burmese railway, and Margaret was utterly captivated by the beautiful people and their fabulous architecture. The humidity made clothes stick to the body as if one had just stepped out of the shower fully dressed, but no matter. The tropical forest covering the mountains north of Mandalay was too beautiful for words.

Margaret and Charles stayed at an American mission school in Thandaung (Tantabin), and, even though the butterfly-hunting was not good, the boisterous company of the children was so enchanting that they stayed for over a month. It was good just to spend some time together, far away from the miseries of their own world – this journey was as much about reviving their relationship as anything else.[3] From Thandaung they travelled east, to the genteel pleasures of a colonial hill station at Maymyo, complete with botanical gardens and English-style brick houses. It was the most important British garrison town in Burma, and Margaret's patriotic heart swelled with pride to see the 'well-washed red necks' of the South Staffordshire Regiment at the barracks church on Sundays.

The climate was almost ideal at Maymyo, with warm sunny days and cool nights, and Margaret and Charles spent happy times riding through the light jungle on the surrounding hills, 1,000 metres above the fetid rice fields on the plain. But Margaret's money was much shorter in these post-war years, and though they lived comfortably enough they were unable to explore as much as they would have liked. They still had a long way to go before reaching their intended destination in the Philippines, so they left Burma for Bangkok, sailing all around the Malaysian peninsula instead of travelling the more interesting route overland. In fact, by the time they reached Bangkok Margaret's money ran out altogether, and she had to borrow money from Charles so they could reach Hong Kong and her next letter of credit.

It took nine days by Danish cargo boat to reach Hong Kong via the South China Sea, but their cabins were comfortable, and Margaret was profoundly grateful that Charles was taking care of her once more. She was sixty years old by now and suffering very much from nocturnal 'heat waves' brought on by the menopause, yet Charles still cared enough to steal passionate kisses whenever she let him. 'But we are together – Charles and I – after long years of separation, and, after all, that is all that really matters,' she wrote. As for her own feelings, she claimed to feel nothing more than the 'attachment of a mother'.

They were forced to make Hong Kong their home for no less than five months, the time it took for Margaret's next letter of credit to reach them, but their enforced rest was an excellent opportunity to breed butterflies, and China's interior was off limits for exploring anyway. The political situation was extremely unstable, and the news was full of appalling massacres and the wholesale destruction of towns and villages. Mainland China was in the grip of competing generals and warlords, all fighting for supremacy and a chance to expel their common Japanese enemy.[4]

They hated their cheap Kowloon guest-house, across the bay from Hong Kong, and the suffocating summer temperatures. Prickly heat rashes tormented them, and for once Margaret wished for cold weather. But there were compensations, too: the sight of a million twinkling lights reflected in Hong Kong harbour was mesmerizing at night, and they loved taking trips up the city's funicular Peak Railway, to stroll down into the city hunting tropical swallowtails off shading citrus trees. Hong Kong really was a remarkable achievement, said to have been built on nothing but bare rock, which was hard to believe, given the profusion of tropical plants everywhere.

But when Margaret's money arrived at last they gladly endured two days of rough seas to reach the Philippines, every naturalist's El Dorado even today and a world away from the killing fields of China. While the American occupation of the Philippines was by no means welcome, it had brought stability to the island nation and Filipinos enjoyed a great deal of influence in the running of their country. America's attitude was bene-volently paternalistic compared to their Spanish predecessors, and the atmosphere in Manila in 1923 was one of peaceful cooperation, if not exactly friendship.[5] It was certainly not a dangerous country for tourists at that time, and Margaret and Charles were free to travel wherever they wished.

Their first base was on Luzon, home to the capital city and also the largest island of the Philippine archipelago. A local entomologist at the Manila Bureau of Science had recommended the American College of Agriculture at Los Baños as a good collecting base, so they travelled the short distance south to the foothills of Mount Makiling and were delighted to find a comfortable American guest-house as well. Shortly after their arrival, Charles caught a vigorous female Birdwing butterfly (*Ornithoptera rhadamantus*) which delighted Margaret by laying over thirty eggs on the net of her cage, and their days were soon dominated by the need to find fresh vine leaves for their incessantly hungry caterpillars.

Margaret and Charles were to spend a whole year in the Philippines, and it was extraordinarily successful, both personally and in entomo-logical terms. They found or bred no less than 114 butterfly species, including the rare *Vanessa benguetana*, which had never been bred before; and Margaret was also the first person to breed the uncommon Swallow-tail *Papilio semperi*. 'The full-grown larva is an exceedingly handsome creature,' she noted of that species in *The Entomologist*, 'very dark velvety brown, conspicuously ornamented with a number of bright vermilion-red spines, tapering to a point tipped with black.'[6]

To Margaret's profound joy, she and Charles became a team once more, and she was deeply touched whenever he left a handwritten message of love for her to find on her pillow at night. He would sign himself 'From your old boy Charles' and called her 'Sweetheart', which was indeed charming for a woman whose hair had gone completely grey.

They spent Christmas 1923 in Manila, but they were still capable of having violent rows as well, especially in the oppressive environment of an overcrowded tropical city. Margaret felt deeply left out when she saw others surrounded by expectant children on Christmas Eve. 'Why was not I like those well-dressed American women, going about with a lot of happy children, or grand-children as it would be by this time?' she wrote sadly. 'I loved the wild life I had chosen, but sometimes I feel a longing for what my fate might have been otherwise, something so very different to what it really is.' It was the price of freedom.

Away from 'civilization', though, life was always sweet. When Margaret and Charles had the chance to live with a native family in a simple bamboo house on Polillo Island, east of Luzon, nothing could have been finer. No hardship was too much in return for the life of a lepidopterist, and Margaret enjoyed nothing more than a few cigarettes after a hard day's butterfly work. 'I love to sit here in the evening,' she wrote of those happy times, 'when the day's work is done, often thinking of lands far away, places I have visited and known on this wonderful planet.' Charles would join her then, to sit in darkness and talk or just be silent, the way only people at peace with each other can be.

Sadly, they would not today recognize any of the places they visited then but especially not lovely Polillo Island. Despite the fact that it is in one of the world's highest priority regions for the conservation of threatened species, it has lost almost all of its original forest. Only three isolated patches remain, the rest of the island denuded for timber or covered in coconut plantations in the past sixty years.

In fact, according to the latest research, 71 per cent of all Philippine butterflies have no stable population within a protected area, and over 150 unique species are about to be lost for ever.[7] Margaret could never have imagined such a catastrophe, but her unique study of the life-cycles of tropical butterflies represents a major resource for modern-day conservationists who are trying to protect the last fragments of primary forest in the Philippines or, where that is not possible, to cultivate the all-important food plants Margaret discovered for her caterpillars in order to establish captive breeding programmes. Her pioneering work in breeding tropical butterflies, along with her personal diaries, represents the most important legacy Margaret has left us, and modern scientists have recognized this by naming a Philippine butterfly in her honour: *Euploea phaenareta margaretae*.[8]

While they were in the Philippines Charles received news that his Syrian wife had fallen on her head and lost her mind. He wished the woman he had been forced to marry in his youth, and who had been ruining his chances with Margaret for over twenty-five years now, could have died instead. His father's cousin was Head Patriarch of the Greek Church in Damascus by this time, and he wrote requesting a divorce once more. Margaret no longer cared if they got married or not, but she let Charles persuade her to set off in opposite directions once again, and they booked their tickets around the globe: he to Damascus via Suez and she to London via Vancouver and Montréal. The fact that she had to cross the entire North American continent was a minor detail, made easy by the trans-Canadian railway.

'What a glorious country Canada is (in the summer!),' she wrote, 'the grand beauty of the Rocky Mountains was at once soothing and elevating: elevating because it raised one so far above the sordid sorrows of our poor, human lives – soothing because its very grandeur made those wretched sorrows seem so small and insignificant.'

Margaret's lofty sentiments never made her lose sight of reality, though, and she was not above a bit of smuggling when it suited her. At Liverpool customs she nervously presented her trunks stuffed full of Filipino cigars but had the presence of mind to divert attention by admitting to her less valuable supply of cigarettes. So it was a rather smug Margaret who got on the train for London. Not only had she completed a journey of some 10,000 miles, crossed two oceans and a continent, but she had also succeeded in importing cigars worth £2 each, for which she had paid less than half in Manila.

Margaret aged sixty-six, from the frontispiece to her diary of 1928

BUTTERFLIES
1928–1940

❀21❀
BEREFT AT SIXTY-SIX

I T WAS VERY hard to be alone in London, but Margaret kept busy
with setting and packing butterflies for collectors and museums in
America and England – a lucrative business for her now – and
occasionally she was persuaded to network in the entomological
world. On one memorable occasion she spent the day at Lord Walter
Rothschild's famous estate at Tring, where she was astounded to find that
he had almost two million butterfly and moth specimens. Her own 16,000-
strong butterfly collection seemed paltry in comparison, a 'drop in the
ocean', she wrote enviously.

She was pleased for Charles when he wrote to say his uncle, the Bishop,
had dissolved his marriage at last. Apparently Bishop Neimy thought English ladies made very good wives and thoroughly approved of his nephew's
plan to marry Margaret, though she was deeply frustrated when he also
wrote to say he must remain in Damascus for the tourist season to earn
money for his mother. As 1924 passed into 1925 and still he would not
come she became depressed and resentful, allowing self-pity to take hold.

'And as to Charles,' she wrote disconsolately, 'I felt now he did not care
a damn about me, in fact I did not believe he cared for anything on God's
Earth except his mother . . .' She got so carried away with this thought she
actually sent Charles an ultimatum: either he promised to meet her by
April or May that year or she would expect never to see him again. 'But I
think you will be pleased to stay on with your mother indefinitely,' she
wrote petulantly.[1]

As soon as she posted her letter she wished she could have had it back,
but it was too late, and Charles did what no woman in distress ever wants
from her lover: he took her at her word. 'I am very sorry . . . you think I do

not care of you any more, my dearest. You making big mistake indeed,' he wrote from Damascus. 'How can I forget my old and best friend and my lover for many years. I am no doubt in great fix between you and my old mother. I do not know what to do. I cannot hurt the feeling of my poor old mother and leave her which she have nobody or any soul look after her.'

It was a pitiful situation. He was clearly torn, but Margaret continued to feel resentful, not least because she was still paying him a wage, which was contributing to the care of his mother, and she had also promised to let him spend every tourist season in Damascus as long as his mother was alive. There was a sister in Damascus, too. Why did she not take care of Mrs Neimy, who had been pulling her 'dying stunt' for years now? But it was no use; Charles refused to leave Damascus, and Margaret was forced to accept the situation.

Meanwhile, she moved her studio from the noise and bustle of Kensington to leafy Fellows Road, in Hampstead, where she could house her collection in a spacious and light room. It even had enough space for her piano and was so perfect that when the owner suddenly decided to sell the studio and adjoining house she bought the lot for £2,400, much against the advice of her lawyers. Her trust fund was worth half what it had been before the First World War, but Margaret did not care. She could earn up to £7 for just one butterfly specimen now and did not need to use her capital for living.

Once her butterflies were safely settled at Fellows Road she booked herself a passage to West Africa and tried not to contemplate the awful news emanating from Syria, where the French were bombing Damascus in response to a Druze insurrection. She had to believe Charles would have the sense to leave if things got really bad, and she set off to lands unknown, ever the stranger abroad.

She took a German boat from the Woermann Line, because it was the only one allowing a stopover in the Canaries, and was pleasantly surprised by the friendliness and courtesy of the German crew. The Canaries were the last point at which Charles could have joined her from Port Said, and Margaret could not resist trying to bend fate just one last time. But he did not come, and Margaret was forced to swallow her disappointment and carry on alone.

Margaret's West African expedition ranged from plague-infested

Nigeria to the mountains of Cameroon, from miserable Sierra Leone to the delights of French cooking in Conakry, and along the way she survived three violent bouts of malaria and falling in love with a German plantation manager. The entomological results of her journey were spectacular, and she was thrilled to discover so many species new to her. On the other hand, her time in West Africa was deeply marred by the news of her sister Geraldine's death from tuberculosis, like so many of her other siblings, and also the continued inability of Charles to leave Syria on account of his mother. As if that were not enough, the news from America was also bad. Arthur sent wild letters accusing Mollie of infidelity, and Margaret was very sorry to read that she had taken herself and the children away to her parents' house. The rift was so bad that even the children had taken against their father, but Margaret had long ago lost patience with her brother and there was nothing she could do for him anyway.

By the time Margaret left West Africa for the Canaries she was a frail sixty-five-year-old woman, weak from malaria and dysentery and beginning to feel that death would be preferable to the miserable life she was leading now. She had not seen Charles for nearly three years. But the longed-for news came to her at Las Palmas at last: he was free to be with her once more, for someone had been found to take care of his mother.

'Poor man, or rich man, I don't care, it is *you, you dear self* that I am longing to see again,' she wrote reassuringly, and her old heart was young again. She could only hope he would feel the same and that the dentist in Marseilles would have her dentures ready before her darling arrived for their reunion. Her illnesses in Africa had resulted in the loss of her last three remaining teeth. She need not have worried about her own shrivelled appearance, however. Charles had also been ravaged by illness, and Margaret was shocked to find he, too, had a new set of front teeth, all of pure gold! The hotel receptionist entered his nationality as American, assuming that only they could afford such a thing, and Margaret was grateful she had nothing worse to worry about. They were like young lovers again, strolling in the parks of Marseilles and planning their future together.

How gratifying to be told by the maid at her Finchley boarding-house that a gentleman was there to see her and then to wander up to her studio in Hampstead, where Charles would read the paper while she set her butterflies. *Together*, just that one word made her happy, and she tried not to resent the money she was sending to Damascus to pay for the old woman, his mother. But their time together was not destined to last. A Mr Longsdon commissioned Margaret to collect butterflies for him in the West Indies, which was an opportunity for earning money too good to be missed. Margaret and Charles agreed it was for the best, though it was also very painful to separate again so soon after their reunion.

If only he could have come with her – but the British authorities would not allow it, if he wanted to have his imperial naturalization finalized. Perversely, they refused to accept his years of residency in Australia and insisted that he remain in England for one year, without interruption, before giving him the papers that would finally allow Margaret to marry him as a British citizen. It was profoundly unjust, but Margaret and Charles had been waiting to get married for over twenty-five years now. They could manage one more. And so Charles waved goodbye to Margaret at Victoria station, flashing his gold teeth with an encouraging smile, and she waved and waved until she lost sight of him. How she wished he could have come with her!

How much more she would have wished it had she known what a terrible mistake it was to leave Charles alone in London. The winter of 1927 was one of the harshest on record. Never before had he experienced an English winter, and now he had to do it alone, with no one to care that his knees were aching with rheumatism or to alleviate his loneliness. It was too much, and he jumped at the chance to escape the cold with his own commission for work. A man he met in a bar hired him for a trip to Egypt, and Margaret was unable to make him reconsider, despite being just months from getting his papers in order. Did he not want their dream of marriage to come true at last? She implored him but too late. The next letter she received from him informed her of his departure, and it was a lonely and disconsolate Margaret who returned to an empty studio six months later. She could not believe she had left her darling for a job, and it was a decision that was to haunt her for the rest of her days.

All her life Margaret was plagued by uncertain outcomes, and now she was faced with the worst one of all: the death of the most important person in her life, the circumstances of which have remained an unsolved mystery to this day. But when she first returned to London everything seemed quite promising. There were several letters from Charles waiting for her, and in June 1928 she sent him funds for his return journey from Damascus. He wrote to say that he had a malarial fever, and Margaret worried that she had delayed too long before sending him money. 'What did I care that I was selling those wretched *Polydamus* at three pounds apiece to Lord Rothschild and Joicey. Money was nothing to me without Charles,' she wrote miserably.[2]

Her forebodings increased as the intervals between letters became longer and longer and their contents more pitiful until, finally, she received just a short note telling her he was 'very danger ill', and she could not help feeling she was about to face the most terrible loss of her life. Waiting for news was agony, and Margaret blamed herself fiercely for leaving Charles alone in London. If only she had not done it! If only she had sent money as soon as she had known he was ill! If only . . .

'Yes, I felt it was all my fault, and that added tenfold to my torture,' she recalled, though it was by no means all her fault. He chose to leave London knowing full well what he was giving up, and he must also have known how terrible it would be for Margaret to return and find him gone. They had both chosen actions painful to the other – as so often before – and there was nothing to be done about it. Guilt was not the issue, though Margaret could never see it that way.

When at last a Syrian-stamped letter arrived with an unknown handwriting on it, Margaret knew at once what it meant.

'Dear Madam,' the letter read, 'We are sorry to inform you that Charles is dead after 2 weeks sickness.'

It was the end for Margaret, too. He was her rock, and now he was gone. She could hardly fathom how her own heart refused to stop beating, and at sixty-six she really felt she did not have the strength to face this awful loss alone. She sent for her last surviving sister. Evelyn arrived that same afternoon and tried to comfort Margaret with the idea that grief would probably not last long. Soon they would all be dead!

Margaret threw herself into work, as if keeping busy would somehow cheat time into healing her more quickly. But the healer was not tricked so easily, and the pain and incessant memories plagued Margaret's every waking moment. When she sat down to set her butterflies, it reminded her of the time she had caught them with Charles. When she entered her studio, she waited for his call. When she went to bed, she remembered their evenings together. There was also a steady stream of distressing letters from Damascus which did nothing to ease the pain of having missed her darling's final moments, not to mention his funeral.

It is almost certain that he died of malaria in a Damascus hospital on 7 July 1928, but Margaret received conflicting letters from his mother, sister and a supposed friend she had never heard of, about the circumstances. The most upsetting were from his sister, Poling Neimy, the very same who had moved to the other side of Damascus to shirk her duties with their mother as long as Charles was alive. She wrote as if her brother and his wife were still very much a family, however dysfunctional, which came as a shock. According to her, this wife had been very cruel to Charles, abandoning him when he became ill and also taking their *five* children. She had refused to take care of her husband, taunting and humiliating him to such a degree that he even had a heart attack. Certainly the sister thought this woman had hastened Charles's death, but what she really wanted to relate was that he had promised Margaret would continue supporting his mother and sister after he was gone!

It was too awful. Not only did Margaret have to contend with her grief, but she also had to face up to the idea that Charles had deceived her throughout their entire twenty-seven-year relationship. The wife had been no secret, of course – but the children? Did they really exist? If they did, why had Charles never admitted to them? Why had he told her he was divorced? So many unanswered questions tormented Margaret, yet she never for an instant thought of going to Damascus to find out more. Pride and bitterness prevented it. She would not fall prey to scheming or give anyone the pleasure of seeing her wail at Charles's tomb. He had died among his own people, and she felt very strongly that it was best not to investigate further, not least because she had no faith in getting straight answers from anyone. It was her money they wanted, of that she was sure. Sadly, Margaret's instincts were unfailingly correct on that score, because it was not long before she also began receiving begging letters from his wife herself.

It hurt very much to think that Charles had lied to her for so many years, that their plans to get married had been a fiction all along and that he had lived a double life with her. Of course, Margaret had led a double life herself but not like this. It hurt even more to think that there had been children. According to one letter there was a son of twenty-two, which meant that Charles had gone back to his wife around the time of her engagement with the Vice-Consul in Turkey. It was possible, yet his wife's letters implied there were young children, too, which was as upsetting as it was confusing. Margaret thought she had 'tangible reasons' for knowing that he could not have fathered any children lately, perhaps alluding to his genito-urinary illness in Australia, but there could never be answers to these questions. Only one thing was certain: Margaret would never send money to anyone in Damascus, and she quickly terminated all correspondence with Syria.

'That this wife existed, and was, and always had been, a very decided factor in Charles' life I scarcely now felt any doubt,' she wrote sadly. 'As to the children, they may have been his, or they may not. I should never know, nor should I ever be able to sift the matter to the bottom and arrive at anything near the real truth. But strange as it may seem, the knowledge that beyond doubt he had been more or less deceiving me all these years was a thing, now in my miserable loneliness without him, I felt positively grateful for, as it could not do otherwise than mitigate the bitter sorrow I was feeling for his loss.'

Margaret needed the anger to fire her will to live, but it was very hard. 'Reader, are you weary of me?' she wrote at last. 'If indeed you have come with me thus far through the long years of my strange and stormy life . . .'

Yet her life was by no means over.

❧ 22 ❧

SOLACE IN LATIN AMERICA

T
HERE WAS NOTHING like work and travel to take the mind off private grief, and Margaret left London as soon as she could, setting off for South America on an ancient boat from the Nelson Line. She looked forward to discovering the well-known hunting grounds around Rio de Janeiro, though it was inexpressibly sad to think it would be without Charles, and she felt his loss especially when the Rio customs men insisted on unpacking all her luggage and then leaving her to reassemble it alone. Such discourtesy would never have happened with him at her side.

Rio soon cast its spell on her, nevertheless, and she was thrilled with the view from her room at the Hotel Internacional: a magnificent panorama that stretched from the ocean to the distant mountains, with the famous Sugar Loaf reaching up out of the city. The butterflying was superb as well, and she was up at 5.30 each morning to keep up with her work.

'I find it very hard to have no one to help me now,' she wrote to Riley at the Natural History Museum, who had commissioned her to collect for him.[1] She found it even harder in the evenings, with no one to talk to when everyone else was sitting down to share a meal or enjoy the sunsets. She was still receiving letters from Damascus, each in a different handwriting but always claiming to be from Charles's wife and a cruel reminder of her loss. The letters insisted that Mrs Neimy had been married to Charles for over thirty years and that she and her children were now left destitute. But Margaret refused to see these letters as anything other than attempts at extortion and did not answer. Perhaps those children really did exist, but they were certainly not infants, as the letters claimed. After all, the oldest was supposed to be a son of twenty-two. She vowed to herself not to yield and felt a profound anger with Charles for dying before her and for leaving her with these bothersome letters.

A fortnight in Rio turned into the best part of six months as Margaret learnt to love the city and its environs, and the entomological riches to be found were so extensive that it was hard to pull herself away. But at last she headed north, travelling to the coastal town of Recife and onwards, to Belém do Pará in the mouth of the Amazon river. She had a letter of introduction for Mr Miles-Moss, the British chaplain there, who was also a renowned entomologist. He was a stout little man given to wearing ragged dungarees instead of a cassock, but Margaret quickly warmed to him and felt a great admiration for his detailed knowledge of local flora and fauna. He was a very fine artist, too, and Margaret noted in her diary that his drawings of caterpillars were the best she had ever seen – high praise coming from her. All in all, they had much in common, including a love of music, and Margaret was almost happy again, based at the Grand Hotel in Belém and filling her collecting boxes with dozens of new species.[2]

It was impossible for Margaret to remain in the city, though. She had to get right into Amazonia, and she took it into her head to follow Tomlinson's route into the rainforest, travelling over 2,000 miles up the rivers Amazon and Madeira, to Porto Velho and beyond.[3] It was there, as she was working out of Porto Velho, that the magic of the South American rainforest truly revealed itself to her, and she could never get enough of seeing the river banks teeming with butterflies as they sucked moisture from the mud. Her companion in this remote region was a young Englishman called Mr Harding, who would have been happy to see the entire rainforest chopped down for firewood, but Margaret admonished him with prescient wisdom that if his wish came true the entire region would be reduced to desert from the lack of rain.

The only routes into the jungle in these remote areas were either the many tributaries of the Madeira river or the railway tracks laid for the timber trade. The Madeira–Marmoré railway, built by the British out of Porto Velho, was one such route, and Margaret persuaded the local engineers to let her use it in return for making up a fourth at bridge for them. In this way she was able to reach deep into virgin forest without arduous treks on foot, and she was delighted when her new friends allowed her to stay in a remote rest house at the end of the railway line at Guajará-Mirim. She was on the border with northern Bolivia now, and it pleased her to think she was crossing another frontier just by taking a boat across the river.

She still hated getting on water, but in spite of the danger from whirlpools and piranhas she managed to overcome her fears to do excellent work. In fact, she discovered several new butterflies, two of which she allowed Riley to name after Charles. 'Poor Mr Neimy,' she wrote to Riley, 'how pleased he would have been.'

The remote jungle along the Bolivian border is the traditional home of a native Indian tribe which was understandably hostile to the invasion of its land by destructive foreigners, but the first Margaret knew about it was when she suddenly found herself alone one day. Her guide inexplicably vanished while she was exploring a particularly good hunting spot, and she only discovered why on her return when he explained that the Indians had killed several white people there recently. Margaret thought it was disgraceful of him to leave her to face poisoned arrows in the back alone, but there was no suggestion she would have stayed away had she known. She was a brave woman, and she was also far too old and detached from life to worry about being killed.

Excepting Mr Miles-Moss, the men Margaret encountered on her Brazilian journey were altogether a great disappointment, and she was especially irritated by Mr Harding, who disapproved of her smoking. A Mr Twiss annoyed her even more by showing the same prejudice even while he himself used a pipe. 'But smoke I did,' she noted grimly, determined not to take any notice of people who thought they could tell a grown woman in her sixties what to do. She was thrilled, therefore, when she met a German woman after her own heart, an enthusiastic smoker and a naturalist, too, who was collecting birds for the Museo Nacional in Rio. Margaret jumped at the chance to spend some time in the forest with Frau Snethlage instead of those tiresome men, and they quickly became great 'chums', as Margaret called it.

'We made a little expedition the next day,' Margaret remembered fondly, 'she with her gun, I with my net, and she shot about half a dozen poor little birds, which made me feel very unhappy, though of course I disguised my feelings, and pretended to be very pleased.'[4]

Margaret was even more unhappy when her new friend had to leave. Emilie Snethlage's company had done her good after the many months of hunting alone, without a soul-mate to share her passion. Sadly, the friendship was not destined to last either, because Emilie died of a heart attack just weeks later.[5]

Almost a year passed before Margaret thought of returning to England, by which time she had travelled literally thousands of miles up and down the Amazon river, including all the way to Teffé, where the great naturalist Henry Walter Bates had once made his home. She owned his famous book which spoke of the fabulous wealth of butterfly species around a natural lake there, of the kaleidoscope of colours quivering in every sunny glade, and she was determined to see for herself. He had written of seeing no less than eighty species from twenty-two different butterfly families around the lake, and Margaret was delighted to find Teffé had changed very little in the eighty years since Bates had been there. She even had a comfortable place to stay with some French nuns, but, frustratingly, the butterfly-hunting was no good. It was too late in the dry season, and the insects she captured were in such poor condition that they were not worth keeping. She was especially disappointed not to catch even one *Agria*, those lovely giants of the butterfly world, whose wings flash red and black and blue in the forest canopy. Instead, she reluctantly paid over the odds in Belém for some specimens for sale, knowing full well she would double her money in England.

But when her collecting boxes were full it was time to leave, not least because there were several museums and collectors impatiently waiting for her treasures. So she returned to England and a damp squib of a summer on the SS *Hildebrand*, reflecting there was very little to recommend old age, especially alone. Her sister Evelyn was her only occasional companion now, and together they visited their cousin Skye on Park Lane, a sporty eighty-six-year-old. Other members of the family were not so tough. Florence Curtois was very ill with breast cancer, Dering and Lisle were both dead, and Margaret Curtois was 'no use to anyone', suffering from Alzheimer's disease. Margaret was nowhere near retirement or death, however, and her collecting in Brazil had been so successful that she decided to return the following year. The physical hardships of travelling in the jungle were many, but to Margaret they were always preferable to the dreary confines of her empty studio.

Roughing it on the Essequibo river was much more interesting than living in London, and she enjoyed the uncomplicated company of enterprising planters and missionaries. But times had changed dramatically in Amazonia since she had left the year before, and the 1930 revolution in Brazil cut Margaret off from all her contacts there. She was unable to return to Brazilian territory, and, though British Guyana was politically more stable, a slump in the diamond trade meant that every settlement was swamped with destitute miners, which posed its own danger. Margaret was appalled to see such human suffering in one of 'our colonies', recalling in her diary the pathetic sight of starving men arriving by boat with nothing but the clothes on their backs and a small bundle of tools. 'Never have I seen a more forlorn sight,' she wrote of the sick and impoverished men pouring out of the jungle.

Five months in British Guyana yielded just one store box of butterflies, which was very unsatisfactory indeed. She had eleven boxes to fill, and so she set off for Venezuela, via Trinidad, to try her luck on the Orinoco. But that, too, was a disappointment, because the river banks around Ciudad Bolívar, where she came to collect, were bare and lifeless. Wholesale destruction of the rainforest had already occurred here, and the arid treeless landscape was devoid of all wildlife, including butterflies. Margaret had spent a small fortune to reach this hell-hole, and she was furiously disappointed. When the local Consul was not even able to guarantee her protection should she venture further, she cut her losses and decided to pay an even greater fortune to leave by booking herself on to her first flight on an aeroplane.

As the plane soared up into the sky, Margaret was relieved to be leaving the sordid mess of Ciudad Bolívar behind her, though whether she would live to see another day she was unsure. Tucked in behind the pilot and another passenger, Margaret found herself soaring into the chill air in an open plane, a ferocious wind in her face and her ears blasted by propeller noise. It must have been absolutely terrifying, yet in her diary Margaret simply records that she hoped it would not be her last flight as well as her first! But no matter how much money she spent to reach different locations in Venezuela, the result was always the same: frustration and trouble, disgusting accommodation and even worse food. No ordinary traveller would ever have put up with such hardships, but Margaret had the motivation of finding rare butterflies to sustain her, and even though her Venezuelan expedition was a failure she did meet some very interesting people.

Her most intriguing encounter was with escaped convicts from the dreaded penal colonies off French Guyana. 'I once had a long talk with one of these men,' she noted, 'a most harmless looking little Frenchman. I could not think that his crime had been a very ghastly one. He seemed smart too, and really did know quite a lot about butterflies, mentioning several genera by their scientific names . . .' Perhaps it was Henri Charrière, 'Papillon' himself, who boasts in his famous book of cheating wealthy butterfly collectors. A particular rarity sought in the Amazon were butterflies that were both male and female – gynandromorphs – where one side of the wings show the colour and patterning of the male and the other show those of the female. Charrière used to manufacture these specimens with some careful cutting and sticking and sell them to anyone who fell for it.

An encounter from the other end of the social spectrum came on the small boat taking Margaret out of Venezuela, for on board was none other than Lady Walpole, a well-known adventurer and travel writer in her day, known as Dorothy Mills. Margaret was flattered when she asked if she was the 'woman scientist' she had heard about further up the Orinoco, and the two women hit it off, despite their very different styles: one dowdy and practical, the other famously glamorous and well dressed.[6]

They parted company in Trinidad, where Margaret collapsed with exhaustion. It had been a very arduous and frustrating journey, and she ended her account of it railing against nature. She had, by now, begun each and every day with pain throughout her body, followed by a violent heat wave for over twelve years. 'Surely I am beating all records?' she complained bitterly, noting this was no doubt nature's way of getting rid of the superfluous female. A year away from her seventieth birthday, she had reached the end of 'the allotted span of human life', though her body did not seem to think so.

23

A STRANGER IN A
STRANGE LAND

ALL SHIPS BETWEEN England and Amazonian ports once
stopped in Port of Spain on the island of Trinidad, so it was
an ideal resting place. For Margaret it was also a place that
brought back happy memories of collecting with Charles,
though she used a different base now, more in tune with her solitary status:
the guest-house of a monastery, high up on the island's northern range.[1]

'The order is a strict one,' she wrote of the community at Mount St
Benedict; 'no female is allowed to enter within its sacred precincts',
though that did not stop her making friends with a certain Father Maurus,
a keen entomologist who accompanied her on many forays into the jungle.[2]
Margaret was astonished how he could manage the rocks and steep tangle
of the forest in his cassock, but she was even more mystified that a man so
committed to nature had willingly 'incarcerated' himself in monastic life.
She did not approve of men locking themselves up together, and she
found the religious atmosphere of St Benedict unfathomably disturbing;
though that might have had more to do with the wild letters she was
receiving from her brother Arthur at this time. For months now he had
been begging her to visit him in Covington, and reluctantly Margaret
decided to return to England via the USA – an immense detour,but one
she felt she had to make, if not for the sake of her wretched brother then
for his children.

Arthur had taken it into his head that Melville was not his son but the
result of an affair between Mollie and her sister's seducer, whose name was
also Melville. It was a terrible accusation that had torn the whole family
apart, and Margaret found Arthur holed up at the O'Gara Hotel in Covington, more decrepit than ever. 'The poor thing seemed quite overcome with

emotion at the sight of me,' she wrote sadly, 'and from that moment I was glad indeed that I had given up everything to come to him.'

At first Margaret was appalled to think Mollie had allowed herself to get pregnant by another man, but when she thought on it she realized it could not be true. 'Had I not been there for four months with them,' she remembered, 'and seen Mollie and Melville as a baby, born only eleven months after another boy, who had died in infancy.' Arthur himself had told her at the time how much Mollie had grieved for that dead baby. It seemed inconceivable she would have joined with her sister's boyfriend just months after the death of her child. 'Arthur did not seem to realise what a cruel injustice he was doing to this boy [his son Melville],' Margaret wrote, 'and I felt sure in his own mind, he was merely saying it to spite Mollie all he possibly could.' It was her duty, Margaret decided, to establish Melville's paternity once and for all, and she made up her mind to find Mollie at Hot Springs, where she was now living with Melville.

At least the boy had his mother. Poor Lee had been packed off to live on a remote farm, separated from his mother, yet not cared for by his father either. Margaret was desperate to see him – he had been such a beautiful baby – but he did not come to Covington, and Arthur had no explanation. In fact, he was virtually enslaved to his uncle Peter on the farm, and Margaret was shocked to find the conditions her nephew was living in when she arrived by hired motor car. The beautiful boy she had once held in her arms had grown into a cowed teenager of nineteen who could barely look at her. It was heart-breaking.

'And the boy would be as beautiful as a Greek God, had he been brought up in refined surroundings, instead of amongst a mob of Virginian farmers,' she wrote, outraged. It was intolerable to see a member of her family reduced to a virtual serf. At least her brother was the architect of his own misfortune, but his son deserved better. Lee's condition was unworthy of the Fountaine lineage, and Margaret was determined to help him. But how? Arthur was utterly destitute, and her own funds were also extremely limited these days.

Going by Margaret's studio portraits, it would be easy to imagine her as a dour old spinster without a humorous bone in her body. But this was never so, and this is nowhere more obvious than in her dealings with young people. They loved her wherever she encountered them, and many a harassed mother trying to entertain bored children on ocean crossings was grateful for Margaret's company. She never lost the sense of fun and mischief she had been born with and had a natural empathy with anyone who showed the same. Melville, too, would one day have fond memories of his aunt beating him at pool in the local haunts in Covington.

To Margaret's surprise, she received a call from Mollie, acting just as if nothing was wrong at all and inviting her to visit. Even stranger, Arthur encouraged her to go, and so she did, setting off by hired motor car once more, to find herself introduced to a very thin, tall boy of fifteen. 'This is Melville,' said Mollie, after giving the astonished Margaret a friendly hug, and the boy's sad, pathetic smile melted her heart in an instant.

Of course he was Arthur's son – anyone could see that, Margaret thought, not least because he looked so much like his dead aunts, especially Florence. Nevertheless, as soon as a quiet moment allowed she questioned Mollie regarding his paternity and was very glad when her sister-in-law solemnly swore he was his father's child. But Melville's situation upset Margaret even more than Lee's, for not only was he nothing but a dish-washer in the hotel where his mother also worked but he regularly cleared up after black customers, a degradation too far for Margaret's imperial heart. He was the descendant of a 'long line of noble ancestors', after all, and it was her duty to remove Melville and his brother from the miserable lives they seemed destined to live.

Taking charge of her nephews' lives was easier said than done, however. The acrimonious split between Arthur and Mollie had resulted in the boys taking sides, Lee choosing his father and Melville his mother. Negotiating the minefield of hurts and resentments, not to mention monetary issues, required a level of diplomacy Margaret was by no means used to, and she found it very hard not to show her feelings. What on earth made Lee stick with his father? she wondered. He had been virtually sold to his uncle Pete Oliver, and when he was allowed to visit Arthur he had to sleep in the same bed at his hotel so his father could save money.

If Arthur's accusations against Mollie were public knowledge it was no wonder the boys had become estranged, but Margaret did her best to bring them back together, and, little by little, she succeeded. It was a small victory, but after four months in Covington Margaret left the brothers in happy possession of a Ford roadster, and Lee had been removed from the farm and installed with his mother's sister instead. She left by six-seater plane from the airport at White Sulphur Springs, feeling a deep affection for her nephews and determined to remember them in her will.

'No early Victorian lady in her Sedan Chair could have travelled in greater comfort or safety,' she noted with satisfaction about her flight to Washington, DC. She loved travelling by aeroplane, convinced earthly travel was a thing of the past. 'Washington from the air was a sight to be remembered,' she thrilled, 'and by and by we passed over Baltimore and Philadelphia, and how much did I love to find myself up there in the blue sky away from all the gay frivolities and sordid miseries of those crowded, populous cities.'

It took just four hours to reach New York from West Virginia, and Margaret was delighted to book herself into the Cornish Arms once more. She just had time for a short visit to her old friend Kollmorgen before catching the next boat back to London. 'Margaret, just think how lucky you were that I was already married when we first met,' he teased her, 'otherwise you might have found yourself married to a German!'

She preferred to think she might have married her good butterfly friend Mr Roland-Brown. He had always been the heart and soul of meetings at the Entomological Society in London, and Margaret missed him very much. 'He might perhaps never have died from over-work during the cursed War,' she once wrote, if she had been there to take care of him.[3]

But Margaret did not return to England after all. The world depression that was inaugurated by the Wall Street Crash of 1929 claimed another victim as Britain left the Gold Standard in October 1931, and Margaret's and millions of others' funds were reduced to a fraction of their former value overnight. Luckily for Margaret, she had just cashed a substantial letter of credit, so her short-term situation was fine, but she was deeply sorry to see her country so publicly humiliated. Suddenly she found herself feeling defensively patriotic and imagined that hotel staff and shopkeepers were less courteous now, knowing she was British.

She decided to sit out the European winter in Cuba. 'I had neither friend or acquaintance on the island,' she wrote sadly, noting that it was now three years since Charles had left her to face old age alone. She still felt the pain very much, especially since the American woman who was supposed to accompany her could no longer afford to; nor could many others, and the glamorous reception rooms and lovely deck of the large Ward Liner from New York remained silent and unused. No more than twenty-two passengers were on board, a small band of lucky escapees from the human misery unfolding for millions of unemployed and hungry people. The world was in sharp decline in many ways, and Margaret was astounded to see the spread of sugarcane plantations across Cuba. She was on a flight heading for the eastern end of the island, but the tropical vege-tation she and Charles had explored just twenty years before had gone. It was 'as if it had never been', and Margaret could hardly believe her eyes. Yet she found herself spending some of the happiest times of her career in eastern Cuba that winter, successfully breeding many butterflies and even becoming a trusted adviser to the local farmers. It seems that their cab-bages were being eaten by caterpillars, and Margaret was called in to help solve the problem. She advised watering the plants with saline solution every evening and was delighted when a fine crop of cabbages emerged not much later in the season.

Guantánamo was an obscure little village then, with a comfortable hotel and one of the friendliest entomologists Margaret had ever met living near by. 'The longer I stayed in Guantánamo, the more I liked it,' Margaret wrote in the early months of 1932. 'Everybody was so awfully nice to me,' she remembered, and life as a lonely old woman was not so bad after all. Coming up to her seventieth birthday, she rode 45 miles in just one day, galloping most of the way home and feeling as strong as ever.

'I think Browning must have been suffering from loss of memory when he wrote "Oh to be in England, now that April's here,"' Margaret wrote, when she returned home at last. Her studio was freezing, and it was not much fun dragging buckets of anthracite up from the coal bunker each day. Her grandmother had always rung for a footman if the drawing-room needed warming, and even Margaret's own mother would have thought carrying coal too physical. But these minor hardships were insignificant in the greater scheme of things, and Margaret did not have time to brood on her reduced circumstances. She was far too busy working with her butter-flies and enjoying modern treats, such as the occasional 'talkie' in a West End cinema. She also attended some more traditional entertainments with her sister Evelyn, such as the races at Ascot, and could not help noting that there was very little sign of the straitened times. The ladies' gowns 'swept the grass as in the old days of Queen Victoria', and the horses were as sleek and beautiful as ever.

The real highlight of the year for Margaret, however, was the Entomological Congress in Paris. Even better, Thomas Cook had negotiated a 50 per cent rebate for delegates attending by air or rail, and Margaret jumped at the chance to reach Paris by aeroplane. 'The trip by air to Paris was indeed perfect,' she recalled happily. The plane took off on a damp grey morning, but soon it was cruising above the clouds in brilliant sunshine, and Margaret was entranced by the magical beauty of the white mounds beneath her, 'like rolling billows of glistening snow'.

It was thrilling to float into Paris and book herself into the Palais d'Orsay, feeling fresh and relaxed for the nine days ahead, and Margaret was amazed to find herself the object of a great many admirers.

'Is this Miss Fountaine?' cried an American entomologist. 'Oh! I have always wanted so much to make your acquaintance!'

Margaret had never heard of him but was delighted nevertheless.

'I had no idea I was so famous!' she laughed with her old friend Professor Poulton.

On another occasion a young Russian refugee took her hand and insisted on telling her how thrilled he was to be meeting the 'celebrated lady traveller'. Margaret was again delighted, even more so for the fact that he was so handsome. 'I assured him the pleasure had been quite mutual,' she wrote in her diary.

Margaret may have been past seventy, but that was no reason to stop working, though few of any age could have kept up her pace. A look at her final sketch book of caterpillars at the Natural History Museum shows just how much she packed into an age most people call retirement: each meticulously drawn egg, caterpillar and chrysalis is annotated with the date and location where it was found or reared, and from this we can see she travelled to Madagascar, Kenya and Uganda in 1933, Kenya, Uganda and Tanzania in 1934 and back to Tanzania and Uganda in 1935. Always, she remained receptive to the world around her, never ceasing to think up new ways of reaching her quarry. In Uganda, for example, she was astonished to find there was not a single horse in the country, so she bought a car instead. The fact that she did not know how to drive it was no hindrance at all. She simply hired a driver, though finding a local man who knew how to drive cars was much harder than buying the vehicle in the first place. Once Ernest had been found, however, he became her trusted chauffeur throughout East Africa, driving her from the Upper Nile to the Budongo Forest, above Lake Albert, and from Kampala to Nairobi.[4]

In fact, in terms of her butterfly work the 1930s were the most productive time of her life, a time when she perfected her study of caterpillars into a prodigious breeding programme that benefited museums and collectors from London to New York and revealed the life-cycles and eating habits of many tropical butterflies, for which there was no previous information at all.

'I don't suppose Miss Fountaine left any notes,' a researcher wrote to the Keeper of Natural History at Norwich Castle Museum in 1951. 'It is distressing to think just how much information she took with her and never published.'

In fact, many others benefited from her generous gift of information, publishing the results of her research in their own papers. For example, the renowned expert on African butterflies V.G.L. van Someren used Margaret's pioneering studies for his work on African *Charaxes* butterflies, and Norman Riley, at the Natural History Museum in London, also used much of her source material for his own work. Perhaps if she had spent more time at home in her studio she would have written up her observations herself, but she was simply too busy and never minded giving her unique knowledge to others. She was neither proud nor competitive about her work as a lepidopterist, secure in the knowledge that those who counted in the entomological world of her day accepted her as one of them.

Margaret received news of her brother Arthur's death while in Uganda, and though it came as no surprise it was still a cause for regret. 'Never again would that poor, broken down old gentleman be seen sitting hour after hour in the Depot, watching the trains passing through Covington,' she wrote and made a mental note to visit her nephews just as soon as she could find the time and money.

Her chance came the following year, and she was delighted to travel by modern air-conditioned train from New York. Lee and Melville were grown young men by now, and the more Margaret knew of them the better she liked them, though not Lee's young wife, Frances. A diminutive eighteen-year-old, she was overbearing and uncouth, and Margaret could not help thinking her handsome young nephew could have done better than end up in a one-room hovel with this girl.

'The more I saw of Lee, the more my heart went out to him,' Margaret wrote sadly, 'so irresponsible, so easily influenced for good or bad, but with such a dear, lovable nature, that I just longed to be able to do more for him than I did.'

Margaret did a great deal, however, not only buying the young couple a six-bedroom farm with 175 acres of land but ensuring that what was left of Arthur's money went into a trust fund for his sons and not to his money-grubbing ex-wife.

Thankfully, Margaret never lived to hear what the young people did with her generous gift, for they sold it soon afterwards and divorced after producing two children. Melville, meanwhile, made a more successful life for himself, marrying in 1943 and bringing up three sons of his own. Sadly, even Margaret's efforts at reconciliation between the brothers was a failure in the long term, for they drifted apart, and the last Melville knew of Lee was in the 1950s, when he moved to Florida with a second wife, taking their mother with them. They never saw each other again, and the Fountaines of Virginia have no contact with their cousins in Florida.

Margaret left her nephews with a lump in her throat, the more so because she knew in her heart that she would never see them again. But autumn in America was no good for Margaret's aching bones, and she was soon back in the tropics, hunting and breeding butterflies on her beloved Trinidad. The monastery had recently refurbished its guest-house, and Margaret felt more at home there than anywhere else in the world. It was her refuge, just as it had been for the founding fathers of St Benedict. Meanwhile, the papers and radio were full of the Spanish Civil War, and Margaret was appalled to read that Franco had mined the Bay of Biscay. 'How am I going to get home, if in addition to the normal terrors of the sea will be added the fear of mines?' she asked herself.

Strangely, the bad news from Europe did not stop her booking her return passage on a German ship, and it must have been a very odd sensation celebrating the coronation of King George VI and Queen Elizabeth on that vessel. Margaret always enjoyed a good joke, though, and everyone was having a field day with Edward and Mrs Simpson. Her favourite was the one about Edward giving up being First Admiral in the British Navy to become third mate on an American tramp, and she was rather pleased with her own effort, too: 'Esau gave up his birth-right for a mess of pottage, whereas Edward VIII had given up his for a tart!' she recorded with a smirk.

But no worldly affairs could keep her from her butterfly work, and London had to do without her almost as soon as she had deposited her latest specimens. There were still places to go and species to find, and she spent 1938 travelling the length and breadth of Vietnam and Cambodia, even while the papers were full of the possibility of another war in Europe. It seemed incredible to Margaret that any government could contemplate a repeat of the carnage that had taken place just two decades earlier. 'What an intolerable muddle Europe is in,' she wrote, blaming an incompetent League of Nations for failing to reach fair agreements with Hitler and Mussolini.

Margaret was in London for the last time in the summer of 1939. It was the last time she went to a photographic studio to get a picture of herself for the frontispiece of her latest volume of private diaries and the last time she left instructions with her lawyers that the black box containing them should remain sealed until 1978, one hundred years after they were begun. She was as neat and meticulous about her private record as she was about her butterfly collection. Nothing was left to chance, and she slipped back to Trinidad just in time to escape the Atlantic blockades of the Second World War.

'I really think I am rather a wonderful old woman for my age,' she had written to Norman Riley the year before, and so she was.

POSTSCRIPT
The Lost Bequests

When I first arrived at the Castle Museum in Norwich I was told that, though Margaret left her butterfly collection and paintings to the Norwich and London museums respectively, she had decreed that her library should be given to the youngest member of the Royal Entomological Society in the year of her death – 1940. This was Denis Cowper, and his whereabouts were now unknown. He emigrated to the USA the year before Margaret died, and no one knew what had become of him. This was a shame because if any scientific notebooks ever existed to substantiate Margaret's methods and expertise they were presumed to be among her books.

It is this lack of specific information about her methods which has led the most eminent leaders of her profession to assess her as 'perhaps one of the greatest collectors of the twentieth century' but not a great entomologist. If anything, she is remembered for her eccentricity and astounding journeys, for her endurance and single-minded dedication to her subject, but not as someone who made a significant contribution to our understanding of butterflies. Yet, as Michael Salmon says in his wonderful book about butterfly collectors, 'personal eccentricity is an inescapable part of the history of entomology', and if that were an obstacle to recognition, then half the great Victorian naturalists would have to be removed from the roll of honour.

Norman Riley, the renowned Keeper of the Department of Entomology at the Natural History Museum in London, wrote in his unpublished memoir of her that 'naturalists, and particularly the kind who take pride in building up a valuable collection, are notoriously bad at recording their observations for the benefit of others. We all have known entomologists whose compendious knowledge was freely available to us by word of mouth but who never put pen to paper. Miss Fountaine was one such', despite her twenty-two articles for *The Entomologist* and *The Entomologists' Record*.

Her butterfly collection was never going to attract much attention in a provincial museum in a remote corner of the country, and her art books remain filed in a draw in the Natural History Museum. Public interest in vast collections of dead insects evaporated a long time ago, and in fact the Norwich Castle Museum has never included the Fountaine–Neimy Butterfly Collection in its permanent displays. You have to make a special appointment to see it.

The Second World War and the emergence of a more scientific approach to natural history in the latter part of the twentieth century have meant that Margaret's achievements have been marginalized, though modern entomologists may come to value them once more, especially those working in conservation and taxonomy.

'It would be nice if one could find notebooks, but Bill Cater's journalistic contacts in the USA failed to find any trace of Denis Cowper in the late 1970s,' Tony Irwin, the Natural History Curator in Norwich, informed me during our early discussions. If a *Sunday Times* journalist as experienced as Bill Cater, who edited Margaret's diaries for publication, had come up with nothing, there seemed little hope that I would succeed. Yet I was working almost thirty years later, and information technology had developed a spectacularly useful tool: the internet. Research that would have taken months and years in previous eras could now be done at the press of a button.

A year after beginning my research, Tony and I were talking about those possible notebooks once more, wondering what might have happened to them, if they ever existed and who on earth the youngest member of the Entomological Society in London was in 1940. All we had was a name, gleaned from the legal correspondence connected with establishing the age and identity of this person, but that was all.

Since he had just emigrated to America in 1940, we had no idea if Margaret's library had ever been forwarded to him or if they had simply remained with his father, who received the packages from the solicitors in London after the Second World War in 1945. Perhaps they had long ago been thrown away in some house clearance or been dispersed to a variety of second-hand bookshops . . . It was a tantalizing thought, but there seemed no realistic way of pursuing the matter.

Tony suggested an open appeal in the relevant internet chat rooms – a long shot, to say the least.

'Why don't we just type "Denis Cowper" into Google and see what we come up with?' I suggested.

Within hours we had found our man. We were sure it was him. He was a cactus specialist from Belen, New Mexico, who had died in 1974, four years before Margaret's diaries were revealed.

The thrill was intense, but Margaret's books and papers were still agonizingly out of reach. If only he could have lived a little longer perhaps the publication of Bill Cater's edited diaries might have brought him out. Had he even kept Margaret's bequest? Had he given it away, sold it or maybe left it to his children? There were many questions without answers, and we tried not to mention the unthinkable: that these precious items might have been safe and sound until so very recently, and no one knew about them. Were we just a few decades too late? The torment of those thoughts was almost intolerable.

We discovered an old friend of Cowper's, who not only remembered him fondly but also recalled Margaret's library and papers! They had spent some hours studying them together, but, being cactus men, there was little they were interested in – or, at least, little that David Eppele was interested in. It was he who informed us Cowper had died in 1974, but he had no idea where his widow might be or if she was even still alive. Apparently he had tried to gain access to some notebooks himself after his friend's death but had had no luck with Cowper's widow. He doubted she would be much help, even if she were alive, he wrote, since mutual friends had told him at least five years ago that she was suffering from dementia. (When confronted by Cowper's widow, he denied ever having made these claims, insisting we must have been in contact with an impostor.)

The torment! The closer we got the more likely it seemed we were just too late. Could it be that the books and papers had been safe and sound until these past few years? Could it be they were thrown out just recently? Or had they been left to the Cowpers' children? Had they cared to have them, or had they disposed of them, and where were they now? The questions just kept on flying around in my head, and no doubt Tony was wondering why he had not attempted an internet search sooner.

'Why didn't you?' I could not help myself asking him.

'I believed Bill Cater when he said his colleagues in the States had failed to trace him.'

It had not occurred to Tony to attempt a Google search until I suggested it in June 2004, almost thirty years after the diaries had been opened and at least ten years since the internet had been in common use, but there was no use wishing for what was past. The good news was that we had come so far in such a short time. Within days Tony had accessed a curator at the University of Albuquerque who not only knew of Cowper and his cactus work but found a phone number for his widow. Even better, she phoned her and prepared the way for us to contact her.

No, she was not senile, and, no, she had not thrown away her husband's library and papers. All had been in storage for the past thirty years! Hurrah!

'Let's open a detective agency!' I joked.

We agreed that Tony would phone her that very day, 9 June 2004, and tomorrow I would know if there would be any point in getting on the next plane to New Mexico.

A long conversation across echoing transatlantic telephone lines established that Denis Cowper had died in tragic circumstances and his widow had found herself unable to dispose of any of his things for the past three decades since his death. Every now and then she had considered doing something about all those boxes, but so far she had not been able to face it. Our phone call, however, might prove a catalyst for her, and she agreed to think over our request to see Margaret's books and papers.

In the meantime, it was good to know that Denis Cowper had been proud of owning Margaret's bequest, and from what we had learnt so far it seemed he was a worthy recipient: someone equally passionate and energetic about his natural history work, someone Margaret would have enjoyed meeting. She, too, had spent happy times hunting butterflies in the American South-West. They would have had much to talk about.

Denis Cowper turned out to be larger than life, a character worthy of his own biography, whose achievements and personality are still remembered today. A man of many talents, he not only ran a highly lucrative commercial cactus farm in the 1960s, selling seeds to collectors all around the world, but he was also a full-time attorney of law. He came close to becoming a district judge as well but narrowly failed to win this politically elected post. Perhaps it was because he switched from the Republican side to campaign with the Democrats, though his widow insists it was because they lived outside the hub of things in Albuquerque, remaining on their farm in Belen.

He was born in London in 1922 and educated at Westminster School and then in Switzerland, and his parents had ambitions for him to become a Member of Parliament. He spoke at least nine languages fluently, including German, French, Italian, Spanish and Russian, and became the youngest Fellow of the Royal Entomological Society when he was just fifteen, after discovering a new species of grasshopper.[1] His teenage notebooks from that time record he paid £2 2s. for his first subscription in 1937 and furthermore that his butterfly trading that year brought him a deficit of £9 8s. Business was clearly in his blood, though, and by the time he ran his cactus farm there were only profits.

His parents sent him to America on the last boat before war broke out, in 1939, ostensibly to study law at Harvard, but saving their only son from battle may also have had something to do with it. He rewarded their sacrifice by becoming the youngest person to hand in a perfect entrance paper for Harvard, and he thrived on his own, when the cheques stopped coming during the war years. He took it all in his stride, working in restaurants to pay his way and leaving Harvard with not only a law degree but a life-long passion for cooking – a talent his widow still sorely misses, never having learnt the art herself.

But the 'disastrous genius' – as his parents liked to call him – was no Perfect Peter. The big wide world of America was much more fun than war-torn Europe, and Denis disappointed his parents by refusing to return to their chosen destiny for him in the Westminster Parliament. Instead, he headed west to California and finally to New Mexico, where the climate was ideal for someone with a bad chest and a passion for cacti and butterflies.

His widow was surprised to discover that she was his fifth wife – she had always thought she was his fourth. But casting her mind back over his eventful life for me, another name came to her from distant memory, and we established there had indeed been five of them. The first was a Sioux Indian woman, who went out to buy bread one day and never returned, leaving him with two small daughters. The second produced a son, while the third was a Mexican girl he sent home after just one month. His fourth wife produced another son, but the marriage ended in divorce. By the time he married for the fifth time he was still only thirty-seven, but in Jodye he had met his match. 'Denis certainly wore the trousers in our relationship,' she told me fondly; 'I just told him which ones to wear.'

They were each other's perfect mate, partners in everything, both inside and outside the home. They met at law school, so she understood and supported his work, and she also learnt to share his passion for succulents, taking off with him to hunt cacti whenever possible. The best places were Indian reservations, and Jodye recalled how they were often thrown out for digging up plants. They had many adventures together travelling all over the world, from Russia to Africa, Europe to South America. But their favourite place was always the American South-West and Mexico, where they drove many thousands of miles in their pick-up truck to hunt exotic butterflies and plants.

When they took off for the jungle near Puerto Vallarta on Mexico's Pacific shore, they had no inkling of the tragedy awaiting them. It was December 1974 and just another perfect holiday. Denis and Jodye had spent hundreds of hours in jungles together, both confident in the environment despite the dangers, so Jodye had nothing to fear when she kissed her husband goodbye. They would meet back at their pick-up truck at the end of the afternoon and she watched his strong, handsome frame of six feet three inches stride off into the gloom. It was the last time she would see him alive.

For ten days Jodye struggled with reluctant Mexican officials to find her husband. Nobody wanted to get involved, and she had to use all her powers of persuasion and money to force the local police chief into action. A tiny woman of five feet, she was – and is – nevertheless a formidable presence, and this, combined with her fluent Spanish, soon ensured that teams of police and army were sent into the forest. She even paid hundreds of dollars a day for a helicopter to search from above, but with every passing day hopes of finding Denis alive diminished. Jodye's fourteen-year-old son flew in with his grown-up sister to offer moral support, but there was no comfort for the agony of waiting, and Jodye faced the added burden of having to be strong for her son, her only child by Denis.

Single Copy 10¢

The News - Bulletin

| 64th Year | Thursday, December 5, 1974 | Sixth & Baca | Belen, New Mexico |

Belen attorney reported missing in Mexico jungle

Belen Attorney Denis Cowper was still reported missing late yesterday in a jungle near Puerto Vallarta, Mexico, five days after he was last seen by area inhabitants.

Cowper, 127 Ventura Rd. in Los Chaves, was last seen Friday morning butterfly-hunting at the edge of a tropical jungle outside Puerto Vallarta, a Pacific coast city in the Jalisco state of Mexico located about 1,300 miles south of Belen.

Mrs. Josephine Cowper, the attorney's wife and the owner of the Credit Bureau of Belen, has hired search planes, a helicopter and ground searchers in an attempt to locate her husband.

"This is an absolute nightmare. I need some kind of help from the United States," Mrs. Cowper said by telephone. She added that only 16 Mexican soldiers were hunting for her husband and that helicopter costs were running her $400 per day.

Mrs. Cowper told Pope shortly after 3 p.m. yesterday that searchers still had not located her husband. She may now seek the assistance of blood hounds to locate Cowper.

Her daughter, Mrs. Francine Moore, Belen, and Tom Newboldt, an investigator for the Cowper, Bailey and Pope law firm, flew Tuesday to Puerto Vallarta to assist Mrs. Cowper.

Cowper left Nov. 22 in his four-wheel drive automobile on a trip to Mexico to pursue his hobbies of cacti and butterfly collecting. Mrs. Cowper flew to Puerto Vallarta on Nov. 24 to join her husband in what was planned as a two-week vacation.

Though the truck was located, Mrs. Cowper said "a piece of the key was in the ignition and we can't understand that."

John Pope, Cowper's law partner, says the 32-year old attorney apparently left for the day last Friday to seek butterflies in the jungle. His wife became alarmed when he did not return that night and a search began in earnest last Sunday. Jalisco state residents found the attorney's vehicle that same day. Others said they saw Cowper enter the jungle with his butterfly net.

"He speaks German, French, Italian, Czech, Russian and Spanish," Pope adds.

"Mexican Spanish and several Indian dialects."

Cowper has sought butterflies in the wilds, including Mexico, many times. Pope declares. His collection may be one of the finest in the state as he trades varieties with lepidopterists throughout the world.

"Denis has discovered several new genii, including one he named after his step-daughter, Francine," Pope says.

The attorney also has collected thousands of cacti for his New Mexico Cactus Research Company. He has written numerous articles on cacti for national and international publications.

The attorney practiced law with Tibo Chaves for 24 years until he dissolved the partnership last August and formed a new firm with Pope and Lance Bailey of Socorro.

"Sen. Joseph Montoya called the Governor of Jalisco on Monday and asked him to give all the assistance he could to the search," Pope said. "The military is also taking part in the search. However, neither the military, aircraft or ground-searchers have yet been able to locate Cowper. Pope says. "Josie

DENIS COWPER

is optimistic," he adds.

Mrs. Cowper, her daughter and Newboldt are staying in Puerto Vallarta. The Cowper's 14-year old son, Denny, has been staying with his grandmother, Mrs. Epifano Chaves, in Belen.

Her focus now was firmly on finding her husband's body and taking him home, but the longer nothing was found the less willing the Mexican authorities seemed to be to help. Jodye even began to suspect foul play. She was watched wherever she went, and every time she tried to call the USA from her hotel the connection failed. Drastic measures were called for, and she climbed down the drainpipe from her hotel window to make a phone call elsewhere. She even paid a man on the street to give her his clothes to make her less recognizable, and then, at last, she succeeded in contacting her friend, the Governor of New Mexico, who offered to send bloodhounds.

The dogs found Denis in no time at all. The stench of his body after several weeks in the moist heat of the jungle was appalling. 'To see the man you shared your bed with for fifteen years look like that was so terrible,' his widow told me. 'No one should have to see their loved one like that.'

It was no longer possible to tell how Denis died. The papers in New Mexico suggested that he died of a heart attack, since he had already suffered one eight months previously. But Jodye has never been able to believe that entirely. She remains haunted by uncertainty and the fact she was not there when Denis died.

265

'Too many memories,' she said sadly one day, and it felt horribly inappropriate to ask about Margaret's things in the warehouse. But, even at seventy-seven and weakened by emphysema, Jodye insisted she was ready to help me.

'I thought I had let him go,' she explained, 'but I never have.'

Now was the time to sort his possessions and make peace with the past. Sadly, the challenge was almost too much. Her body was letting her down now, and breathing dust in the storeroom sent her gasping for her oxygen bottles back home.

For five hours her nephew valiantly climbed the mountain of boxes and furniture stored ceiling high in an unventilated room. Sweat poured down his face as he unpacked and packed container after container, but it was hopeless. There were simply too many boxes. At one point my heart skipped a beat as he unearthed three handwritten journals. They appeared to be precisely what I was looking for. But no. The faded words *Westminster School* embossed on the covers soon revealed them as the teenage butterfly notes written by Denis – a precious find for Jodye but less so for me.

Poor Jodye, she felt so guilty for having failed to clear the storeroom before my arrival and the fact that I appeared to have flown halfway around the world for nothing. But her health had declined dramatically since we had first been in touch, and she was clearly in no position to carry any boxes herself, much less hunt through the legacy of an entire lifetime. I assured her my visit had by no means been a waste of time. Not only had I solved the mystery of where one of Margaret's bequests had ended up, but – with Jodye's help – I had also discovered Denis Cowper, an individual as extraordinary and fascinating as Margaret herself.

I knew from Jodye that none of Margaret's books contained handwritten annotations, so there was no need to set eyes on them myself. As for her possible butterfly journals, Jodye could not recall ever seeing those, and it is entirely possible they were lost a long time before she even met Denis. He moved all over the USA before he settled in New Mexico, and there is every chance some of his possessions did not survive the many marriages and house moves that occurred. Legal correspondence in London shows that Margaret's bequest was stored in numerous boxes at the Royal Entomological Society during the Second World War, and at least one was lost in the post when they were all sent to Cowper's father in

London in 1945. No inventory for those boxes survives, but Margaret's scientific journals could well have been in the one that was lost, if they ever existed at all.

Uncertain outcomes plagued Margaret's life, and they continued even after her death. When she wrote her last will and testament she intended to be generous to both public institutions and private individuals. Thus, in addition to her major bequests to the Natural History Museum in London and the Castle Museum in Norwich, money was also left to the Royal Entomological Society and the South London Entomological Society, as well as to those charged with carrying out the instructions in her will. Her most important private gift was to her American nephews, Lee and Melville Fountaine, who were to inherit her very substantial Hampstead property, along with its contents of furniture, pictures and personal effects.

Margaret's uncle Edward had set her free by leaving her a share of his fortune, and her dearest wish had no doubt been to do the same for her nephews. Unfortunately, however, they were never told of the true extent of their inheritance. Instead of gaining a house that is worth several million pounds today, they received her paintings – much treasured but hardly life-changing. Why were they not told? It has been suggested that the lease on the Fellows Road property may have been due to expire in the early 1960s, making the house impossible to sell after Margaret's death. Perhaps the executors therefore felt it was not worth mentioning. It may also have suffered severe bomb damage or have been requisitioned during the Second World War. There are answers to be found, but that is another story.

APPENDIX I
Insects Named After
Margaret Fountaine and Khalil Neimy

Margaret was always extremely reluctant for her name to be used in the naming of the dozens of new species of butterfly she discovered. She refused permission many times. Nevertheless, a few butterflies were named in her honour during her lifetime. None of them is a valid species; rather, they are varieties, forms or aberrations. The modern nomenclature is in brackets, where known. There could well be more named after her since her death, but this is the present state of knowledge. Thanks are due to Tony Irwin and Colin Treadaway for the information.

Colias fountainei Aigner, 1901 (*Colias aurorina heldreichi* f. *fountainei*); described in *Rovartani Lapok*, Budapest, Vol. 8, p. 30.

Nordmannia fountaineae Aigner, 1906 (*Thecla ilicis* var. *mauretanica* ab. *fountaineae*); described in *Rovartani Lapok*, Budapest, Vol. 13, pp. 69–75.

Pieris fountaineae Verity, 1910 (*Pieris napi* ab. *fountaineae*); described in *Rhopalocera Palaearctica*, London, p. 331, pl. 59, f. 21.

Strymon fountaineae Arg. (this may be a typo-derived duplication of *Nordmannia fountaineae* Aigner, as *Strymon* and *Nordmannia* are closely related genera and have shared species in the past).

Fountainea Rydon, 1971; described in *Entomologist's Record and Journal of Variation*, Vol. 83, p. 339.

Charaxes margaretae Rydon, 1980, described in D'Abrera, *Butterflies of the Afrotropical Region*, p. 396.

Mylothris nubile fountainei Berger and *Colias alfacariensis fontanei* Reissinger, 1989; may be patronyms of Margaret or someone else. Butterflies named in the latter part of the twentieth century were probably in honour of Dr M. Fontaine, who collected mostly in West Africa and published several papers in the 1980s.

Kenneth J. Morton named a dragonfly in Margaret's honour, a new species which she discovered for him in Algeria: *Ischnura fountainei*; described in *Entomologists' Monthly Magazine*, 1905, Vol. 41, pp. 145–9.

In Margaret's day the *Euploea phaenareta althaea* butterfly was thought to be a species in its own right, but today it is accepted as a subspecies of *phaenareta*. Five are now recognized on the Philippines, and in recognition of Margaret's contribution to the knowledge of Philippine lepidoptera one of them is named in her honour: *Euploea phaenareta margaretae*, described in *Entomologische Zeitschrift*, Frankfurt am Main, 1988, Vol. 21, pp. 313–20. She would not have approved, but she might have been pleased.

After Khalil Neimy's death, Margaret allowed two butterflies she discovered along the Rio Madeira, in the Brazilian Amazon, to be named in his honour:

Ceratinia ninonia neimyi; described by N.D. Riley in *The Entomologist*, 1931, Vol. 64, p. 35.

Chiomara khalili sp. nov; described by N.D. Riley in *The Entomologist*, 1934, Vol. 67, pp. 185–6.

There are two invaluable websites for researching butterfly names, past and present:

http://internt.nhm.ac.uk/jdsml/perth/lepindex/

This is the British Museum Natural History's Global Lepidoptera Names Index.

http://www.funet.fi/pub/sci/bio/life/intro.html

This site provides links to historical butterfly names.

APPENDIX II

Known Scientific Articles That Have Drawn on Margaret Fountaine's Work

Cock, M.J.W., 'Margaret E. Fountaine: An Early 20th-Century Butterfly Collector in Trinidad', *Living World* (Journal of the Trinidad and Tobago Field Nature Club), 2004, pp. 43–9

Rydon, A., 'The Systematics of the Charaxidae (Lepidoptera: Nymphalidae)', *Entomologists Record and Journal of Variation*, Vol. 83, 1971, pp. 219–33, 283–7, 310–16, 336–41, 384–8

Vane-Wright, R.I., 'The Coloration, Identification and Phylogeny of *Nessaea* Butterflies (Lepidoptera: Nymphalidae)', *Entomology Series*, British Museum (Natural History), Vol. 38, 1979, p. 2

APPENDIX III

Fountaine Family Tree

(compiled by the author)

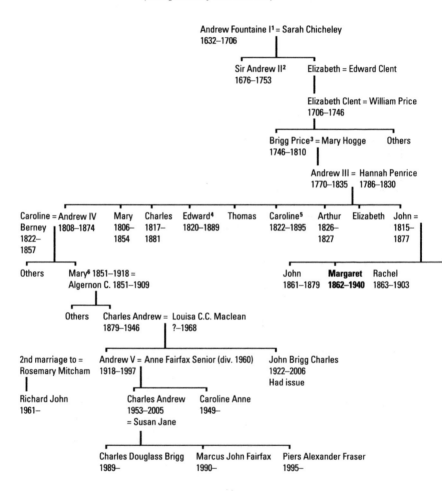

1 Bought Narford in 1690 and began building Narford Hall in 1702.

2 Died without issue and left Narford Hall to his sister.

3 Assumed by Act the name and arms of Fountaine.

4 Left his money to Margaret and her sisters.

5 Married Sir John Bennett Lawes (1814–1900), executor of Edward's estate and trustee of the Fountain sisters' money. She was the mother of Margaret Fountaine's favourite cousin, Skye.

6 Married her first cousin.

7 Married Rev. Atwill Curtois. Their eleven children all died without issue.

The American Fountaines

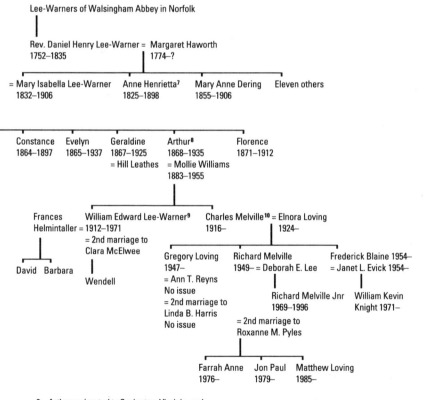

Lee-Warners of Walsingham Abbey in Norfolk

Rev. Daniel Henry Lee-Warner = Margaret Haworth
1752–1835   1774–?

= Mary Isabella Lee-Warner   Anne Henrietta[7]   Mary Anne Dering   Eleven others
1832–1906   1825–1898   1855–1906

Constance   Evelyn   Geraldine   Arthur[8]   Florence
1864–1897   1865–1937   1867–1925   1868–1935   1871–1912
                          = Hill Leathes = Mollie Williams
                                          1883–1955

Frances   William Edward Lee-Warner[9]   Charles Melville[10] = Elnora Loving
Helmintaller =   1912–1971   1916–   1924–
                       = 2nd marriage to
                       Clara McElwee
                                                       Gregory Loving   Richard Melville   Frederick Blaine 1954–
David   Barbara   1947–   1949– = Deborah E. Lee   = Janet L. Evick 1954–
                       Wendell   = Ann T. Reyns
                                                       No issue   Richard Melville Jnr   William Kevin
                                                       = 2nd marriage to 1969–1996   Knight 1971–
                                                       Linda B. Harris
                                                       No issue   = 2nd marriage to
                                                                         Roxanne M. Pyles

                                                       Farrah Anne   Jon Paul   Matthew Loving
                                                       1976–   1979–   1985–

8 Arthur emigrated to Covington, Virginia, and
   married Mollie Williams in 1910.

9 Moved to Florida in the 1950s. Nothing is known
   of his descendants.

10 The family is still in Virginia.

Notes

Chapter 1. *Childhood in Norfolk*

1. According to Charles Fountaine, the only mark left by Margaret's father is the duck decoy he built on the Narford estate. The information about John Fountaine's shooting skills comes from the introduction to *Love Among the Butterflies*.

2. For more on Sir Andrew Fountaine's Grand Tour see Andrew W. Moore's *Norfolk and the Grand Tour*, Chapter 2, pp. 27–8.

3. *The Battle of the Books*, published in 1704, was Swift's satirical contribution to the debate raging at the time on whether the Ancients or Moderns produced better authors and philosophers. Sir Andrew Fountaine was responsible for the design and production of eight plates to accompany the publication, though it seems only one was used in a later edition, entitled *A Tale of a Tub* (1710). Jonathan Swift also mentions dining with his friend Andrew Fountaine in his *Letters to Sally*.

4. The library and art collection of Narford Hall have been somewhat depleted by sales to finance extension and restoration, in particular by the four-day sale that took place in 1884, which caused a national scandal. The majolica collection at Narford was the largest in existence outside the Medici Court in Florence, and a syndicate was formed by wealthy patrons to buy as many items as possible for the nation. For a detailed account see Andrew W. Moore's article in the *Burlington Magazine*, June 1988.

5. Volume I of the diaries, p. 7.

Chapter 2. *Unladylike Behaviour*

1. Quotes are from Volumes I and II of Margaret's diaries, pp. 9–503.

2. Unpublished memoir of Margaret Fountaine by Norman Riley held at

Norwich Castle Study Centre, Natural History Department. Norman Denbigh Riley (1890–1979) spent almost his entire career, from 1911 to 1955, at the Natural History Museum in London and was one of the foremost museum entomologists of the twentieth century. He also co-authored the hugely influential *Field Guide to the Butterflies of Britain and Europe*, Collins, 1970.

Chapter 3. *The Secret Passion*

1. Quotes are from Volumes II and III of the diaries, pp. 558–604.

2. Sir John Bennet Lawes (1814–1900) became immensely wealthy through patenting the earliest forms of chemical fertilizer in England. He began manufacturing in Deptford in 1844, and his Rothamsted Experimental Station on his estate in Hertfordshire is the oldest of its kind in the world, still operational today. He was a larger-than-life character, ahead of his times in many ways – one of the earliest employers to offer his workers a cooperative savings bank and other social security benefits. See Macdonald Hastings's biography of Sir John's daughter, *Diane: A Victorian*, Michael Joseph, 1974.

Chapter 4. *Misspent Youth*

1. Quotes are from Volume IV of the diaries, pp. 644–823.

2. M.A. Titmarsh (W.M. Thackaray), *The Irish Sketchbook*, 1842, published by Chapman and Hall, 1863, Chapter XIV, pp. 163–70.

Chapter 5. *Flight to the Continent*

1. Quotes are from Volume IV of the diaries, pp. 947–64.

Chapter 6. *Music and Men*

1. Quotes are from Volumes IV and V of the diaries, pp. 1031–1208.

2. In 2004 Sotheby's held a violin made by Giovanni Battista Guadagnini (1711–86) for offers in the region of £180,000–250,000.

3. Dr Bruno Galli-Valerio (1867–1943) was to become a renowned scientist and alpinist, publishing a variety of books and pamphlets on subjects as diverse as first ascents in the Italian Alps to zoonosis (the transfer of disease from animals to humans). He was nominated but not honoured for the Nobel Prize in Medicine in 1935, when he was Professor of Hygiene at the University of Lausanne.

Chapter 7. *Sicilian Adventure*

1. Henry John Elwes, FRS (1846–1922), was a traveller, horticulturalist and butterfly collector. His two most noteworthy books were *The Trees of Great Britain and Ireland* (1906) and *A Monograph of the Genus Lilium* (1877–80). Today his estate is well known to snowdrop enthusiasts, who flock there each spring to enjoy over 140 varieties in bloom (Mr and Mrs H.W.G. Elwes, Colesbourne Park, Colesbourne, Nr Cheltenham, GL 53 9NP; hwg@globalnet.co.uk).

2. James Edwards (1856–1928) was a Norfolk entomologist whose original expertise was in beetles. He worked as a curator and private secretary to Henry John Elwes from 1891 to 1922. He published many articles with Elwes and in his own right in journals such as *The Entomologist*, and he also made important contributions to the *Transactions of the Norfolk and Norwich Naturalists Society*.

3. The Norwich Entomological Society, founded in 1810, was the first provincial field club to be entirely dedicated to entomology. It also distinguished itself by allowing members' wives to accompany collecting expeditions, which was unheard of in the grander clubs in London.

4. See *The Aurelian Legacy* by Michael A. Salmon for more information on the early English butterfly collectors.

5. *European Butterflies*, p. viii. William Francis de Vismes Kane, MA, JP, DL (1840–1918), was a member of the landed gentry in Ireland and lived at Drumreaske, in the parish of Tydavnet, Co. Monaghan. He wrote *A Catalogue of the Lepidoptera of Ireland* (1901) as well as *European Butterflies* (1885).

6. Watkins and Doncaster was founded by William Watkins in Eastbourne, where his house, the Villa Sphinx, was renamed 'The Villa Stinks' by the neighbours, owing to the persistent smell of mothballs. The firm moved to 36 The Strand in 1879, in partnership with Arthur Doncaster, who was deaf and dumb but managed to conduct business with a slate and chalk hung around his neck. The business moved to Welling, Kent, in 1956 and still supplies specialist equipment to naturalists all over the world (www.watdon.com).

7. William Swainson (1789–1855) wrote *The Naturalist's Guide for Collecting and Preserving All Subjects of Natural History and Botany*, Baldwin and Cradock, 1822.

8. Quotes are from Volumes IV and V of the diaries, pp. 1219–74.

9. Emilio Ragusa (1849–1924) published a great many articles between 1887 and 1924 in Italian journals such as *Il Naturalista Siciliano* and *Bollettino del Laboratorio di Zoologia Generale e Agraria*.

Chapter 8. *Among the Austro-Hungarians*

1. Dr Otto Staudinger (1830–1900) was one of the best-known European lepidopterists in the nineteenth century, whose immense collection of butterflies formed the basis of his commercial business. He also published two important reference books (the *Katalog der Lepidopteren Europas und der angränzenden Länder*, and the *Katalog der Palaearktischen Lepidopteren*) and many other highly respected works on European and exotic butterflies. His surviving collection was acquired by the Natural History Museum of Berlin in 1907.

2. 'Two Seasons Among the Butterflies of Hungary and Austria', *The Entomologist*, Vol. 31, 1898, pp. 281–9.

3. Quotes are from Volume V of the diaries, pp. 1280–1333.

Chapter 9. *Lady on a Bike*

1. Thomas Humber started out making the early type of bicycle known as penny-farthings and founded his company in Coventry in the late 1880s, where he made the famous Humber cycle. The Humber Company also went on to produce popular motorbikes and cars.

2. Quotes are from Volumes V and VI of the diaries, pp. 1336–1409.

3. Ludwig Aigner (1840–1909) was a German writer and publisher who made his life in Budapest and who took an interest in entomology in the latter part of his life. He used the pen names Abafi Lajos and Abafi Aigner Lajos, and in his most important butterfly book, *Die Schmetterlinge Ungarns*, which was published in 1907, he claimed to have discovered the very white female variety of *Colias chrysotheme* that Margaret found almost a decade earlier. However, he did have the decency to consult Margaret in the naming of it, and thus modern scientists know this butterfly variety as *Colias chrysotheme hurleyi* Aigner-Abafi, in honour of Margaret's beloved nanny.

4. See L. Higgins and N. Riley, *A Field Guide to the Butterflies of Britain and Europe*, p. 133.

Chapter 10. *Rough Rides in Greece*

1. Henry Charles Lang (d. 1909) originally qualified as a medical doctor but chose to enter Holy Orders instead and was rector of All Saints Church in Southend from 1892 until his death. He was also a respected authority on European butterflies, and his most important publications were the two volumes entitled *The Butterflies of Europe*, the second of which was beautifully illustrated by Horace Knight. Reverend Lang was elected a Fellow of the Entomological Society of London in 1900.

2. *The Entomologists' Record*, Vol. 14, 1902, pp. 29–35 and 64–7.

3. Quotes are from Volume VI of the diaries, pp. 1416–1517.

4. Diane, Sylvia and Lilian were Sir John's granddaughters by his formidable daughter Caroline Lawes (1844–1946), known to all the family as 'Skye', who was also mother to twin boys and another daughter.

Chapter 11. *The Dragoman Lover*

1. Quotes are from Volume VI of the diaries, pp. 1523–1651.

2. Mrs Nicholl (1839–1922), whose full name was Mary De la Beche Nicholl, was a well-known butterfly collector and climber of mountains, whose friend, Mr Elwes, named at least one butterfly after her. Her own collection went to the Swansea Museum in Wales. For more see Hilary M. Thomas, *Grandmother Extraordinary*, Barry, Stewart Williams, 1979.

3. Much of the Middle East, including modern-day Iraq, Syria, Lebanon, Palestine, part of Arabia and most of North Africa, belonged at this time to the Ottoman Empire, which existed from 1300 to 1922. Khalil Neimy was therefore a Turkish subject when he met Margaret.

4. Though Khalil Neimy grew up an Arabic-speaking Turkish subject in Syria, he was a Christian of Greek parentage; hence his allegiance to the Greek Orthodox Church.

Chapter 12. *Deceit and Betrayal*

1. Quotes are from Volume VI of the diaries, pp. 1610–51, and Volume VII, pp. 1661–1740.

Chapter 13. *Turkish Delight*

1. Quotes are from Volume VII of the diaries, pp. 1742–1804. Skye (Caroline Lawes) was the only grand relation Margaret had a significant bond

with. She was the daughter of Margaret's beloved uncle by marriage, Sir John Bennet Lawes, and as independent and talented as her cousin. A great shot, writer and society hostess, she was eighteen years older and a trusted confidante, yet outlived Margaret to become 101. For more see Macdonald Hastings, *Diane: A Victorian*, Michael Joseph, 1974.
2. 'A Butterfly Summer in Asia Minor', *The Entomologist*, Vol. 37, 1904, pp. 79–84, 105–8 and 184–5.

Chapter 14. *Midlife Crisis*
1. Quotes are from the diaries, Volume VII, pp. 1806–1927.
2. 'Algerian Butterflies in the Spring and Summer of 1904', *The Entomologist*, Vol. 39, 1906, pp. 84–9 and 107–9.

Chapter 15. *Free to Roam*
1. Quotes are from Volume VIII of the diaries, pp. 1960–2038. Watkins and Doncaster was the major supplier of entomological kit and still is. See notes to Chapter 7 for further information.
2. Bosnia-Herzegovina was still part of the Austro-Hungarian Empire at this time; hence the German-speaking institution, which would have been the top hospital in Sarajevo for moneyed expatriates.

Chapter 16. *A Naturalist in Africa*
1. Quotes are from Volume VIII of the diaries, pp. 2040–2126.
2. Her four sketch books are kept in the Entomological Library at the Natural History Museum in London, available to see by appointment.
3. See John Feltwell, *The Illustrated Encyclopaedia of Butterflies*, for an introduction to butterfly conservation issues.
4. For more see I. Migdoll, *Field Guide to the Butterflies of South Africa*, New Holland, 1988.

Chapter 17. *American Odyssey*
1. Quotes are from Volume VIII of the diaries, pp. 2145–2214, and Volume IX, pp. 2240–76.
2. What she did not mention, but the renowned Russo-American entomologist Nicholas Shoumatoff recalled many decades later, was that she was the first collector to catch a specimen of *Chlosyne pantone* since its

discovery in 1886. None was found again until 1936, during his own collecting trip to Cuba. 'She had a fabulous record for picking up the rarest species,' he said.

3. 'Five Months' Butterfly Cllecting in Costa Rica in the Summer of 1911', *The Entomologist*, Vol. 46, 1913, pp. 189–95 and 214–19.

4. For more information, see John Hewetson, *Memoirs of the House of Hewetson or Hewson of Ireland*, Mitchel and Hughes, 1901. Bono (real name Paul Hewson), of the music group U2, is also a relation. Music has a long tradition in the Hewson family.

Chapter 18. *Australian Exile*

1. Quotes are from Volume IX of the diaries, pp. 2344–94.

2. The house Margaret and Khalil had built for them was blown down by a cyclone in 1920.

Chapter 19. *Painful Separation*

1. Quotes are from Volume IX of the diaries, pp. 2409–83.

2. The Lorquin Natural History Club was founded by Fordyce Grinnell Jr in June 1913, originally to encourage young boys. By 1927, however, it had evolved into the Lorquin Entomological Society and has since had many distinguished members. It exists to this day.

3. She refers to the butterfly in question as *Euchloe pima* in her diary, now known as the Pima Orangetip, *Anthocharis pima*.

4. A total of 550,000 Americans died during the ten-month period of the influenza epidemic in 1918, but other countries suffered far, far worse. Twelve million people died of influenza in India alone. In fact, the influenza pandemic of 1918 killed over twice the number of people who died in the First World War.

Chapter 20. *The Lonely Lepidopterist*

1. Quotes are from Volume X of the diaries, pp. 2496–2631.

2. Since 1989 Burma has been known as Myanmar and Rangoon as Yangôn.

3. Margaret would no longer find Tantabin a happy place to stay. These days it is a major army training post surrounded by terrified native villages trying to survive under the constant threat of kidnap and enforced labour.

4. China was crushingly defeated by Japan in 1895 and dominated by it until the Second World War. By the 1920s a combination of massive natural disasters and an orgy of slaughter had reduced the country to virtual anarchy, without a central government of any kind.

5. US President McKinley had recognized Philippine aspirations for independence as long ago as 1899, and prior to the Second World War there was general consensus that it was only a matter of time before it would be achieved.

6. 'Amongst the *Rhopalocera* of the Philippines', *The Entomologist*, Vol. 58, 1925, pp. 235–9, 263–5; and Vol. 59, 1926, pp. 9–11, 31–4, 53–7.

7. F. Danielsen and C.G. Treadaway, 'Priority Conservation Areas for Butterflies in the Philippine Islands', *Animal Conservation*, Vol. 7, 2004, pp. 79–92.

8. H. Schröder and C.G. Treadaway, *Entomologische Zeitschrift*, Frankfurt am Main, Vol. 21, 1988, pp. 313–20.

Chapter 21. *Bereft at Sixty-Six*

1. Quotes are from Volume X of the diaries, pp. 2640–2759, and Volume XI, pp. 2772–2842.

2. J.J. Joicey was a wealthy collector and patron of lepidopterists who founded the private Hill Museum in Whitley, Surrey, which survived until the 1930s.

Chapter 22. *Solace in Latin America*

1. The Riley–Fountaine correspondence is held by the Entomological Library of the Natural History Museum in London.

2. Arthur Miles-Moss (1873–1948) left his entomological writings and art work to the Natural History Museum in London.

3. H.M. Tomlinson (1873–1958) was a journalist and writer who wrote the bestseller *The Sea and the Jungle*, which recounts his experience of travelling up the rivers Amazon and Madeira employed as purser on a tramp steamer in 1909/10.

4. Quotes are from Volume XI of the diaries, pp. 2827–2952.

5. Dr Emilie Snethlage (1868–1929) was the most eminent female bird collector of the early twentieth century and was hugely instrumental in advancing Brazilian ornithology. Director of the Museu Paraense Emilio

Goeldi from 1914 to 1922, her best-known work is the *Catalogo das Aves Amazonicas*. Born of an impecunious pastor, she, too, inherited enough money to set her free, earning a PhD in 1904, sixteen years before universities in her own country granted women that right. She was as tough as Margaret any day, even amputating her own finger once, after being mauled by a piranha.

6. Lady Dorothy Mills (1889–1959) was the first Englishwoman to enter Timbuktu after crossing the Sahara and wrote several travel books on Africa. She met Margaret during her final journey, which resulted in her book *The Country of the Orinoco*, published by Hutchinson in 1931.

Chapter 23. *A Stranger in a Strange Land*

1. Mount St Benedict was founded in 1912 by three Benedictine monks fleeing an anti-clerical government in Brazil. It is the oldest monastery in the Caribbean, and its guest-house still welcomes visitors from all over the world.

2. Quotes are from Volume XI of the diaries, pp. 2957–3014, and Volume XII, pp. 3072–3201.

3. Henry Roland-Brown (1865–1922) was a poet and entomologist and one of the most popular officers of the Entomological Society. He died prematurely of heart disease, weakened by the strain of being a Commissioner for Civil Liabilities in London during and after the First World War.

4. Margaret's own descriptions of her adventures in Africa and Indo-China can be found in *Butterflies and Late Loves*, edited by W. F. Cater.

Postscript: *The Lost Bequests*

1. Denis found a *Calliptamus italicus* (Italian locust) in Swanage, Dorset, which was exhibited at the Royal Entomological Society on his behalf in December 1936. This foreign species may have been imported with foodstuffs or plants and is not known to have been spotted since.

Bibliography

Ackery, P., 'Books, bravado and butterflies: tales from the Natural History Museum', at *www.nhm.ac.uk/entomology/features/butterflies/butterflies.html*

Adams, W.H.D., *Celebrated Women Travellers of the Nineteenth Century*. London, Swann Sonnenschein, 1883

Aitken, M., *A Girdle Round the Earth: Adventuresses Abroad*. London, Constable, 1987

Allen, A., *Travelling Ladies: Victorian Adventuresses*. London, Jupiter, 1983

Allen, D.E., *The Naturalist in Britain: A Social History*. London, Allen Lane, 1976

Anon, *A Few Words of Advice on Travelling and Its Requirements Addressed to Ladies*, 4th edn. London, Thomas Cook and Sons, 1878

Barnes Stevenson, C., *Victorian Women Travel Writers in Africa*. Boston, Massachusetts, Twayne, 1982

Birkett, D., *Spinsters Abroad: Victorian Lady Explorers*. Oxford, Blackwell, 1989

Bolingbroke, V., *Frederick William Frohawk*. Faringdon, Oxfordshire, E.W. Classey, 1977

Chatfield, J.F.W., *Frohawk: His Life and Work*. Marlborough, Crowood Press, 1987

Cook's Tourist Handbook on Switzerland, 1895

Cook's Tourist Handbook on Palestine and Syria, 1891

Cunnington, W., *Feminine Attitudes in the Nineteenth Century*. London, Heinemann, 1945

Davidson, L.C., *Hints to Lady Travellers*. London, 1889

Delamont, S., and Duffin, L., *Nineteenth Century Women*. London, Croom Helm, 1978

Dyhouse, C., *Girls Growing Up in Late Victorian and Edwardian England*. London, Routledge and Kegan Paul, 1981

Early, J.E., 'The Science of Work, Life, and Text: Margaret Fountaine's Captures/Capturing Margaret Fountaine', *Women's Writing*, Vol. 2, No. 2, 1995

Eggeling, W.J., *When I Was Younger*. Self-published, 1987

Feltwell, J., *The Illustrated Encyclopaedia of Butterflies*. London, Quarto, 1993

Fisher, R., *A Field Guide to Australian Butterflies*. New South Wales, Surrey Beatty and Sons, 1995

Fountaine, M., edited by W.F. Cater, *Love Among the Butterflies*. London, Collins, 1980

Fountaine, M., edited by W.F. Cater, *Butterflies and Late Loves*. London, Collins, 1986

Frawley, M.H., *A Wider Range: Travel Writing by Women in Victorian England*. London, Rutherford, 1994

Galton, F., *The Art of Travel*. London, Murray, 1893

Gates, B.T., *Kindred Nature*. Chicago, University of Chicago Press, 1998

Gates, B.T., and Shteir, A.B. (eds), *Natural Eloquence*. Wisconsin, University of Wisconsin Press, 1997

Gilbert, P., *A Compendium of the Biographical Literature on Deceased Entomologists*. London, British Museum, 1977

Hampson, K. *et al.*, *Wildlife and Conservation in the Polillo Islands*. Glossop, Viper Press, 2003

Hastings, M., *Diane: A Victorian*. London, Michael Joseph, 1974

Heilbrun, C.G., *Writing a Woman's Life*. London, Women's Press, 1988

Higgins, L.G., and Riley, N.D., *Field Guide to the Butterflies of Britain and Europe*. London, Collins, 1970

Hughes, K., *The Writer's Guide to Everyday Life in Regency and Victorian England 1811–1901*. London, Writers' Digest Books, 1998

Irwin, T., 'Of Butterflies and Broken Hearts', *Antenna*, Vol. 2, No. 3, July 1978

Johnson, K., and Coates, S., *Nabokov's Blues: The Scientific Odyssey of a Literary Genius*. New York, McGraw-Hill, 2003

Keay, J., *With Passport and Parasol: The Adventures of Seven Victorian Ladies*. London, BBC Books, 1989

Keenan, B., *Damascus: Hidden Treasures of the Old City*. London, Thames and Hudson, 2000

Kirby, W.F., *Familiar Butterflies and Moths*. London, Cassell, 1901

Lang, H.C., *The Butterflies of Europe*, Vols I and II. London, L. Reeve and Co., 1884

Longford, E., *Eminent Victorian Women*. London, Weidenfeld and Nicolson, 1981

McKay, J., *Brilliant Careers*. Brisbane, Queensland Museum Publications, 1997

Middleton, D., *Victorian Lady Travellers*. London, Routledge and Kegan Paul, 1965

Migdoll, I., *Field Guide to the Butterflies of South Africa*. London, New Holland, 1988

Monteith, G., *The Butterfly Man of Kuranda*. Brisbane, Queensland Museum, 1991

Moore, A.W., *Dutch and Flemish Painting in Norfolk*. London, HMSO, 1988, for the Norfolk Museums Service

Moore, A.W., 'The Fountaine Collection of Maiolica', *The Burlington Magazine*, Vol. CXXX, No. 1023, June 1988

Moore, A.W., *Norfolk and the Grand Tour*. London, HMSO, 1985, for the Norfolk Museums Service

Moore, A.W., and Crawley, C., *Family and Friends: A Regional Survey of British Portraiture*. London, HMSO, 1992, for the Norfolk Museums Service

Moss, M., *A Trip into the Interior of Peru*. Lima, Charles F. Southwell, 1909

Polk, M., and Tiegreen, M., *Women of Discovery*. London, Scriptum Editions, 2001

Pratt, M.L., *Imperial Eyes*. London, Routledge, 1992

Richardson, A. (ed.), *Women Who Did*. London, Penguin, 2002

Ring, J., *How the English Made the Alps*. London, John Murray, 2000

Robinson, J., *Wayward Women*. Oxford, Oxford University Press, 1990

Russell, M., *The Blessings of a Good Thick Skirt*. London, Flamingo, 1994

Ryall, A., 'Forstillelse Er Frihetens Pris. Margaret Fountaine Selvbiografi', in *Erobring og overskridelse*. Oslo, Unipub Forlag, 2003

Sackett, T., *British Life a Century Ago: Images from the Francis Frith Collection*. Salisbury, Frith Book Company, 1999

Salmon, M.A., *The Aurelian Legacy*. Berkeley, California, University of California Press, 2000

Sheffield, S. Le-May, *Revealing New Worlds*. London, Routledge, 2001

Sheffield, S. Le-May, *Women and Science: Social Impact and Interaction*. Santa Barbara, California, ABC-CLIO, 2004

Sheldon, W.G., 'Margaret Elizabeth Fountaine', *The Entomologist*, Vol. LXXIII, September 1940

Stenton, D.M., *The English Woman in History*. New York, Schocken,1972

The Complete Book of British Butterflies. London, Ward Lock, 1934

Timpson, J., *Timpson's English Eccentrics*. Norwich, Jarrold, 1995

Tolman, T., and Lewington, R., *Butterflies of Britain and Europe*. London, Collins, 2004

Trollope, J., *Britannia's Daughters: Women of the British Empire*. London, Hutchinson, 1983

Vane-Wright, R.I., *Butterflies*. Washington, DC, Smithsonian Books, 2003

Vismes Kane (de), M.F., *European Butterflies*. London, Macmillan, 1885

Williamson, A., *The Golden Age of Travel*. Peterborough, Thomas Cook Publishing, 1998

Younis, A., *The Coming of the Arabic-Speaking People to the United States*. Staten Island, New York, Center for Migration Studies, 1995

Margaret Fountaine's published work
In *The Entomologist*

1897 Vol. 30, pp. 4–11: 'Notes on the Butterflies of Sicily'

1897 Vol. 30, pp. 296–7: (Note) 'White Female of *Colias Chrysotheme* Near Vienna'

1898 Vol. 31, pp. 281–9: 'Two Seasons Among the Butterflies of Hungary and Austria'

1902 Vol. 35, pp. 60–63 and 97–101: 'A Few Notes on Some of the Butterflies of Syria and Palestine'

1904 Vol. 37, pp. 79–84, 105–8, 135–7, 157–9, 184–6: 'A Butterfly Summer in Asia Minor'

1906 Vol. 39, pp. 42–3: (Note) '*Melitaea Desfontainii* and *Melitaea Aurinia* var. *iberica* in Central Aragon'

1906 Vol. 39, pp. 84–9, 107–9: 'Algerian Butterflies in the Spring and Summer of 1904'

1907 Vol. 40, pp. 100–103: 'A Few Notes on Some of the Corsican Butterflies'

1908 Vol. 41, p. 90: (Note) 'Bird Chased by a Butterfly'

1911 Vol. 44, pp. 14–15: 'An Autumn Morning in the Alleghany Mountains'

1911 Vol. 44. pp. 153–4: (Note) 'Remarkable Aberration of *Terias Elathea*'

1911 Vol. 44, pp. 403–4: (Note) 'Note on the Roosting Habits of *Heliconius Charitonia*'

1913 Vol. 46, p. 112: (Note) 'The Audacity of a Bird'

1913 Vol. 46, pp. 189–95, 214–19: 'Five Months' Butterfly Collecting in Costa Rica in the Summer of 1911'

1917 Vol. 50, pp. 154–6: 'List of Butterflies Taken in the Neighbourhood of Los Angeles, California'

1921 Vol. 54, pp. 238–9: (Note) '*Pyrameis Gonerilla* in New Zealand'

1921 Vol. 54, p. 290: (Note) '*Coenonympha Pamophilus*, Vars.'

1925 Vol. 58, pp. 235–9 and 263–5 'Amongst the *Rhopalocera* of the Philippines'

1926 Vol. 59, pp. 9–11, 31–4 and 53–7: 'Amongst the *Rhopalocera* of the Philippines'

1935 Vol. 68, p. 163: (Note) 'Remarkable Tenacity of Life in the Egg of a Butterfly'

1938 Vol. 71, pp. 90–91: (Note) 'Rapid Development of a Tropical Butterfly'

In *The Entomologist's Record and Journal of Variation*

1902 Vol. 14, pp. 29–35 and 64–7: 'Butterfly Hunting in Greece, in the Year 1900'

In *Transactions of the Entomological Society of London*

1911 'Larvae and Pupae of South African *Rhopalocera*'

In *The Pall Mall Magazine*

1904 Vol. 14, pp. 253–8: 'The Butterfly Hunter: In Search of a Long-lost Rarity'

Index